Maria Dimitrova

Sociality and Justice

Toward Social Phenomenology

Maria Dimitrova

SOCIALITY AND JUSTICE

Toward Social Phenomenology

ibidem-Verlag
Stuttgart

Bibliografische Information der Deutschen Nationalbibliothek
Die Deutsche Nationalbibliothek verzeichnet diese Publikation in der Deutschen Nationalbibliografie; detaillierte bibliografische Daten sind im Internet über http://dnb.d-nb.de abrufbar.

Bibliographic information published by the Deutsche Nationalbibliothek
Die Deutsche Nationalbibliothek lists this publication in the Deutsche Nationalbibliografie; detailed bibliographic data are available in the Internet at http://dnb.d-nb.de.

∞

Gedruckt auf alterungsbeständigem, säurefreien Papier
Printed on acid-free paper

ISBN-13: 978-3-8382-0945-6

© *ibidem*-Verlag
Stuttgart 2016

Alle Rechte vorbehalten

Das Werk einschließlich aller seiner Teile ist urheberrechtlich geschützt. Jede Verwertung außerhalb der engen Grenzen des Urheberrechtsgesetzes ist ohne Zustimmung des Verlages unzulässig und strafbar. Dies gilt insbesondere für Vervielfältigungen, Übersetzungen, Mikroverfilmungen und elektronische Speicherformen sowie die Einspeicherung und Verarbeitung in elektronischen Systemen.

All rights reserved. No part of this publication may be reproduced, stored in or introduced into a retrieval system, or transmitted, in any form, or by any means (electronical, mechanical, photocopying, recording or otherwise) without the prior written permission of the publisher. Any person who does any unauthorized act in relation to this publication may be liable to criminal prosecution and civil claims for damages.

Printed in Germany

Table of Contents

Introduction 7
Method or the next step:
From Existential toward Social Phenomenology 35

Chapter One: *Sociality: The I and the Other* 53
   1.1. Ontology and/or ethics. Is ontology fundamental? 53
   1.2. How to think *humanitas* of *homo humanus*? 57
   1.3. Subjectness 67
   1.4. Time and death 86
      a) Existential Time 87
      b) Historical time 90
      c) Eschatological Time 96
   1.5. In the beginning was the Word ... with the Other 100
   1.6. Heidegger and Levinas on the path to language 109
      a) Martin Heidegger 109
      b) Emmanuel Levinas 113
      c) Heidegger and/or Levinas 119

Chapter Two: *The Other and the Third One* 123
   2.1. The Third One 123
   2.2. The Ethical and the Political. Justice and the State 145
   2.3. Kant and Levinas on the Categorical Imperative 172
   2.4. Paul Ricoeur on justice — virtue and institution.
      Revision from Levinas' perspective. 185
   2.5. Jean-François Lyotard: prescription, description and norm....192

Chapter Three: *From the Command to the Norm* 209

   3.1. Replacing the prescription
(the command, the order, the appeal) with the norm 209

   3.2. The neo-liberal notion of justice 222

   3.2. The Communitarian notion of justice 234

Conclusion 243

Index 253

Introduction[1]

In modernity, people began to identify themselves through their belonging in society striving to go beyond provincial borders and following a new sense of cosmopolitanism, i.e., of universality. They aspired to find the general essence of all people on the planet and to spread this kind of humanity amongst humankind. Modernity allowed efforts to be directed firstly at establishing what it is that applies to "everyone". In modern philosophy, the basic social relation was expressed by the formula "the individual and society", ignoring the intermediary role of communities and the irreducible diversity of individuals. In postmodernity this main opposition between individual and society remains, but efforts are being made to restore the rights of particular community, groups, and individuals which in previous epochs were ignored or renounced in the name of the protection of the totality.

Zygmunt Bauman explains that the freedom of "the universal man" in modernity was understood by replacing the colourful diversity of parishioners, family and other local people with "citizens". The citizen is a person with attributes which are bestowed upon him or her by a sole and undisputed authority, acting in the name of the united and sovereign nation-state. The postulate of human essence as a universality of reason corresponded with the ambitions and actions of the modern nation-state in its battle mediating between localised authority figures and individuals whom it wished to subdue. This was a battle against local customs, labelling them *superstitions*; local languages, calling them *dialects*; local markets, describing them as anti-competitive, and, local regulations which were linked to primitivism of the tradition. All had to concede and

---

[1] I would like to express my gratitude to my Ph.D. students, Mr. Paul Carroll and Mr. John de Geus for the proof-reading of the English text with hope that they will write their own books which will exceed the one of their professor.

subordinate themselves to the common currency of centralized government. The rule of state power spread across all subjects of the territory within its jurisdiction.[2] Of course, the legitimacy of a modern state is conferred with reference to reason and declared universal. So reason itself becomes identical to and identifiable with the state's interest; in turn, becoming indistinguishable with the interest of what Pierre Bourdieu calls "state nobility".

However, to recognize only those directives that can stand the test of universality is a task doomed to fail. Universality means ex-territoriality and ex-temporality implying a rejection time and place related to particular claims which, by virtue of their limitations, come into conflict with each other and also with the proclaimed universal interest:

> While promoting ostensibly universal, yet by necessity home-grown and home-bound standards, the polity finds itself opposed and resisted in the name of the selfsame principle of universalism which enlightens and/or ennobles its purpose. Promotion of universal standards then looks suspiciously like suppression of human nature and tends to be censured as intolerance.[3]

Universality (or civilization, where civilization is understood as the pursuit of the ideal of universality) protects itself through its self-empowerment and by alienating those who were not sufficiently universalised (civilized) by exercising pressure and coercion upon them. When standards of universalization were already adopted, and the mandated central authority felt unchallenged, it began to introduce different policies, allowing the inclusion and recognition of the previously unrecognized and excluded. Usually this was implemented, and is still implemented today, through techniques of integration and/or of pluralisation. The principle of universality, which until then was being promoted by overcoming many difficulties and obstacles and demoting the various local and particular differences, began to be seen as a principle of totalitarianism

---

[2] Zygmunt Bauman. *Postmodern Ethics*, Blackwell, 1995, p. 39
[3] Ibid., p. 41

where the state forcibly unifies, homogenizes and excludes.[4] It was believed that these totalitarian tendencies could be corrected by embracing ethnic or cultural diversity and perhaps even replacing them with more pluralism in all spheres of public life. Pluralism, however, despite of any tolerance and respect for diversity which it can bring, as a negation of unity, is only a reaction, led, perhaps under protest, by the discourse which privileges totality. Pluralisation opposes totalitarianism by presupposing it. Diversification and recognition of differences take place against a backdrop of universalisation and usually establishes a second, reflexive level of discourse, which cannot take place without recognition of totality, embedded in its foundation.

Pointedly, modernity proclaims the inclusion of all people into a presupposed citizenship and the equality of all citizens within the state. This is done by neutralizing differences. Many see the hidden roots of this neutralization in the tendency of the market to give quantified expression to qualitative characteristics through valuation. Qualitative differences are reduced to their monetary equivalence so that the natural movement of capital leads to homogenization, depersonalization, unification etc.[5] Nevertheless, although this tendency is maintained today (due to the logic of capital), a critique of homogenization has arisen proclaiming that general rules and laws which apply equally to all, as suggested in early modernity, do not sufficiently take into account individual or group characteristics. It is evident that differences are of utmost importance first of all for the marketing. In a globalizing world, the politics and culture of differences are in opposition to the culture and poli-

---

[4] According to most theorists, under totalitarianism there can not be real private life due to the state intervention in every aspect of the life of individuals; it is often omitted that under totalitarian rule life is always incurably dual—official, public, parade, on the one hand, and private, dissident, informal, on the other.

[5] For example, differences between women and men were neutralized in order for women to be included in the economic life as a workforce equal to men.

tics of unification and strive to replace them. In reality, however, as Bauman stresses, globalization processes go hand in hand with those of localization.⁶

As globalisation develops, the first indications to seize the attention of analysts are the openness of identity and the "fluidity" of the whole. Individuals and groups are understood as identification-processes and not as something pre-given or determined by static individual and/or group features which units them formally in a closed substantial whole. They are grasped rather as temporary "identifications", constructed and relatively mobile. Indeed, contemporary communities, unlike earlier ones, are based on pluralism as their own immanent principle to a much greater degree than before. Nowadays societies are multi-racial, multi-national, multi-ethnic, multi-cultural, etc. In such an environment of pluralisation, fragmentation, hybridization, universality as a symbol of humanity and human rights, if not entirely obsolete, is not sufficient on its own.

Formal justice which classifies particular cases under an universal law, is already unsatisfactory.⁷ In debates on the topics of universality and particularity, of formal equality and special rights, two different concepts prevail, often rendering mutually exclusive interpretations of the problem: (1) from the liberal perspective, according to which the citizen is an autonomous person whose rights and obligations are guaranteed and realised through public institutions and, (2) on the other hand, from the communitarian perspective, defining citizens through their membership in the community and their attitudes towards its values. In both cases, the relation between the individual and society remains, and

---

6 See Zygmunt Bauman. *Globalization: The Human Consequences*. Polity Press, 1998.
7 To continue with the example given above, it is believed that female workers should be granted special rights with regard to motherhood. In the same way the specificity of the group is considered for people with disabilities, immigrants, ethnic minorities, etc., receiving status and rights tailored to their needs and capabilities.

what has to be negotiated is how the particularity and universality of individuals and different groups can be reconciled in favour of their joint participation in the whole of society.

In this work social relation is perceived not as a connection between the individual and society (as this relation was habitually articulated and society was thought, and still is thought, as a totality stretching far beyond the individual), but is seen primarily as a relation of one individual *to* another. This does not mean that group and inter-group relations are ignored. Rather, we begin at the premise that the individual *in concreto* enters into relations with other individuals, and only then is connected *in abstracto* (i.e. through principle, by law, through the general notions, standards, norms) and therefore, indirectly, to social institutions, community, society and humanity as a whole.

This book will discuss an approach where the main relation is the interpersonal connection and in order to understand the whole, we proceed from intersubjectivity. The ultimate goal is not the understanding of the totality or of the individual within totality, but one's own responsibility for the Other as the primary human attitude toward him — on the base of it is composed totality. The whole is placed at the service of the Other (not of man in general, but the Other in its uniqueness); however, this service is always personalized as the totality itself cannot respond and act; always the individuals respond to other individuals, think and act. However, the I and the Other are not equal and intersubjectivity is not a reciprocal nor symmetrical relation. To quote Levinas, I always have one more responsibility than the Other. The responsibility for the Other is constitutive for my Self, while the responsibility of the Other for me is his own business. Totality, the state, society and community, obtain and update their meaning if the I, which embodies them as "individualized society" (a famous phrase of Pierre Bourdieu) behaves responsibly towards the Other. However, what does behaving responsibly mean?

This is a topic discussed throughout the text. For sure, goodness, responsibility and sociality represent the very selflessness of the relation to the Other wherein the loss of my identity and the achievement of a new one as a process of self-identification is a side effect of the communication. We can nevertheless state that it is due to one's responsibility that the Other has the opportunity to become a Self too (as in relation to the Third one). Only with the appearance of the Third do reflection and knowledge of relations emerge, followed by their institutionalization and transformation into possible values for "everyone".

Notwithstanding, all institutions and mechanisms of society are products of technology and namely as such are subordinated to the people. We support the thesis that the state machine, and any other public organisation, must be personalized in order to work. In the totality of society the I is exactly such a personalization, a subject bearing on his shoulders all the credentials, knowledge, competences etc. bestowed upon him by institutionalization. Still, for the I to be an I, it must use all the resources at its disposal to respond to others. The resources in any situation are utilised not just to take care of myself, i.e. of my own needs, interests, preferences, etc., but first of all to address to the needs of the Other. These resources are provided by society as a whole.

The human relationship between the Other and I begins with speech but before its beginning I hear the *call* from the Other (albeit a silent one). The I responds to this call not only with words, but above all with deeds. Words motivate actions and give meaning to practices that henceforth also matter for the Third and for each and every-one-else.

The advantages and disadvantages of social and political discourse in a pluralistic society are explicated and observed in the continuous debate between liberals and communitarians. The starting point for this work, however, is the notion that diversity as a philosophical category together with the principle of pluralism, become meaningful because of their implicit or/and explicit opposition to unity and totality. Pluralism's standing is fuelled by the criticism of the whole and, as such, is the negation of identity, of the principle, and of universality. Yet in its quality of negation and reaction, pluralism is a prisoner to this same principle. Pluralism cannot go beyond the framework set out by the boundaries of the whole and remains in the shadow of the concept of totality.

Departing from primarily empirical observations, both communitarians and liberals recognize that the universalist point of view ignores particularity and diversity of differences and is both illusory and utopian, leading to unattainable imaginings; such an universalism is also unjust—a finding that helps both communitarian and liberal critical pathos unfold. People inevitably examine emerging problems and participate in the course of events, influenced by their life-experience as well as by their perception of social reality. According to Bourdieu, their story is the unconscious which appears in public as different habitual practices. These differences are not only the result of a clash of interests and the employment of different tactics of self-defence, but are also the product of their socioeconomic and cultural backgrounds which determines different perceptions and understanding of public relations and order as well as differing motivations of their thought and (in)action. When preference is given to particular differences, we can easily fall into the trap of fragmentation. In fragmentation and heterogeneity, with even greater force than in unification, we find the exclusion of individuals and groups defined as different by empowered some private interests, claiming, however, to be "common" and even "universal". In a pluralised society, people are not forced "to improve, develop, elevate, perfect themselves" according to some universal standard in the attempt to catch up with the "more improved, developed and perfected" groups and societies, but are left to "be what they are". A large number of these groups, however, are factually in the position of being the weaker, marginalized, suffering from deprivations, often repressed and without the right to voice their opinion and therefore also lacking many other rights. Pluralized, fragmented and atomized social environments immediately benefit powerful groups (as is clearly seen for example in disputes over the minority rights). Both concepts of citizenship, liberal and communitarian, insist that it is necessary to take into account the individual and/or group needs and desires to meet our moral obligation to arrange group and individual interests in accordance with the common good making sure that everyone is provided with the opportunity for participation. As Bourdieu critically notes, monopoly over the universal continues to gain supporters and to legitimize itself with the values of neutrality and universal recognition. Hence the age-long issue of monopolization of the right to speak on behalf of a group and of the privileged perspective appears. Even when the emphasis is not put on the "common goal", but placed instead on differences, where everyone contributes precisely according to their particularity to the shared work, the shared meaning is constituted by the commonality of them all. If we resign from the common, it is not clear how the principle of justice could be conceptualized and implemented. Inevitably the question arises whether, how and why people should be treated differently and conversely, the question of whether, how and why people should be put under a common denominator. This work is not a rejection of the categories of "whole", "total", "private", "single", "similarity", "difference", "equality", etc., but rather, it is an attempt to present a different logic of relations between them. This seems more appropriate in articulating social constructions and opens other opportunities for discourse in the field of social and political philosophy.

In this text, we will show as a weakness the conceptions of both communitarians and liberals in their attempts to define social bonds as unifications or oppositions inside a presupposed totality. Within this totality the individuals or groups are preconceived as monads, but open to conversing with one another. Their conversation is always mediated by the common language. Social coherence is perceived firstly as belonging to a type based on shared characteristics, i.e. a relation to others with whom one feels affiliated or "the same", unlike "the others" in respect of whom we emphasize our essential difference. These distinctive similarities or differences as a sign of solidarity or conflict make people recognize each other or group together. The essentialist approach is hence maintained even when insisting that group affiliation is a matter of free choice (liberalism) or interactive recognition (communitarianism). It could be argued that the alternative to the essentialist approach is to be sought by identifying individuals and groups being in a network of relations of responsibilities and not in their definition as substances according to a principle (such as repeatability, universality, law, similarity, etc.). The premise that essence is not predetermined and insurmountable, but acquired and transient because of the roles we perform or, perhaps, as the task of self-constitution that everyone sets, does not break with the substantialist or essentialist approach. Inevitably, in the process of ongoing self-constitution and self-assertion, people are free (although their freedom is limited) to determine the group to which they belong and therefore the qualities they possess, but this kind of self-identification presupposes, without explanation, preserving the opposition between "mine" and "other", "own" and "other, "my rights versus yours". This also leads to the issue of identification through ownership (own and other's), and thus participation in the creation of or/and in the division of totality. Hence even if human essence is not "facticity", but "openness", there is a new conflict in addition to that of the universal/particular, i.e. whole and part—the problem of "the otherness and mineness". Thus a categorization of our relations and interactions comes forth which, to a certain extent, is more fundamental than the division between universal/particular or common/individual. Both in theory and in practice, the universal/particular division involves separation of mine from the other's. Inside the totality, even when it is in the process of its becoming, alienation from the mine-ness and the difficulties in integrating the other-ness (to accept and assimilate otherness or at least recognize, tolerate or ignore it) impede communication and interaction. From a philosophical perspective it seems the category of "otherness" is the one that creates problems.

Both communitarians and liberals define otherness in relation to the principle (the norm, the majority, law, etc.) or through mutual commensurability (which also presupposes *a priori* common standard, common measurement unit etc., even when one of the comparable entities is used as such and is imposed on the others). The starting point is the law of identity and after experiencing the peripetia of the play with otherness, there is a return to it. As others have been originally excluded from the class of the same, it is very difficult to find the way back to cohesion and inclusion in an extended community (whether a community of representation, recognition or common practices). This simply shows that neither liberals nor "defenders of community" have cut the umbilical cord with early modern ways of thinking. Such a conclusion applies both to those who today consciously uphold the continuation of the project of modernity and to those who relentlessly oppose it. The reflex of absorption of the alterity and its integration into the whole, with which the Self is identified (as a part or as an outsider), has been preserved in many even to this day. It emerged in modernity's discourse and reached its profound justification in Hegelian philosophy where the Other is assimilated, based on the identity of opposites (differences), as it occurred and still occurs *de facto* in society. Those who oppose such an assimilation reach at most neutrality towards otherness, tolerance to others and eventually indifference to differences. Today, on the one hand, diversity is promoted and encouraged, yet on the other hand, due to the preliminary opposition of viewpoints, new attempts are being made to collectivize differences by uniting them into a cohesive whole by fusing horizons. This is attempted through dialogue, consensus, demand for tolerance, monitoring of human rights, recognition, etc. Well, sometimes people with a pretention to be open-minded tend to abandon cohesion which for them is not obligatory: let differences remain differences and others remain others, let us rejoice in diversity and enjoy variety, but on one condition—differences should not create problems for us and must obey the universal law and the constitution adopted "in the name of all".

Serious philosophical criticism of universality stems not from the attack of totalitarianism, as is usual in the field of politics, but rather from elsewhere, i.e. from ethical considerations. As summarized by Bauman, the fact of the matter is that moral impulses and restrictions were neutralized in modernity and perceived as irrelevant[8], hence men and women were given the opportunity to perform inhumane deeds without ever feeling inhumane. After a review of the literature on these topics it could be concluded that by challenging modern ideals in terms of the antinomies attained in postmodernity, most philosophers' and theorists' attention hovers mainly around ethical issues.

We try to defend herein a new understanding of primary sociality, and hence of primary community based on the **responsibility** of the I in relation to the Other and not on the **affiliation** of individuals to the whole. The I is in the process of identification through the responsibilities it undertakes. This presupposes a new conception of subjectivity and freedom as well of the protection of human rights, based not on our group or individual selfishness, but above all on the responsibility for the rights of the Other, which is the authentic concern for him. It is not about responsibility which is sought after by virtue of reflection and court proceedings, when acts have already been performed (e.g. judicially), but rather about the sensitivity and the preliminary consideration of what my deeds would mean to others in my relationship with them.[9]

---

[8] Zygmunt Bauman. *Life in Fragments*. Blackwell, 1995, p. 197
[9] Responsibility precedes freedom of the subsequent action and it is thus different from arbitrariness, understood as pure spontaneity and therefore irresponsibility.

Some may argue, and rightly so, that this is the Kantian approach to universalization, which requires the maxim of my behaviour to comply in advance with the others so that it becomes an universal law for everyone's actions. There is, however, an essential difference: for Kant the Self is the starting point, while in our proposed approach we start with the Other and thereby follow Levinas. Clearly, such a perspective cannot be sustained unless we rethink our conceptions of communication and dialogue, justice and law, morality and citizenship. It is important to understand this change in perspective, which can be summed up in the words of Levinas as "we" is not the plural of "I", because the Other is not another I for me; the Other is "I" only for himself. He exists by himself, is significant for himself and is not just the bearer of the significance that I attribute to him. The Other is not perceived as negativity—as enemy, rival, boundary, barrier to the freedom of the Self; on the contrary—he is perceived as positivity. What does this mean? What constitutes the positivity of the Other with his otherness is a topic at the centre of the entire analysis at hand. Even in this foreword we could state that the positivity of otherness is not evaluated in accordance with the possibilities it opens for me, i.e. is not assessed in the light of instrumental thinking in which the Other is reduced to his usefulness for my Self. It is also necessary to rethink the concept of community in disagreement with what is already assumed in philosophy:

1. Community is not made up of the multiplication of transcendental subjects whose only commonality is the fact that each one is constituted as self-consciousness through "I think which is accompanies all my ideas and representations";
2. In a community we do not treat the Other with respect for the sake of some abstract humanism, i.e. according to the universal law (Kant's imperative), but in view of his empirical or historical presence in all

his particularity and moreover—in all his singularity. In early modern philosophy and German idealism the Other's particularity is the boundary of mine;
3. Community is not the universal substance-subject, i.e., that which has historically become whole, wherein self-consciousness is the distinction that is not actually distinction, as any difference is created by the absolute subject to distinguish itself from itself (Hegel).

These forms of understanding of community and human co-existence are being opposed by both liberals and communitarians, starting from the empirical differences to find a theoretical, moral and/or legal basis to reconcile them. Both liberals and communitarians want to see in the Other a partner despite him being my frontier and, in fact, namely because the Other is my frontier. Let's remind ourselves that albeit interpreted differently nowadays, reconciliation is the last chord since Hegel's philosophical symphony. But even as per the noblest and most generous motivation towards the Other, when efforts are focused mainly on ensuring the recognition of his otherness, liberals and communitarians put the Other at best on my level, beside me, next to "me", "shoulder to shoulder with me" (which of course is not below or after me). Unfortunately, in these efforts their ultimate refuge is egalitarianism. Liberals and communitarians believe that to achieve equal opportunities for the individual and group autonomy respectively, differences should be reduced to mutual recognition. The thought of the Other being superior to me (or us) is not allowed, because it almost instinctively identifies with a relationship of domination and subordination. Conversely, in this work we maintain Levinas' conception that the Other is one to whom my existence is in service (even when I do not want this consciously) and that this kind of attitude is not slavery to, but responsibility for, the Other. This is the way in which the existence of the Self, who is "for the Other" acquires a social dimension. The I becomes "Self" due to its answers to others. Only in this manner can sociality transcend naturality and sense can transcend non-sense. Here the Other is Transcendence, but

> [the] Other is not transcendent because he will be free as I am; on the contrary his freedom is a superiority that comes from his very transcendence. ... he overflows absolutely every idea I can have for him.[10]

The freedom of the Other is not a limitation on my freedom as in the interpretation of community as a formal centralized entity. In the social whole, according to the usual individualistic-atomistic conception, the individual has more freedom when least restricted by others and accordingly, when being able to impose most limits on their freedom. Freedom defined as independence from others—from their customs, beliefs, prejudices, community attachments and tradition in general—stems from the beginning of the modern epoch, unfolding later in the concept of autonomy, where the subject itself sets the law which it must follow. However, since the whole always has limits, everyone experiences the Other as a constraint and an obstacle. So one's autonomy is inevitably opposed to the others'. The more independent the individual is, the greater his ability to achieve his chosen objectives, the wider the scope of his activities and the more successful his self-realization. But since the opposite side, the other individual also seeks its maximum realization within the space of their interaction, the expansionist claims of the One clash with those of the Other. Thus one's freedom is inevitably an obstacle to the freedom of the Other and vice versa. To be honest, however, let us point out that today's neo-liberal and communitarian concepts aim to underline the relations of cooperation, not competition and this topic will be discussed in more detail in the third chapter.

In this work, the category of freedom, understood as autonomy, will be deprived of the privileged position it has acquired. The concept of

---

[10] Emmanuel Levinas. *Totality and Infinity*. Duquesne University Press, 1992, Pittsburg, p. 87

heteronomy has been thrown "overboard" by Kantian philosophy. Here Kant's definition of self-determination is re-examined for the purpose of the rehabilitation of heteronomy. The very autonomy of the Self is understood differently, specifically as a response to a heteronomous request by the Other. And the notion of heteronomy is also changed as it is not anymore understood as despotism over the individual but as the Other's appeal to me. It is more accurate to say that protecting the freedom of the Other, and his right to be his Self, empowers me as an autonomous subject to act, i.e. to "respond to and for the Other." My behaviour acquires its importance and focus not according to the law which I establish for myself but in response to the presence of the Other. Otherwise my expression of freedom would be just a rash act of spontaneity, a whim, and falls under the rubric of arbitrariness and the instrumentalisation of others. Even the Kantian categorical imperative cannot be a cure for these two malignant mutations. If the Kantian imperative requires universalization of the maxim I follow, being the expression of my will and claiming to express the rationality of humanity in general, then it should extend to others as equally valid for them. However, such a claim for postulating an universal moral law imposed by me on everybody else would represent a danger rather than a solution. It is necessary to take into account the demands and the situation of others in advance as they motivate my behaviour accordingly — not just in their capacity of noumenal beings, but in response to their otherness. The question is how such consideration is possible and/or realistic.

If we assume, as proposed here, that autonomy should be the answer to heteronomy—heteronomy, identified with the call of the Other which questions the spontaneity of my will—the issue appears whether we give up all normativity and the very concepts of freedom and justice as they are understood by Kant and in modern discourse in general. Isn't the principle, protecting the individual autonomy of all individuals, the precondition for any legislation and any justice? This work gives a negative answer to these questions, not, however, by rejecting these categories. The ambition advocated here is the promotion of a new understanding of them.

Aristotle believed justice to be the highest virtue and injustice the greatest evil man could commit against his fellow citizens. However, whilst agreeing with Aristotle on this point, we ask ourselves whether our life together can have another more fundamental and important meaning, different from that to which we are accustomed, namely, that the polis is the whole in which we all participate (according to our status of free citizens and our functions in the system) and it is only this participation which gives sense to individual human life. The question is whether such an inclusion exhausts the meaning of "togetherness". This paper argues that the constitution of togetherness as an interpersonal relation preceded its organization into a unity, as unity implies sameness or uniformity according to a certain pattern of categorization, while togetherness owes its creation to the very differences that exist before the establishment of unity. Moreover, unity itself might impose a new kind of tyranny—universalization, homogenization, depersonalization. Depersonalization however could be overcome if the resources of such a formal unity allow for the Self to support the Other in his otherness, and not to enter into confrontation with him. Then, through the responsibility for and cooperation with the Other an authentic totality appears in contrast to the mere formal totality.[11]

Aristotle believed our sameness was the result of our participation as free citizens in making decisions concerning the polis.[12] A point to be

---

[11] Only just then, the Self moves aside of its position to be the performer of a social role into such formal totality and could find itself reflecting upon itself (that is, upon its answers) but rather as a by-product.

[12] As is known, free citizens at that time were actually not all, but only a small group of the male population and their freedom was the highest privilege. Totality as such is always constituted by the privileged perspective of some who claim and /or identify themselves as common representation.

made here is that before our participation in the hierarchy and the organization of the whole of the polis, we participate in interpersonal relations that are primary when compared to institutional and organizational links. Or better, they are the base of them. The primordial need for communication between different individuals (e.g. between child and adult, worker and employer, employee and client, doctor and patient, etc.—not only between those with equal status as free citizens and the operators of the system) is driven precisely by their differences. At first they are not depending on a particular whole. Before being mediated, the human link is immediate: because one needs the other, they meet. The second party is necessary for the first party precisely because it has something to give to the first party, taking into account its specific condition as needing—advice, favour, protection, security, information, etc. Namely this alterity creates the primary community between them which is further expanded due to repetition, regularity and regulation, i.e., institutionalization. But the institutionalization is demanded when the third, the forth and each one in his turn can enter into the similar relationship—then it can be structured in order to facilitate and make more effective their contacts. However, if the relation between the One and the Other is organized and institutionalized, it can be beneficial but can also abandon its original function and become an obstacle to such contacts.

* * *

Probably the pioneer of such an innovative understanding of togetherness, prioritizing the interpersonal, is Martin Buber, whose main theme is dialogue. Philosophy before him was monological, unlike the new trend founded by him which emphasized the dialogical form of human history and culture.¹³ The basic movement in monological life is reflection, where the I retreats into itself. Buber insists that although the alterity of the Other touches my soul, it is in no way inside it, so as to allow the different one to exist only as my experience just being "part of myself."¹⁴ In philosophy based on the dialogic principle, the "I–Thou" relationship is separated from the "I–It" relation and meeting with the Other is the event which marks the beginning of togetherness. Only afterwards does this event drive the reflection of the Self, so that "I-Thou" can become the "I-It" relation.

In the tradition of the older idealistic philosophy, where only the subject-object relationship is present, the object (It) has an ambiguous status: it is transcendent in relation to the knowing Self; whilst on the other hand, as a result of the activity of consciousness, it is transformed into immanence, into an idea. This duality has given rise to the creation of many different theories of the subject-object relationship, but is nevertheless adopted as a model in monological philosophy. In these theories every thought and movement of the Self is reflection and self-reflection, and language is simply an additional factor, considered only as a means of expression and objectification of inner experiences. However, in his philosophy of dialogue Martin Buber examines language and communication in a different manner. The most important for language is addressing the Other as "Thou". The "I-Thou" creates the world of the relationship, while the "I–It" is the experience. Experience is the world of the

---

[13] Some might say that ancient Greek culture was dialogical, but this can be argued for dialogue then, in Plato's version at least, was "midwifery" of truth, a task impossible without the meditation of ideas. Socrates is the one who led a dialogue by asking questions, and henceforth he received from the interlocutor only what seemed known to him already and in the question itself contained. What comes to the inquiring one as if from outside, actually comes to him from within and is understandable there, so it is rather remembering. This is how Plato defined thinking.

[14] Martin Buber. Dialogue. *Between Man and Man*. Routledge (London& New York: 1993), p. 26–27.

Self—it is "in the Self" and not between the Self and the world, because the world does not have a share in experience. The world is studied but it does not invest in this experiential learning anything of itself and nothing is returned in tribute. Buber argues that the event of the meeting "I–Thou" is reciprocity, incompatible with the act of cognition. Plus that in Buber's works, the I in the "I–Thou" and in the "I–It" relation is not the same "I".

In Levinas' works "I" and "You" are not equal and reciprocal (as one might claim upon reading Buber). The basic speech as "I-Thou" is the condition for the occurrence of any language, and the "I–It" relationship is a derivative of it. The "I-It" relationship is also language, but—as is perceived here, unlike Buber's position—it is the language, denoting things in the world, that is residual and the dependent on of the "I–Thou" relation.

In the dialogic line of philosophizing the subject-subject relationship precedes as well as transcends (both chronologically and logically) the subject-object relationship. For the purposes of this work, however, such a statement would be extremely botched. To understand what constitutes its weakness it is necessary to take into account the concept that dialogue is not a reciprocal relation between equal subjects. That is Levinas' lesson: there is no original equality between I and Thou. More likely, the formulation "I-Thou" is maybe inadequate. The relation between the Other and the I started precisely because of the original inequality and difference between the two. For Levinas, all social connections arise from the moral relation between the Other and me, which is asymmetrical and non-reciprocal, even when—as with tyranny, despotism and all other forms of violence against the Other—in this asymmetry and non-reciprocity, morality is seemingly rejected. Moral responsibility, in its most extreme and exaggerated form, is substituting the Other by me.[15] The fundamental difference between the Other and myself—the difference from which all other differences originate—is precisely my exclusive responsibility, which does not cease to face the alterity of the Other. The moral "I" does not cease to question what, how and why the other is the Other and how to respond to his otherness but this means to question my own identification and responsibility. The moral subject, according to Levinas, by its responsibility weaves the net of closeness and togetherness.

Unlike Buber's conception which remains substantialist (although not the beings but the meeting is substantiated), for Levinas my identity is not born from my participation in the space of the meeting or the community anymore, but from my identification (being the chosen one) as sole and irreplaceable bearer of responsibility for the Other (others). The Self takes this responsibility as it fall on to him without any expectations of sharing, reciprocity or reversibility of the relationship (although this can happen, but is not determining factor in the interpersonal relationship; sometimes it is presumed that, in totality of society, taking risks and responsibility will be compensated with the mediating function of the state, by the justice of institutional order, due to tradition or custom etc.). Togetherness does not imply equality, multiplication and a collection of elements indifferent to one another, although aggregated on the basis of their similarity; it implies non-in-difference of the One towards the Other precisely because they are not equal, equivalent and interchangeable at the very beginning of the social relationship.

In the dialogical line of philosophizing there are other branches besides the one of Buber and Levinas, but as a rule they remain supportive of totality. Two of them are the hermeneutics of Hans-Georg Gadamer which largely reproduces the Hegelian logic and favours the creation of

---

[15] Levinas believes that hyperbolization, i.e. bringing something to the possible extreme, is the most appropriate method by which one can delineate the meanings of human relations in their pure form.

Sociality and Justice: Toward Social Phenomenology 27

a common horizon in the dialogue and the theory of communicative action of Jürgen Habermas, which relies on consensus. Although they emphasize openness in dialogue, these paradigms are based on the old division of part/whole, i.e. particular/universal, with the premise that unity and totality represent a higher achievement. The relationship between mine and not mine replaces the relationship between the Other and me. Hence individuals acquire the status of elements or stages in the process of speech and only in the light of the result of the conversation do they obtain adequate significance. Buber states that:

> ... [according to the] reigning modern perspective ... in the end, only the so-called objectives, or rather collectives are real, and individuals are given meaning only as workers or tools for collectives.[16]

Conversely, it is held here that individuals have significance, created in communication without resorting to the teleologism of unity. The Other is the beginning of communication (not I, nor every one, and neither the universal transcendental subject) and he has a significance which is not obtained from his participation in the totality but itself makes this social totality possible, understandable and meaningful by the provoking (to be more precise—by the investing) of sociality in the I. The I as "individualized society" allows and helps the Other to be admitted to the conversation. But because of the remoteness and elusiveness of the Other, on the one hand, and the position "here and now" (which corresponds to the present, including protention and retention, using the terminology of Husserl) of my I, on the other hand, we participate differently in the interaction. The Other and my I play a completely different role in the drama of human being-here.

Thus, this work does not follow the stances and solutions in Habermas' critical theory or Gadamer's hermeneutics, but rather relies on

---

[16] Ibid., p. 83

achievements in phenomenology. In the phenomenological paradigm after Husserl's *Cartesian Meditations*, the division is no longer based on the principle "I and the Totality", present throughout entire modern culture, but on the transcendental asymmetrical intersubjective relation. This is, as already pointed out, a different categorization which sets a new depth of philosophical discourse not only by not giving up, but rather developing the tradition of Continental philosophy.

The goal of this book is, by building on the work of Levinas, to show a new perspective in the phenomenological paradigm which does not focus on the self-reflection of the thinking subject, but on his sociality as a "responsibility for the Other." The conversation may be taken as a model, in which the features of social bond are primordially exhibited. The difference between saying and said (Levinas) creates the matrix of all other relations. Sociality, however, occurs in interpersonal relation of the One to the Other and not just as a common characteristic inherent, "by nature" or *a priori*, equally in all individuals in the human kind. To convert the asymmetric and non-reciprocal relation into a symmetrical and reciprocal one we need the Third. Then in the true sense of the word we can talk about the social relation between them. The presence of the Third alongside the Second invokes the question of institutionalization and justice, which is central to any humanitarian discourse and every society. Here the Third is a name for "everyone", for third persons—he, she, they—who are excluded from the immediacy of the relationship, establishing the narrow space only between the Other and me. The Third suggests mediation. This is, as we know, already problematized in a certain way territory, at least since Hegel.[17]

---

[17] Hegel himself has even gone as far as to declare that any immediacy is actually mediacy, i.e. that immediacy is always a platitude as long as it is considered as a pure result, that is, not in view of the road or the method by which it is achieved.

This new perspective in philosophy relying on intersubjectivity can be called **social phenomenology**. It tries to restore the rights of immediacy, not as a cognitive category of sensation and knowledge, as it is traditionally conceived, but as a moral category for the primordial relation to the Other. Broadly speaking, we support the thesis that morality as responsibility for others is the "alpha and omega" of the human way of being, even when everything in the human world has turned against morality and people question its sense.[18] The thing is however, that morality is not a necessity that can be satisfied or not—we are used to hearing that morality is a highly spiritual need. We attempt to show that morality— not as a moral code, different for different communities and epochs, but as responsibility—is the deepest root of any human association. Society as an entity with all its branches, institutions and relations would have died without morality. Justice, before becoming a category of social philosophy, is an ethical category, absolutely unavoidable in the vast area inhabited by more or less distant others. They are multitude (sometimes completely foreign, unknown and anonymous) and responsibility in such a plan is implemented only through the establishment and maintenance of just institutions in the scale of the whole society. But justice ceases to be justice if we stop to ask whether it is just enough, i.e. how far it stands from moral holiness. Justice inhabits firstly the space between one, the other and the third, and then, it settles in their relation to the law.

* * *

The field of the intelligible, the meaningful to which we adhere by in our everyday life and the tradition of our philosophical and scientific thought, is characterized by seeing. The structure of seeing which has as

---

[18] Throughout this text, unlike in Hegelian philosophy, there is no distinction between the categories of morality and ethics—they are used as synonyms.

its object or theme the seen (the so called intentional structure) is found in all forms of perception and thus intentionality is present in any reasonable approach to everything in the world, including in the way human beings interact. "Intentions" also play a decisive role between beings that speak between themselves or, as we say, see one another[19] or know each other by paying attention to the other, putting their knowledge in some kind of language form. This is the ordinary way of understanding language. It is necessary to take into account, however, that in speaking, knowledge and seeing, we resort to signs which being communicated to others, go beyond the pure ego-logical summation of the signified into representation or theme. Here arises the problem of the motivation of this communication carried out through the use of signs. Is language important only by what is said, that is, by the sentences in different moods, by the content of the statements, instructions and descriptions, by the pure relaying on information that can be recorded and objectified in language forms after being said? Is it not important through its other functions where not just ideas and messages matter but the most significant is the contact with the Other, which in all forms of speech and action, as we will see later, is of paramount importance.

The stake for modern philosophy throughout its existence is truth. "I think" was the certainty of the "I". Thinking about thinking, all this tradition which is broader than philosophy and characterizes the culture of modern times, suggest that thought as such leads us to the deepest interiority declared as the beginning and therefore as the principle, i.e. subjectivity. Speaking is also interpreted as one of the activities of the I, being the subject. But today we see how speaking leads us onto other paths, guiding us to that "outside" which "commands" speech and where the speaking subject seems to disappear because of the said. As if modern philosophy anticipates the danger looming over traditional attitudes,

---

[19] In the long tradition of European philosophy seeing and understanding are often identified.

Sociality and Justice: Toward Social Phenomenology 31

when the experience of language takes the place of the self-evidence of "I think". Language requires two people—the one who emits signs into circulation and the one that should receive them, i.e. the addressing party on the one hand, and the addressee on the other. Due to this shift of focus—from thinking of thinking subject to the other of thinking and the Other in speaking—philosophy begins to finally comprehend, albeit gradually and slowly, throughout the entire 20th century, a language feature that was earlier not noticed: dialogism. True dialogue is quite different from the internal dialogue or monologue as conversation of the soul with itself (Plato), precisely because in conversation with the Other, the interlocutor is not reduced to my idea of him, but is a face to me. This is a relation precisely to his otherness, not to be an object of my perception and seeing; the collocutor is not the one who because of the universal and unifying reason (seeing) is understood as the same as me, like me, the present, a being among other beings, a thing among other things, spatially existent before me. In speech, my attention to the Other humanises him. The Other is present for me in a way in which the I is not present for itself. The Other is different in his own way and this difference calls for my attention and conversation with him.

* * *

If in the early modern epoch priority was placed on knowledge, production and creativity, the epoch of late modernity or post-modernity pays much more attention to communication and its forms. The exclusive primary place thinking and work, and generally human activity occupied in modern philosophy is now reserved to language and communication. If earlier the very process of communication was seen as a kind of human knowledge and practice, now the practice itself, knowledge and even thinking are viewed as a kind of communication. The point is not to remove one of those two moments under the scheme "either/or" (either communication or activity), but to analyse their role in the creation and re-creation of social relations. Of course, people produce their living conditions, public institutions and themselves due to their own activity, ensuring the reproduction of the social totality. But we maintain here that communication, by defining the motives and meaning of human activity, is primary to instrumentality and determination of actions and interactions. Before reifying, objectifying and transcending oneself through his actions, one learns about the existence of transcendence, including the transcendence of the objective world due to his meeting with the alterity of the Other where also the source of all understanding is.

Conceiving himself as a limited being, the individual has always wanted to be correlated with a reality beyond his own boundaries. Looking back through the centuries, we see how the individual was identified with a totality (as its element), precisely because it always exceeded by far the limits of his capabilities. He saw himself as an component of its order and subject to its universal laws, even if—as in Kant, and many philosophers after him—the individual himself was declared the legislator, though no longer of a pre-given totality, but of one constituted and designed by man himself. Any such totality has always been and is still thought in terms of its universal laws or principles—natural, social, moral, etc.—but by whom? By man, identified with the reason, in the stance of an "objective observer", almost having occupied the vacant throne of all-seeing and judging God—this is the conception of early modernity. Even though Kant warns us in *Critique of Pure Reason* of the transcendental illusion, which we ourselves create, but which is inevitable, i.e. the illusion that we can embrace the whole of the experience constitutively, with the help of principles in order to understand it as a totality. Further, in the language of Marx's critique of German philosophy it could be added that people really felt themselves participants in the unity of reality, i.e. subjects to its universal laws, universalizing their own ideas and concepts as well their own essence. Or, put in the aphoristic language of Pierre Bourdieu and from another angle, the universal is always the object of universalized recognition:

> The universal is the object of an official recognition and the recognition universally given to the sacrificing of selfish interests (especially economic ones) universally favours the strategies of universalization, through the undeniable symbolic profits it provides. [20]

However, since faith in the universal turns out to be problematic, since (to quote Buber) the individual feels "socially and cosmically homeless", since he has no hope that by self-reification, he would transcend himself towards universality, the question of transcendence is exceptionally acute. The entire history of the modern West is regarded as a destruction of the piety before Transcendence by destroying Transcendence itself. The problem is that the legitimacy of universally valid norms, imperatives, laws, etc. (which were actually extrapolation of human limitations or of one or another private interest, prejudice, belief or conviction) is put under question. The particular was seen as one or another absolute, expanded to the scale of the universal, i.e. to the principle of the whole. This work maintains the conception that true transcendence is not predominantly the Whole to which one relates as subject to object and in which one is eventually absorbed but that the true transcendence is the other human. Transcendence of the external world—of nature, community, society, the artefacts of culture, etc.—appears and is understood only through the correlation of the I with the transcendence of the Other.

It seems that the first one to reach this insight into the Other's transcendence is Husserl but in his phenomenology the Other is just my *Alter Ego*. The Other's subjectivity is created by analogy with my subjectivity in my own immanence, but is loaded by me with transcendence and with the sign of otherness. Conversely, this work does not support Husserl's

---

[20] Pierre Bourdieu. *Pascalian Meditations*. Stanford University Press, 2000, p. 125

conception about the otherness of the Other, particularly, because the Other is met and not constituted; the I and the Other are in an asymmetrical intersubjective bond in the event of the meeting. This bond, although bilateral, at least in its primary form is not reciprocal and the Other is not derived from and described by analogy with myself. The relationship between the Other and me in the meeting is not the same as the relationship between my I and the Other. The path from the Other towards me is not the same as the path from me towards the Other. It could also be said that in this primordial intersubjective relationship there is no interchangeability.

In the many attempts to articulate this relationship, Emmanuel Levinas' thinking is of extraordinary importance. We should pay tribute to him for the introduction into philosophy of the primordial sociality of the subject, which is neither reduced to nor is derived from the participation of the individual in a preliminary established social totality. The involvement of the individual in the community and society is rather due to this asymmetrical and irreversible relation between the Other and me, where precisely the key to sociality is found.

* * *

When in the history of philosophy a new perspective is proposed, it cannot be represented as a mere clash of arguments "for" and "against", because it would presuppose a tacit prior agreement on paradigmatic coordinates. In philosophy, however, a challenge of an already established paradigm or interpretation of the world (this is the critical function of philosophical thinking), and the proposal for a new understanding (which is the constructive work in philosophy) are inseparable. That is why the history of philosophy is a never-ending conversation between different schools and thinkers who follow and at the same time criticise each other.

But in any newly emerged philosophy, redefining even one of the fundamental concepts leads to shifting of layers, to changing of the relations between them and this requires a new and different reading of all concepts. However, in this way they can become completely unrecognizable to those who adhere to previous systems of meanings. The all difficulty both within philosophical and non-philosophical discourse, stems from the fact that each original philosophy names things in its own and different way (and things can exist for our thinking and speech, as well as for our action, only in so far as they have received meanings or names, in so far as they are designated and indicated) and this sometimes incomprehensible newly emerging language needs inevitably translation, comparisons and often returning to the very beginnings and original sources. Precisely because of speech diversity the presentation of a new perspective requires the hard work of translation, interpretation and commentary. Such is the genre of this philosophical text. It corresponds to what is called "research" in the field of science.

Method or the next step:
From Existential toward Social Phenomenology

The underlying principle in Husserl's phenomenology could be summarized as follows using Levinas' words:

> The thought [le pensé] — object, theme, meaning — refers back to the thought [la pensée] that thinks it, but also determines the subjective articulation of its appearing: being determines its phenomena.[21]

According to phenomenology, everyday thinking and science deal with abstractions built not on proofs but on beliefs. It is believed that objects and other people exist as parts of the world. It is also believed that the

---

[21] Emmanuel Levinas. Nonintentional Consciousness. *Entre Nous: Thinking-of-the-Other.* Columbia University Press, New York, 1998, p. 123

thinking subject in a similar way is a part of the world. Husserl calls taking the world for granted the "natural attitude". The world itself, being totality of all existing things, is approached as a self-sufficient entity. Belief in the existence of the world implicitly underlies every action directed to the objects within the world's horizon. Husserl sees this attitude as naïve. Its naivety consists in a disposition of trust towards the being of the encompassing without any preliminary questions or doubts. Everyday understanding and scientific abstraction likewise, engulfed into their attention towards objects, are unable to see the structure of knowledge itself and determine the proper location of objects within the horizon of consciousness from which they derive their meaning. However, according to Husserl's phenomenological approach, the meaning of the object to which consciousness is directed by virtue of its inner intentionality, cannot be accessed while living in the midst of things with our attention riveted by and we only work with objects and the experiences of consciousness. The question for Husserl is how to understand the fact that something is grasped in cognition and becomes an object of consciousness. Whether objectivity disappears and turns into something subjective? According to transcendental phenomenology, we need to study the life of consciousness itself. Instead of just living life, we must ask ourselves what constitutes its meaning, what kind of intentions are engaged in different types of experience, what is their structure, how do they relate and in general how is our life-world constituted.

Husserl undertook the task of deciding how thinking, although governed by its own laws, is consistent with external reality. His conception of consciousness evokes that we do not experience any mental objects in the form of images or symbols that represent real objects, but we in fact experience the actual objects; therefore, the logic of thinking is not autonomous legislation but corresponds to the shape of being itself. To clarify the meaning of the transcendence of the outside world is to understand the intention of thinking and the way it constitutes the transcendental object. To understand transcendence we must understand the acts of thinking which constitute it. We need to examine what characteristics the actions of consciousness possess when its object is given as really existing and what these actions are, if the objects are present only as phenomena. Consciousness is not just directed at its objects, it places them as existing.

However, the concrete being is not what exists for a single consciousness only and for Husserl the idea of being contains the idea of the intersubjective world. Hence in Husserl's philosophy, the Other appears and with him the problem of world constitution, not from the perspective of the single I, but in terms of transcendental intersubjectivity.

Levinas gratefully acknowledges that Husserl's philosophy was the source of inspiration for his own works. Intentional analysis rediscovered the horizons of meanings that everyday and scientific thinking had forgotten. The intentionality of consciousness, the concepts and the idea of the horizon of meaning played a crucial role in his explorations. Unlike Husserl, who was primarily interested in theoretical knowledge, thought, perception, subjectivity, the process of constitution, etc., or rather, in the epistemological and ontological meaning of existence, Levinas was more focused on what in the tradition of Western philosophy is labelled "practical philosophy." Levinas assigned a primary role to our relation to others and his phenomenology led to a way of articulating philosophical problems that was completely different from Husserl's. Metaphysics, according to Levinas, is neither ontology, nor epistemology but ethics.

Husserl's influence on Levinas took place, not only directly, but also with the mediation of Heidegger's fundamental ontology. Martin

Heidegger was the pioneer in existentialist interpretation of phenomenology[22]. He was the one amongst Husserl's students who modified Husserl most and determined all of its subsequent developments. His book *Being and Time* (1927) marked the beginning of a new era not only in phenomenology but in Continental philosophy in general.

Heidegger regarded metaphysics, i.e. philosophy, not as a doctrine of abstract-positive thinking nor as a dialectical system of speculative thinking, but as a kind of thinking on the meaning of Being, i.e. being as a way of life for the individual and of humanity. Existential-phenomenological philosophy, as we know, deals with the human condition as existing in the world together with others. It is common knowledge that this philosophy as critique of *Das Man* opposes the emergence of mass society with its mass communications, mass industrialization and technologization, mass culture and mass (dis)orientation, i.e. the crisis of the humanity. There is a great temptation according to existentialists to live faceless, indistinguishable in the crowd, to feel comfortable and safe in the anonymity, lost in the complacency of the successful resolution of everyday worries, escaping from freedom and responsibility and relating oneself only with the average standards involving social adaptation. The individual ceases to be an anonymous participant in the human crowd and becomes him/herself thanks to the responsibility which a man from the crowd is trying to escape. The responsibility is the central motif that is common to all phenomenological philosophy. In Husserl's theory it is found as responsibility for scientific truth and in Heidegger's as a responsibility to the truth of Being; Sartre argues that it is the responsibility for the individual's own choices and actions and in Levinas' concept, it is responsibility for the Other.

---

[22] Heidegger is just one of many thinkers classified as "existentialist" when we need to pin them in the herbarium of the historical and philosophical classifications. But neither he, nor the others, except perhaps Sartre and Simone de Beauvoir, agree to be labelled as existentialists.

* * *

Existentialists do not perceive individuality or personality as an obvious fact and provided by nature, but as an achievement; a conception of theirs that was at the time innovative and even shocking, but is nowadays common and has become a template for the everyday perception of things in the understanding of "constructed identity."

"To make of yourself what you want to" is not an understanding of human freedom which was created by Kierkegaard and existentialism but an individualistic formulation of the more general principle of subjectivity inherent in all modern European philosophy. Kant asked, how was it possible for Man as a subject to live according to the law of Reason—legislation which one himself creates for his own freedom. Descartes already demanded that Man relied, not on the authority of Scripture as a measure of all truths, but on his own mind: to rely on his clear and distinct knowledge, by virtue of which he provides evidence of himself and of what is actually existing. In early modernity the greatest European thinkers sought to replace contemplative philosophy with a newly founded practical philosophy to help people become masters and rulers of nature and their own lives. Culture had to prevail over natural instincts and affects, the subject to rule over the objects, society and individuals to learn to live self-consciously. Man had to make a world for himself out of the world, existing in itself. This meant to methodically master being in the name of ideas and values. This era ultimately became the era of ideologies, each of them aiming to explain the totality of the world and then provide rules for its transformation: morally, intellectually and from a practical perspective.

The belief in historical progress is the direct outcome of the confidence of the individual in his own abilities and his desire to control and consciously develop the forces determining human existence. In the late 19th and early 20th century, the belief in the continuous and unstoppable rise of society—a consequence of united individual and collective efforts—had an almost religious influence. Man regarded with new confidence, and even with some contempt, earlier ages with their wars, famine and turmoil, as a time in which humanity was rudimentary and not enlightened enough. Progress seemed indisputable and proven by daily discoveries and innovations in science and technology.

Nevertheless, despite Europe's newly found belief in human progress, it was destined to experience the tragic collapse of its ideals. The outbreak of the First World War and the subsequent years, especially the Second World War, brought with them dramatic changes in the outlook on faith in human progress, in the best case exposing it as naive idealism. The liberal optimistic confidence that Europe and mankind had that they were on the right and infallible pathway to the best of all possible worlds, gradually disappeared. The sights of destruction, mass murders and humiliation, replaced the dreams of a bright future with disappointment, distrust, despair, resentment, fear and uncertainty. The goal towards which all were expected to work in unity—the development of a united Europe—became an empty illusion. Commonly recognized rules of communication between individuals and peoples were annihilated. It became clear that the achievements of technology could be used not only towards but also against people's happiness. The spiritual atmosphere was permeated with enormous skepticism about the ability of culture—a thin shell that could conceal the predatory human nature lying dormant behind it. Hecatombs of dead showed that man to man was a beast, and not his brother, as new European humanists thought. The well-organized bourgeois world with its stately values that previously unambiguously determined the cost of everything, so that all things had lasting meaning—a world in which loyalty to family, home, profession, promises, etc., were a warranty for the stability of connections, collapsed. Lies and corruption spread so widely that they become commonplace.

Sociality and Justice: Toward Social Phenomenology 41

Among the chaos and rampant anarchy, a new organization was constructed out of immorality and cynicism. It began to emerge behind political proclamations, institutions of the state, the symbolism of public life. The expansion of a total and totalizing bureaucracy demonstrated to individuals that if they could benefit from some freedoms and rights, it was through favours granted by those in power. Individuals began to feel powerless not only in view of world events, in which they were drawn against their will but even in the face of the smallest clerk who personified the soulless totalizing social system. Man's dream to become a citizen of a justful Europe and why not of a World Democratic Republic, was replaced by the feeling of alienation everywhere he went. He was "nobody", and "nowhere"—anonymous, useless and alone. Not only were his affiliations to his social communities destroyed but also his former natural everyday identity with his Self. All previous accumulated knowledge and experience, as well the ability to foresee and plan were deemed worthless. The war destroyed all ranks and differentiations that had been valid in peaceful, secure and orderly bourgeois life. In war, each individual was reduced to a "piece of meat", to part of the crowd at which to shoot. In the crowd people were faceless. The respect for the individual that inspired modern European humanists gradually evaporated. In militarized Europe the principle of the subject became false along with the principles of the social nature of man and justice; the thoughts and feelings of the individual, led to the irrelevance of millions of human beings.

Existentialism expressed the ramblings of the "wartime generation" and its disgust of inauthentic existence, the nausea in the crowd which was dumbed down by its supposed truths and its pseudo-security; by life on the edge of nothing and the crisis of human relations. All this preceded the wars. Existentialists spoke their own language, which not only provided an assessment of events by placing them in a new re-examined space; they were also the first to name these events, transforming the lived experience into articulated segmentations and identifications. Existentialist philosophy itself became part of the life situation of this generation, by creating the profile of that time and giving it a defined shape. By the act of philosophizing, which existentialists believed gave everyone the opportunity to rise above the adversity of life and to find meaning even in the inevitable battle with death, they wanted to restore respect towards subjectivity and the individual.

In the years after 1945 there was not an intellectual in Europe who was not involved in the discussion of existentialist themes: the problematic of human existence, absurdity, risk, death and suffering, depersonalization of the individual, collapsed reason etc. Immediately after the war the influence of existentialism reached its peak and spread far beyond the borders of Europe—to the USA, Japan, India and many other countries. However, it was also the time when multiple critical voices were gradually raised, labelling existentialism as a "philosophy of crisis" that enhances and deepens the tragic sense of life and pushes people into the abyss of the impasse. In 1951 the Vatican condemned it with the accusation of preaching frustrating pessimism. In response, many attempts were made to transform existentialism into a positive ideological program. Nonetheless, to claim that existentialists were sensitive only to the "revelations of death" and "the dark side of life," was to misunderstand their position—their pathos was focused exactly on searching for and asserting positive values that reconcile critical thinking with the possibility of affirmative action. Many felt existentialism was "anti-humanism" because the existentialist generation demonstrably gave up the faith of their fathers in "humane ideals." Existentialists ask a truly cruel question: "What is the humanity of these ideals, if following them, as history shows, leads to an increase in violence, to political outrage, to degradation of the individual and human dignity, to wars and the death of millions? Was civilization not built with faith in the so-called "eternal values of mankind", yet in fact fails on terror and power, on abstractions and bureaucracy, on lies and force, as well as on the absurdity that follows from them? Would it not be a modern form of shamelessness to close our eyes to everything that happened and to make another attempt to create yet another metaphysics of "eternal values"?

The modern era is the time of great metaphysical systems. They have been used in modernity as a theoretical basis for various ideologies. Each metaphysics implies that what is, i.e. reality, does not match what it should be, i.e. the ideal; it carries with it the negation of all that is here and now in the name of something then and there. Through metaphysics, utopianism and abstractions attempt to take over living reality. Each metaphysics feels destined to rule out categorical general propositions by using a kind of *a priori* knowledge. It subdivides everything in existence and labels it without even deliberating on its source. "In an era of offensive worldviews—says Heidegger—all relations with the world are limited to the judgement over it." It is of no consequence whether the verdict is pronounced in the name of God, Morality, Reason, Democracy, Unity, Progress, etc. If these categories themselves are not re-examined according to the essence of work, but on the contrary, are examined according to an essence that begins with habitual opinions, these labels thereby rather drive us to misconceptions and the language in which we speak on them, is fake. Labels and classifications are used for introducing order in life and to unify it so as to ensure dominance over it.

By seeking to explain everything in terms of their *a priori* principles, ideologies have a ready answer to any question beginning with "why?". Living according to ideological clichés, however noble they appear, is to live as a slave—obedient and hunched, in agreement with oppression and terror, despite hailing freedom with lofty phrases. Ideological solutions exempt individuals from the burden of their own reflections and choices. To judge according to the values and ideas of metaphysics means to run away from responsibility. Innocence cannot be reduced to living according to established eternal categories of good and evil, duty and freedom, and God and Truth... Truth becomes a dogma, when not subjected to doubt; beauty is reduced to a cliché and becomes obsolete, if no one transforms it; good cannot be identified with custom nor love with fulfilling one's duty.

If gods and scriptures are eternal, it is not because they do not die, but because they are resurrected repeatedly for man. If existentialists renounce the firmly fixed norms and principles for human thinking and guiding action, they do so to the extent considered appropriate and continually stressing that universality is not something self-evident, as was perceived by early modern philosophy. It neither precedes, nor follows experience, but is rather constantly doubted. Existentialists want to restore man's dignity by defending his individuality and choices. Therefore, he is not worthy who hides under the convenience of mastered public stereotypes and in the shelter of habitual petty everyday problems. The dignity of the individual depends on the courage with which he/she stands face to face with the incompleteness, instability, volatility and openness of the human condition. In other words—the courage to stand face to face with death.

When Shestov was accused that all his revelations stem from the touch with death, he warned that it would be a big mistake to use "revelations of death" to extract rules for life. Rules and principles are not full, live knowledge but slim and vague—because of the rules we often forget about life's diversity. Human language is not capable of expressing everything that people experience in such a way that it could be united according to principles and rules. Language and thinking, cultivated by language, pull us towards unilateralism and abstractions. If our eyes must be open about death, it is not to turn away from reality, but rather to learn to see more in it than the rules allow us—to find value even in what we failed to notice earlier.

In response to criticisms of existentialism Heidegger wrote his letter *On Humanism*. Humanism is nothing but reflection and care, for man to be humane and not inhumane. The creature *homo humanus* is determined by thinking, but one thinks—in the proper sense of the word—only if one does not forget Being. Thinking according to ideas and values is for Heidegger sacrilege towards authentic existence. Man keeps the human in himself and does not become, automatically, the weapon of one or another ideology, if he keeps in his mind the thought of Being. The main merit of thought and not just common, hollow, worn out concepts spoken, lies in the fact that it allows existence to be. To think against the values of classical humanism does not mean for Heidegger to declare all existence null and void. The sense of the resistance against early modern ideas and values is very different: it is opposition to the reduction of existence to a mere conglomerate of objects of cognition and judgment—against neglecting such of its actions and characteristics that have slipped so far from the scope of the Reason. Heidegger believed that everything dear and sacred to man disappears if the openness of Being is not illuminated and if, when illuminated, it is not closer to us. Thinking overcomes metaphysics not by rising higher, nor by climbing over it to sublate it by "uplifting" it and including it in a new, richer totality. Thinking overcomes metaphysics by going back to what is closest to Man—Being, i.e. near to the unhabituality of simplicity.

Not just Shestov and Heidegger but all existentialists believe that rules, laws and values, including those of classical humanism, stop serving human solidarity, when they become catechism and a weapon of the Inquisition. Any human solution exceeding its status of personally experienced truth, becomes questionable when it attempts to assign universal validity to itself. Albert Camus pointed out that the history of thought is rather the history of its delusions and repentance than of its victories and truths. Delusions stem from ignorance or from the persistent refusal to acknowledge the boundary, which is inseparable from human nature. This boundary is not something given once and for all, but rather a constant tension. If there is a point beyond which good becomes evil, truth—

a lie, and each definition reveals its absurd side, then there must be some kind of threshold for things and for man. We become aware that this threshold has been passed when there is rebellion. Rebellion reveals the boundary, beyond which, the human having risen above the individual and the human situation, threatens to become a negation of humanity. Man is a being which rebels against what he was and what he is. No metaphysics or ideology can claim to be the path to the best of all possible worlds, in which there will be no more protests. We can trust neither reason nor morality, nor the universal laws of history in which educators saw the engines of progress. In the past, protest drew its strength from the desire to change reality so as to correspond to these ideals. The absolute riot of existentialists, however, arose namely from the distrust in them. The crisis experienced by the existentialist generation led to a new understanding of man: that reason, morality, history definitely set boundaries for him, but man in turn sets a boundary on everything human—on reason, morality, history... It is at this boundary that value and meaning are born. People cannot once and for all see right through the process of the rebirth of meaning, as it is where the mystery of the world is and it increases with the growth of human knowledge.

It seems however, that humanity after existentialism continues to live according to one or another metaphysics. The metaphysics is continuously revived and resurrected with renewed strength and in new forms. In this work, what particularly concerns us is the metaphysics of Levinas, that is, his conception on ethics.

* * *

Kierkegaard is seen as the forerunner of existentialist philosophy precisely because he claimed that a person has to make of himself what he wants to. Nietzsche was also a supporter of the idea that the individual must become what he is, i.e. to become himself. In fact, the idea that man alone is the architect of his own destiny, dates back at least to the time of

Pico della Mirandola and Renaissance humanism. Similarly, the theme of humanism and the identification of the Self as a subject occupies a central place in the work of Levinas, and he offers an unexpected and remarkable new solution: the individual is I, not because he freely chooses himself with victorious resolve, nor because of his own becoming or self-realization, but because his existence acquires a meaning, when it is for the Other. This means that man is himself when he is "for the Other". This is the delineation of humanity and that which is its sociality.

Emmanuel Levinas identifies sociality with the responsibility for the Other. Such an approach, which Levinas himself described as "phenomenology of sociality"[23] furnishes existential-phenomenological philosophy with a social focus. Before him the philosophy of existence was often called the philosophy of the isolated individual, of absurdity and nothingness, of silence and lonely rebellion. In Levinas' theory, however, the individual cannot be understood otherwise than by his relationship with the Other: it does not deprive the Self of his freedom and authenticity, but invests them into him—provokes them, inspires them, expects them, calls them and so on. The loneliness of existence and the encapsulation of the individual into himself as the center is a negation of all categories of humanness; even when abhorring the senseless repetition of clichés and rebelling against the absurd, it is still at the same time refusing to take responsibility for what happens to others. This type of arrogant individualism is an attempt to escape from sociality. It contrasts the unique world of the private individual, on the one hand, to the uniformed world of the universal averaged regulations that are taken for granted, on the other. For example, in Kierkegaard we read:

---

[23] Emmanuel Levinas. Diachrony and Representation. *Entre Nous. Thinking-of-the-Other.* Translated by Michael B. Smith and Barbara Harshav, Columbia University Press, 1998, p.169

> Man is by nature one of the animal creation. Therefore all human effort tends toward herding together; "let us unite", etc. Naturally this happens under all sorts of high-sounding names, love and sympathy and enthusiasm, and the carrying out of some grand plan, and the like; this is the unusual hypocrisy of scoundrels we are. The truth is that in a herd we are free from the standard of the individual and the ideal."[24]

Levinas agrees with Kierkegaard that freedom is a value and that for the sake of freedom the system must be overrun. However, this should happen not for the sake of the Self (as Kierkegaard suggested), but for the Other (Levinas). The lone rebellion of the Single One, the Superman, the Authentic Self, etc. is disdainful of those who comprise with the bulk of the herd, the crowd. In this type of discourse, the Other is negative entity, and between the Self and the Other the logic of confrontation is reproduced. In existentialism the morality of the One is opposed to the herd morality of the others. In Levinas, on the contrary, the Other is taken in his otherness, i.e. in its positivity as a face awakening morality in me:

> The movement of transcendence is to be distinguished from the negativity by which discontent man refuses the condition in which he is established. Negativity presupposes a being established, placed in a site where he is at home... This mode of negating while taking refuge in what one negates delineates the same or the I. The alterity of a world refused is not the alterity of the Stranger but that of the fatherland which welcomes and protects. Metaphysics does not coincide with negativity.[25]

The connection with the world is ontological but the connection with the Other is meta-physical. For Levinas, the metaphysical, moral and social are synonymous. Sociality cannot be understood if one thinks simply and only through the relationship between the individual and society and even less so where society is labelled a herd. In respecting the universal we seem to miss and forget the relation of the I to the Other in the concreteness of their meeting. The relation of the I to the universal is an

---

[24] See S. Kierkegaard, *The Last Years: Journals, 1853–1855* (London, Collins, 1968), p. 31. Cit. by Zygmunt Bauman. *Postmodern Ethics*. Blackwell, p. 41

[25] Emmanuel Levinas.*Totality and Infinity*. Duquesne University Press, 1992, Pittsburg, p. 40–41.

Sociality and Justice: Toward Social Phenomenology 49

I-It relationship. When the I and the Other are in direct contact, face-to-face, as concrete individuals, they are not abstract agents only, performing roles nor functionaries in the system of society, nor representatives of the universal. Levinas focuses our attention on this gap and this slip of our attention—ignoring the fundamental relationship between the Other and me where morality and sociality are present originally.

Metaphorically speaking, the philosophy of Levinas serves as a beacon illuminating most of the topics discussed herein. But if they are identified because of the light he sheds on those themes, it is not with the sole purpose of reiterating his discoveries and arguments in the chronological and/or logical sequence of his philosophy. The achievements in the history of philosophy are taken as a starting point for a meta-physical debate in support of a humanistic approach to problems related to sociality and justice. We have summarized here, under the heading of "humanism", the views according to which people create themselves and their history in their relationships with one another. The question, however, is "how?" Humanism certainly defends individuality, freedom, dignity but the question is how are they connected with sociality and justice.

Levinas managed to propose solution of the whole problematic related to sociality, justice, morality, politics, the state and in general topics that are nowadays within the scope of social philosophy, by deliberately upholding the position of humanism. Humanism as an approach within social philosophy and practice is legitimized in its defence of the individual—not the individual as a repeated unit in the entity of society and in the context of the relationship particularity-universality; individuality is understood herein not primarily as an ontic characteristic, but as created in the moral relation to the Other. The uniqueness and indispensability of the I is invested in it by the responsibility for the fate of others.

Humanism enjoyed a great heritage, passed on throughout the centuries since the time of Socrates (469–399 BC.) until the present. In ancient

Greece its followers insisted on the relation between philosophical reflection and practice as "care of self" (*epimeleia heautou*). It means the care that each of us owes him/herself as attention to whether his own conduct is worthy and virtuous[26]. Humanism focuses more on practical philosophy, coupled with questions about the right course of action and the relations between individuals in the community rather than only with theoretical truths. Practical philosophy is not so concerned with conceptual relations in a system of abstract statements as in the links between theory and life—the life of human beings, which is always and by definition social. The significant question is exactly: what is sociality?

The humanistic tradition in Europe at the time of Levinas, i.e. the entire twentieth century, is represented primarily by Sartre. He is considered the leading thinker not only of the existentialist circle and revolutionary intellectuals in the period culminating in the events of May 1968, but also of all humanistic thinking movements of Western Europe. In the second half of the 20th century, the main debate was precisely between humanists and anti-humanists. In their definitions of society, the former emphasize on individuals and their relationships, and the latter on the determinism of institutions and social structures. Levinas was firmly on the side of humanism. Sartre himself, as Simone de Beauvoir testified in one of her autobiographical works, was attracted by the phenomenology of Husserl and Heidegger through reading Levinas, who first introduced the French-speaking audience to the ideas of his professors from the University of Freiburg. Heidegger's philosophy actually launched both the humanistic, and antihumanistic discourse in France at that time. Levinas occupies a place in a long line of representatives of moralism, which is emblematic of the French type of humanism.

Levinas, however, questioned whether humanism, as it was with its emphasis on "being oneself", had been sufficiently humanistic and his

---

[26] See Thomas R. Flynn. *Existentialism*. Oxford University Press, Oxford, 2006, p. 1

answer to this question was negative. Levinas announced that *humanitas* of *homo humanus* does not consist in freedom in the centre, understood as autonomy, self-assertion and self-realization and my right to be myself; true humanism is concerned primarily about the rights and freedoms of the Other.

According to Levinas, freedom must be preceded by responsibility for the others and "for-the-Other" is the true delineation of humanity. To "caring for one-Self" Levinas opposes "caring for the Other". Such a shift in the focus of attention highlights the analysis of the ratio between "caring for oneself" and "caring for the other", and consequently of the whole problematics about the Self and the Other, as well as the emergence of the Third, i.e. all social problematics, since it is composed initially around these figures and their relations and interactions. Furthermore, if the I, the Other and the Third are the basic categories, which describe the social micro level, it is the foundation for constructing the macro level of social structures and alliances. While sociality is present initially on the micro level of the informal, asymmetric relationship face-to-face, on the level of formal, mediated, reciprocal relations, i.e. the macro level of sociality, we cannot ignore or undermine the concept of justice and social order, encompassing the multitude of individuals in any community, interacting with the mediation of social institutions.

This thesis is structured in three chapters in which we thematize the following:

1. Sociality as a direct, asymmetrical, non-reciprocal, intersubjective relation (micro-level of social relations) is defined in the First chapter.
2. The transition from micro to macro analysis, i.e. from initial sociality to justice is described in chapter Two.
3. Finally, the theories of justice as a reciprocal, institutionalized participation of individuals and groups in the social entity (macro-level of social order) will be discussed in the Third chapter.

Chapter One:
Sociality: The I and the Other

1.1. Ontology and/or ethics. Is ontology fundamental?

With the separation of the social sciences, particularly political science and sociology, social philosophy has become increasingly committed to the justification *a posteriori* of the various conceptions proposed by those sciences, instead of analyzing them in the light of fundamental ontological principles.

> The ontological questions concern what you recognize as the factors you will invoke to account for social life. Or, put in the "formal mode," they concern the terms you accept as ultimate in the order of explanation.[27]

Ontology (even when understood in the familiar manner, as in the above-quotation by Charles Taylor) and social philosophy have followed different paths that diverge and as a result, regrettably, we have nowadays reached the point where we no longer see any common ground between them. Such a discrepancy is not characteristic of the great philosophical schools of the past. On the contrary, the depth of one or another social theory of the past was the product of the ways in which human existence and man's relationship with the world were interpreted.

The fundamental role of ontology is constituted in the understanding that whatever claims are made about the relations connecting or separating existing things, these things, and their relations exist. However, do these assertions relate to human beings? Heidegger insists that the problem of ontology is the meaning of being, which is a dilemma for man only. Raising this question and revealing it is *differentia specifica* of *Dasein*

---

[27] Charles Taylor.. *Debates on Contemporary Philosophy*. Routledge, London, 2005, p. 195 Cross purposes: The Liberal Communitarian Debate

as the being for which being is a problem in its own being. This problem is implicitly solved by all of us on a daily and hourly basis, even when we forget about it, because in order to understand being, according to fundamental ontology, we have to be. Understanding Being coincides with the facticity of the temporal dwelling of *Dasein*. One of the lessons taught to us by Heidegger is that the understanding of existence is not an abstract theoretical attitude to the world, but one that overlaps the whole of human behaviour. Science, affectivity, satisfaction of needs, labour, culture, social life and first of all anxiety about our mortality reveal the understanding of being and truth. Civilization, in its entirety, originated from this understanding—even as the oblivion of being. In short, this is the contribution of Heidegger to the revival of ontology and the search for a fundamental ontology.

However, according to Levinas, there is ambiguity hidden in Heidegger's ontology. Identifying the understanding of being with the fullness of the factual presence in the world risks the dissolution of existence into thinking of it. When philosophy and life are confused, we no longer know whether we care about philosophy because it is life, or we are interested in life insofar as it is philosophy. Heidegger's position seemed to break with classical rationalism. Indeed, in order to understand a life situation one does not need to define and interprete it, but to live it. Heidegger actually stipulated that to understand existence properly and not just reproduce generally accepted conventions that reveal it as much as they hide it, means to exist, i.e. to be in the world as oneself. But is the focus on oneself and such gravitating around this focus a definitive peculiarity, inherent in the I? Levinas calls this I "imperialistic" because its entire ambition consists in making everything its own. This I circles around itself and is closed up on oneself engulfing everything on the way in its self-affirmation (or, conversely, distancing itself from it). Levinas' critique starts from the point that consciousness, the mastering of reality through cognition, even when reality is not perceived from an instrumental point of view, but seemingly *per se*, does not exhaust our relationship with it. The activity of the subject, including cognitive activity, involves intentionality, both coming from him and returning to him. Any cognition of objects captures only that which interests the knowing and acting subject. "Objectivity" is adapted to commonsense and presupposes objectives and intentions of *das Man*. Heidegger stands against the universalization of the instrumental understanding of things in the world, including the instrumentalization of human relationships and the Self as *das Man*. According to Levinas, however, Heidegger's analysis does not abandon intellectualism and the type of theorizing familiar in Western philosophy. The understanding of truth that Heidegger discusses is inevitably a care for survival even when and namely because "it is listening to Being". This care is the deepest motive of the being ecstatically directed toward death. Being oneself is the goal of all goals, the real present tense and implicit instrumentalization of everything existing in the world—not only with a view to the acts, but with a view to "being there". For Heidegger, human beings are drawn in the cognition of truth due to their constant anticipation of death. He interprets truth and our entire factual existence as a function of articulation of the openness of Being. However according to Heidegger, truth exists not because there is a man, but vice versa, since all existence is inseparable from Being's openness (since Being is understandable, comprehensible in unconcealment) there is humanity.

Levinas argued against the primacy of ontology:

> To be or not to be—is that the question? Is it the first and final question? Does being human consist in forcing oneself to be and does the understanding of the meaning of being—the semantics of the verb to be—represent the first philosophy ...?[28]

---

[28] Emmanuel Levinas. Ethics as First Philosophy. *The Levinas' Reader*. Blackwell (Oxford, UK & Cambridge, USA: 1993), p. 86.

For Levinas the question *par excellence* or the deepest philosophical question is not "Why there is being rather than nothing?", but "How being is justified?"

> In this question being and life are awakened to the human dimension. This is the question of the meaning of being.[29]

According to Maurice Blanchot, if Heidegger's question is the <u>ultimate</u> question, encompassing everything that exists (existent as a totality in view of its being), Levinas' question is the <u>most profound</u>, which is however, concealed by ontology.[30] By reducing every relation of human being with what exists to the care for one's own existence and survival, Heidegger privileges freedom and ignores ethics.

Levinas starts from Heidegger's analytic, but believes that human existence is understood primarily through the moral bond between people. Humanity is a response and responsibility for the Other rather than a determination to be and to be myself. For Levinas, it is ethics, not ontology, which is the first philosophy. Ethics is concerned with the possibility of transcending (one's own) being, that is, the possibility of obtaining the meaning of being by subjecting myself to beyond being.

> The first metaphysical question is no longer Leibniz's question — "Why is there something rather than nothing?" — but "Why is there evil rather than good?" This is the neutralization of being or the beyond being. The ontological difference is preceded by the difference of good and evil.[31]

Metaphysics calls into question the intelligibility of everything in existence. Furthermore, it criticizes arbitrary dogmatism inherent in the free exercises of creating some images of the existing world in its wholeness.

---

[29] Ibid., p. 86.
[30] Maurice Blanchot. The Most Profound Question. *The Infinite Conversation*. University of Minnesota Press, Minneapolis and London, 1993, p. 12.
[31] Emmanuel Levinas. Transcendence and Evil. *Of God Who Comes to Mind*. Transl. by Bettina Bergo, Stanford University Press, Stanford, 1998, p. 130.

Sociality and Justice: Toward Social Phenomenology 57

My spontaneity "to be" and to construct ontological pictures is challenged practically and specifically in my meeting with the Other, i.e. with a being that has its own separated existence, subjectivity, imagination, freedom. The world which I inhabited in a carefree manner before the meeting with the other enjoyed the confidence that this is the only correct, universally valid world but it is in fact the world as revealed in my limited particular perspective. The presence of the Other in the totality of the world makes me doubt my spontaneous freedom that takes my singularity as universality. This does not happen until the Other stops to accept my ideas about things as obvious and taken for granted. In the meeting with the Other, my I can be shaken in all its naivety and must abandon its identification with universality:

> The strangeness of the Other, his irreducibility to the I, to my thoughts and my possessions, is precisely accomplished as a calling into question of my spontaneity, as ethics.[32]

This is the serious question about the identity of the I (and consequently about any identity). Whether it should be understood from an **ontological perspective** as a kind of belonging to being (i.e., the totality of the world with its genera and classes) or from an **ethical perspective** as a response that in my very existence as *homo humanus* I give to the presence of others. Where are these others situated? Are they inside or outside of the world, if for the I the world is always a confusion—or better a fusion—of particularity and universality? Is it possible to define something as an essence of humanity?

1.2. How to think *humanitas* of *homo humanus*?

The question of what constitutes the "humanity of man" was not raised originally in Heidegger's philosophy although Heidegger unceasingly

---

[32] Emmanuel Levinas. *Totality and Infinity*. Duquesne University Press, 1992, Pittsburg, p. 43

and importunately discusses it. We do not know when it was first uttered but no doubt people have been asking it since ancient times. In his *Letter on Humanism*[33] Heidegger answers it from the perspective of his fundamental ontology. We pay special attention to this answer, because it is the stepping-stone for a new understanding of sociality. Such an answer has been conceptualised also, although in his own way, in Martin Buber's philosophy of dialogue and continued and developed in the philosophy of Levinas. According to Levinas, the social dimension of our existence does not depersonalize us as in being-with-one-another in Heidegger's philosophy, but is the condition of human identity, which primary is a care of one-for-the-other.

On November 10th 1946, Jean Beaufret asked Heidegger: "How can we restore meaning to the word "humanism"?" to which Heidegger responded in December. Subsequently, in 1947 he rewrote his response and it was published as *Letter on Humanism*. The reason behind this correspondence between Beaufret and Heidegger was Jean-Paul Sartre's essay *Existentialism and Humanism* (1946).[34] Sartre insists that there is no "human nature" or "human essence" which is determined once and for all. Existentialism defines man not by his preordained essence—simply because it, as such, does not exist—but by his actions. Sartre believes that people are judged on their commitments, which are evident in practice. For Sartre human freedom to act is rooted in subjectness, that is, the agency of choice, which is the sole reason for human dignity as well as the only possible foundation of humanism. The focus of humanism is the individual as the author of his own deeds.

Heidegger, however, rejected subjectness and activism as a possible starting point. According to him, humanism underestimates the unique

---

[33] Martin Heidegger. On Humanism. *Basic Writings*. Harper Collins Publishers, San Francisco, 1993
[34] Jean-Paul Sartre. Existentialism and Humanism. *The Continental Philosophy Reader*. Ed. by R.Kearney and M. Rainwater, Routledge, 1998, p. 62–76.

Sociality and Justice: Toward Social Phenomenology 59

position of man as shepherd and guardian of Being. The openness of Being allows the care for being, i.e. caring for the truth of Being, through the articulation of thinking. Thinking is not just *"l'éngagement dans l'action"*, as Sartre believed, but above all *l'engagement* through language and action stemming from the openness of Being. In Heidegger's outlook on philosophy, Beaufret's question; "How can we restore meaning to the word humanism?" implies that this word has lost its meaning and expresses the desire to preserve it. Heidegger himself mentions the various meanings of the term "humanism" associated with the different perceptions of Western metaphysics: Latin, Christian, Marxist, Existentialist, etc. He sees those different ideologemes as more than empty words. The emergence of new "isms" (e.g. Marxism, Existentialism, etc.) signalled that the type of thinking that made Being speaks was already obsolete and had been replaced by thinking as an instrument of education and cultivation. This is a signal that in experiencing the epoch—and consequently conception of humanity of man—we need to delve deeper, to a primordial level. Heidegger himself, in agreement with this view, proposes a new definition of "what humanity means today". Fundamental ontology identifies *humanitas* of *homo humanus* with the authenticity of *Dasein*, i.e. with the understanding of existence as a responsibility for the truth of Being. His letter to Beaufret, however, leaves open the question of the need for a new kind of humanism:

> Should we still keep the name "humanism" for a "humanism" that contradicts all previous humanism—although it in no way advocates the inhuman?[35]

The question of *humanitas* of *homo humanus* becomes central to the work of Levinas. Levinas, however, answers it differently from his teacher: the meaning of human existence is not in the care for the truth of being but care as a responsibility for the Other. For Levinas the former humanism

---

[35] Martin Heidegger. *Basic Writings*. Harper Collins Publishers, San Francisco, 1993, p. 248

of Western metaphysics and culture is not sufficiently humane. It is therefore necessary to consider again what true humanity is. Of course, this is the old and banal question "What is *differentia specifica* of man as a man?" Nonetheless, despite its banality, or perhaps because of it, we should not cease to ask it. Even a small change in the response leads to huge differences in thinking and sensitivity.

Heidegger asks, "What is the humanity of man?", because it is his notion that humanism is the care of man to be human and not inhuman; inhuman means to be out of one's own essence. Levinas emphasizes the originality and fecundity of Heidegger's approach to this commonplace theme. Heidegger really succeeded in revealing an unexpected, but epochal meaning hidden in this repeated question. Heidegger's solution, namely "*Dasein* is the being for which in its own being, being is questioned" is still not the primordial and deepest truth for Levinas. Heidegger "deduces" the personal from the ontological, while for Levinas the personal is the ethical. It is not ontology but ethics which is the beginning of philosophy or rather precedes that beginning. Levinas' radical question is whether the dimension of humanity breaks with Being instead of being the care for it. Can we really talk about human nature and its manifestations, if man is a being reduced to his care to endure? Certainly, this question inevitably leads Levinas to challenge Heidegger's stance, as well as the entire onto-theo-logical tradition.

Sociality and Justice: Toward Social Phenomenology 61

> A philosophy of power, ontology is, as first philosophy which does not call into question the same, a philosophy of injustice. Even though it opposes the technological passion issued forth from the forgetting of being hidden by existents, Heideggerian ontology, which subordinates the relationship with the Other to the relation with Being in general, remains under obedience to the anonymous, and leads inevitably to another power, to imperialist domination, to tyranny. Its origin lies back in the pagan "moods", in the enrootedness in the earth, in the adoration that enslaved men can devote to their masters. Being before the existent, ontology before metaphysics, is freedom...before justice.[36]

For Levinas, if everything human is reduced to ontology, then to be human means to be at the service of Being, to put survival on a pedestal, to be part of the adventure of Being. This would mean then that the individual is subjected to a kind of "faceless destiny":

> The relation with Being that is enacted as ontology consists in neutralizing the existent in order to comprehend or grasp it. It is hence not a relation with the other as such but the reduction of the other to the same. Such is the definition of freedom: to maintain oneself against the other, despite every relation with the other to ensure the autarchy of an I. Thematization and conceptualization, which moreover are inseparable, are not peace with the other but suppression or possession of the other. ... Ontology as first philosophy is a philosophy of power. ... Truth, which should reconcile persons, here exists anonymously. Universality presents itself as impersonal and this is another inhumanity. ... Heidegger finds in Presocratism thought as obedience to the truth of Being.[37]

Levinas argues that thought is obedient to the appeal of the Other. Fundamental ontology is, according to him, the philosophy of power, if only because it maintains the subordination to Being and can legitimize everything through its supremacy. Then, in the realm of *Jemeinigkeit* (mineness) any means would be justified as well as any injustice, domination, violence and even cruelty as long as they serve the purpose of survival and defending oneself.

---

[36] Emmanuel Levinas. *Totality and Infinity*. Duquesne University Press, 1992, Pittsburg, p. 46–47
[37] Emmanuel Levinas. *Ibid.*, p. 45–46.

> Heidegger, with the whole of Western history, takes the relation with the Other as enacted in the destiny of sedentary people, the possessors and builders of the earth. Possession is preeminently the form in which the other becomes the same, by becoming mine.[38]

Levinas' attitude is radically different in comparision with the Heideggerian one. He defends the "nomadic truth", as formulated by Jacques Rolland[39]: If "we are all strangers on this earth,"as written in the Bible, it is empty vanity to identify oneself with one's possessions—with the native, blood, land, with the territoriality "owned" and cultivated by people who, precisely through their identification with it, gain their own meaning. Identification through belonging to any space is not authentic human identification but the way by which we identify objects within their classes and frontiers.

> A person is more holy than a land, even a holy land, since, faced with affront made to a person, this holy land appears in its nakedness to be but stone and wood.[40]

Levinas believes that the humanity of man is not determined by his place under the sun, nor is it in the mastering of objects, nor in power over others but is first constituted in the face-to-face relation with the Other, whereby the I bears responsibility not only for itself but primarily for the Other. My entire Self is not in the service of the system of Being which here and now is the native land (as the self is understood by Heidegger and other philosophers before him—"territorially", in view of his boundaries as *Da*), but in service of thy neighbour being here and now face-to-face where *conatus essendi* of my world is overcome and the vector of existential time acquires a new approach—towards the Other. Generally,

---

[38] Ibid., p. 46
[39] He was one of the first to appreciate the magnitude and completely new perspective of Levinas' philosophy. See.Silvano Petrosino et Jacques Rolland. *La verité nomade*. La Découverte, Paris, 1984.
[40] Emmanuel Levinas. Ethics and Politics. *The Levinas' Reader*. Blackwell, Oxford, UK&Cambridge, USA, 1993, p. 297.

Sociality and Justice: Toward Social Phenomenology 63

if in Heidegger's philosophy *Dasein* is perceived primarily inside of the horizon of being, i.e. spatially and from the perspective of the locus, in Levinas what is central and primary is time as a connection between the Other and me. Time is present for consciousness through space, but "One-for-the-Other" is available as immeasurable proximity even before apprehending it, as well as before any consciousness.

It is often said that Levinas' philosophy is devoted to the problem of the Other, or more precisely, to the otherness of the Other. Yet his thinking is not, in fact, focused on the theme of the Other as such, but on my relation to him. The main problem is my responsibility for the Other which, in its most hyperbolized form, means substituting the Other. [41] By this account, the Self then becomes hostage to the freedom of the Other. The focus in Levinas' philosophy is the moral subject: the Self in the accusative as *me*, that is, the one who is unable to hide behind the mask of the Third and the neutral one.

Within the system of being the Other is either the object of my interest, or a partner in my activity. He or she is already taken in *my* horizon. In the realm of Being, the otherness of the Other is, in the best case neutralized—relations are balanced and brought to reciprocity. They are measured by a common measure—that of the Third[42] and so "*Das Man*" dominates the realm of being. However, according to Levinas there is something he calls "beyond being" or "otherwise than being". "Beyond being" is not non-being, but the moral concern with the Other. The Other for Levinas is not just a participant in the whole of the world of nature, society, history, etc., but the face from which Transcendence is looking

---

[41] Emmanuel Levinas. *Otherwise than Being or beyond Essence*. Duquesne University Press, Pittsburgh, Pennsylvania, 2000, Chapter 4: Substitution

[42] Who is more or less anonymous—the possible Third, i.e., each subsequent one; the grammatical third person can be used in most other languages as a subject of conversation—she, he, they, but also it for a standard rule, institution, the collective body and so on.

at me. As a face, the Other is always outside totality—the cosmos, history, nation, community, society, because they themselves are constituted (as something meaningful) in conversation. Any real conversation suggests the presence of interlocutors, i.e. the I and the others, who thematize beings in the world, but are not themselves thematized. If they are thematized then, on one side, they are still interlocutors but, on the other side, their status is changed and they became the third persons—she, he, they, that is, objects of the conversation.

As already mentioned, Levinas was strongly influenced by his teacher Husserl, who first showed that any transcendence, including the transcendence of the outside world, is already constructed on the assumption of the transcendence of the other Self with its subject-ness—the subject-ness of my *Alter Ego*. Yet for Husserl it is my I that creates the transcendence of my *Alter Ego* as the opposite to my own immanence, while Levinas would not agree to deduce the transcendence of the Other from what to me is inherent—be it as a likeness, or as negation. For Levinas, the Other is not constituted as different from me within myself and by myself—the Other is opposing me, not compared to me, but because he has his own face (i.e. his own existence and subject-ness that exists in itself, not as my constitution and creation). Here Levinas follows Sartre's conception that I encounter the Other but do not invent or constitute him; rather I constitute and invent my Self. Still, the encounter with the Other is not reduced to a simple empirical event. Moral relation to others, although permeating all our empirical relationships, cannot be reduced to their instrumental, informative, aesthetic and other content. The meeting between the Other and me is not just the starting point of reflection—through reflection, the Other is objectified and almost petrified before my eyes. If I approach the Other as a face, i.e. as what is "invisible in the visible", the I is then called to relate to the Other in his dimension of transcendence.

Whether the only definition of Transcendence is that it transcends any definition? Transcendence does not allow being included in our framework of understanding, evaluation and action, i.e. to be grasped in our horizon. Transcendence always goes beyond the idea we can master of it. Transcendence is beyond my ability to understand. Moreover, what would my relationship with transcendence be, if it always eluded me and if I could never encompass it? Furthermore, how could the I make it comprehensible and even make references to it if all human knowledge is seemingly inadequate and incommensurate to it?

Levinas believes that as finite beings, we refer to Transcendence (Infinity). To view myself as a finite being, I should posses some kind of idea of Infinity. If the finite has no alternative, that is, the Infinite, there would be no point in the opposition between good and evil, truth and untruth, etc., because everything would be only transient, non-eternal and meaningless disappearing into nothingness. In such no holds barred and redemption of the finite, i.e. of the ever limited, the slogan "Anything goes!" would be justified. Hence, we can ask ourselves whether such concepts as Transcendence, Immortality, Eternity, Infinity, etc. are not just words whose purpose is simply to create sweet illusions by negating our own boundaries. In this regard, Heidegger's sober reminder that man is a being towards death and that any attempt to overstep our boundaries ends at the boundary of death, is very appropriate and impressive. No doubt, for Heidegger the metaphysical anxiety in front of the nothingness of death is the beginning of the most personal and authentic frame of reference.

However, although he is very convincing on this point, Levinas criticizes it, arguing that the Self has not only his time at risk, but that of the Other too. Of course, my most personal event is my death and no one can experience it for me; but no less personal is my responsibility for the

Other's time and death[43]. My responsibility for the Other makes me unique and irreplaceable. Responsibility for the Other means closeness: the proximity of the neighbour in the face-to-face relation where first the "human, too human" is revealed—the vulnerability and fragility of the individuals. This weakness, vulnerability and orientation towards death, which I read in the naked face of the Other and in the eyes looking at me (ego in the accusative, i.e. me) is overcome thanks to my responsibility and care for this Other. Then the opposition between being and nothingness is surmounted. My concern not just for myself, but rather for the Other's being overlaps with the event of sociality. Caring for others transcends (is superior to) *conatus* of *Jemeinigkeit* and in this way infinity exists, not as exaggerating and extrapolation of the self towards eternity, but rather as a contraction of the self, to make space for the Other, by caring for him and even by supporting his otherness. First, in the face-to-face relationship, and then—in the public sphere as responsibility not only to those nearby but for each other, including the most distant and anonymous. In the public sphere, however, it is not just you and I that are of interest, but each and every one. In the public space individuals are categorized and universalised—reduced to what they are for the sake of law and public institutions.

* * *

As previously mentioned, in the debate between humanists and anti-humanists in the intellectual scene of Europe in the second half of the 20th century, Levinas was fully involved on the side of humanists. However, unlike Sartre, who was considered the intellectual leader of humanists at the time, Levinas announced that *humanitas* of *homo humanus* is consti-

---

[43] In general, Levinas builds on the fact that the Self learns of the existence of death as such first as a witness to the death of the other (no one could witness their own death).

tuted not in my freedom in the first place, or self-realization or self-assertion, i.e. in the right of the Self to be itself; true humanism is concerned primarily with the rights and freedoms of the Other. Levinas emphasizes that freedom must be preceded by responsibility for others and that "for-the-Other" is the very delineation of humanity. Everyone responds to the others by his own "I think," "I do," and "I am", even when not necessarily wanting to. However, activity, thinking, being of the I as a free, autonomous and active subject is preceded and acquires sense thanks to the sensitivity of the Self as a moral subject. The I and the Other are connected by a relation that does not resemble any of the natural relations as between cause and effect, components and systems, function and body. The relationship between the Self and the Other is speech, the word. It is a bond and not mere coexistence; it is ethical and meta-physical and not simply ontological.

1.3. Subjectness

It is necessary to repeat that the problem is not so much about the Other or the otherness of the Other, but the "Self" as a moral subject. The whole novelty of Levinas' work lies in his different interpretation of these two words: "subject" and "moral".

The Greek word for "subject", "*hypokeimenon*", literally means "that which underlies". Gadamer, an undoubted authority of ancient Greek classics, translated it as "that which remains unchanged as it underlies the process of all change."[44] Gadamer reminds us that Aristotle introduced this concept in his contemplations of nature. Aristotle's definition could be applied to anything in the Cosmos and to every living creature, including to every creature which exists as a political/social being, i.e. any rational animal.

---

[44] Hans-Georg Gadamer. Subjectivity and Intersubjectivity, Subject and Person, *Continental Philosophy Review*, 33, no.3 (July, 2000) p. 276.

One may well ask how, from this original orientation, there could develop the modern concept of subject and subjectivity, with its particular connotation.[45]

For Gadamer the answer is obvious. It came through the Cartesian **cogito me cogitare**....[46]

But this answer, albeit obvious for Gadamer, is not obvious for Levinas. Descartes' *cogito* seems to follow the Aristotelian definition that reason is the distinguishing feature of a human being. Descartes believed that reason is a God given ability, but, like the ancients, he associated the human with it and is convinced that it is also an ability we need to cultivate. It is not enough just to possess reason; one has to know, or rather, to learn how to use it. That is why Descartes wrote his *Discourse on the Method of Rightly Conducting One's Reason and of Seeking Truth in the Sciences* and also *Rules for the Direction of the Mind*. It is not enough to know the truth; it is necessary to know how it is achieved. The world as it is presented in my experience within a culture, religion, tradition, and so on, should be questioned and then be proven by logic, i.e. reconstructed/constructed as *episteme* and not *doxa*. Reality, accessible through the sensory, as it appears to us, must be processed by Reason to be raised to the level of truth. The result would be an objective knowledge that can be achieved by anyone who uses reason (universal by definition because it is found in every human being). *Cogito, ergo sum* is the metaphysical foundation of knowledge, representing the world, valid for any reasonable person. The most important aspect of Cartesian philosophy is precisely the figure of the Subject in his capacity as an individual, identified by Reason itself. Descartes believes that we must develop the spark of rationality, which God has put in each of us, in order to obtain mastery over nature. God has provided us with the natural light of reason to be able to distinguish truth from untruth, good from evil. Still, Descartes

---

[45] Ibid., p. 277
[46] Ibid.

Sociality and Justice: Toward Social Phenomenology 69

did not dare to reduce God to the Spirit/Reason in me but rather reserved for God the position of Exteriority. Consequently, the relationship with Transcendence, i.e. God, is still very important in the Cartesian system. Therefore, a logic emerges which Levinas accepted and relied upon: in all ideas achieved by Reason, the Self starts from itself and expands its knowledge towards Infinity; however, the idea of Infinity was not created by Reason, but was invested in it by Infinity itself (that is, by God). It is this idea of infinity reveiled to me, that is, the condition of all ideas created, corrected, verified, abandoned or maintained, divided or united by the Self on his road to Infinity. This road means transcending itself and its own knowledge in Descartes' philosophy and transcending itself and the whole dilemma being-nothingness by my responsibility for the Other in Levinas'philosophy. However, the question remains; how is this idea of Infinity incorporated initially in the mind of a finite human being?

Transcendence as such becomes ever unnecessary in Kant's theory, where God already only has the status of a transcendental idea. Leaving God aside, Kant pioneered the modern conception of autonomy, i.e. of the sovereign subject, source of legislation, which he sets himself to follow. Levinas recognised in Kant the great merit of separating the moral reason from the theoretical—a dichotomy, determined by the prior separation of the subject into the empirical and transcendental. The transcendental subject is in the position to represent the universal human nature compared to the particular nature of every empirical subject.

The tendency to break completely from Transcendence originated in Fichte's idealism. What Fichte's predecessors regarded as an exteriority (for example, Kant's thing-existing-in-itself or the idea of Infinity in Descartes), Fichte already saw as a "not-I" created by the I. Thus, in Fichte's conception, every otherness and every objectivity is constructed as a continuous production of the activity of the I. The model in Fichte's dialectic was developed by Hegel and extended to an all-encompassing system of philosophy and history. Hegel's doctrine is the apogee of modernity whereby he presented the process of alienation (objectification) and sublation of alienation—a process that is endless progress, emancipation, and generally speaking, the story of the development of the all-inclusive totality. It is realised as a negation of the conflict of opposites that are subsequently reconciled by synthesis. As a result of the dialectic of thesis, antithesis and synthesis, historical experience endlessly expands and transforms itself. Individuals pursue their private interests and objectives in the struggle for recognition and as such are children of their time, but the Absolute Eternal Spirit of humanity is embodied, albeit unseen by them, in all their activities and at any time as a cumulative dynamic always at work. Each otherness is welcome as far as it may be included in the whole, i.e. to be recognized as consistent with the principle of the system, that is, the Sameness. The Unity is reproduced again and again, engulfing the Other, which is used as a negation that contributes to the crossing of existing borders; but this negation although welcome, is doomed to be waived and absorbed again by the negation of negation in the Whole, i.e. by returning to the Same, yet on a new and higher level. Sameness, Identity or Absolute Reason is the Subject—the real subject—of the entire human history. Transcendence, i.e. the process of transcending as the ceaseless expansion of boundaries, is embodied in the immanence of historical progress, where going forward entails going back and then reaching synthesis through systematization and elevetion. Construction implies reconstruction and as truth is impossible outside of the scientific system of cognition, so freedom is impossible outside of the state and its legal system. An absolute and true subject is precisely that self-developing system that always eludes us and is recreated again and again, using individuals as its agents. Hegel seems to include and develop all Aristotelian definitions of the subject in his encyclopaedia of human knowledge and history but makes the subject a self-expanding substance. Levinas, on the other hand, shares the conviction, widely accepted nowadays, that Hegel's substance/subject, as in general the Modern Subject, is impersonal (or de-personalized at least). Levinas emphasizes that in German idealism, ethics is reduced to politics. In Hegel's philosophy, morality is sublated in the system of state laws. History is a battle between masters and slaves and in this continuous state of war human beings have no faces: rather they are beings among many other beings, forces that oppose each other. In removing the opposition between master and slave, people have been made equal citizens of the state, which without doubt is a step toward humanization. However, inside the state each of "us" is still as faceless as the other due to this egalitarianism. The individual is in effect seemingly correlated directly with totality. The Citizen is "each of us," subject to the legislation of the republic of citizens, where he has rights and obligations—as does everyone else. The one who is not a "citizen" but his opposition, must become a citizen—such that he would be welcome among us, if he can be assimilated and thus be included in the totality of the state. Levinas believes that the relationship of the individual with Infinity is completely different from his relationship with totality of the State. And he also doesn't agree with egalitarianism: I am laways and inevitably more responsible than the Other.

* * *

Nowadays it is generally accepted that the philosophy of Descartes established the sovereignty of the subject and that it is at the centre of general discourse in modern times. However, if we examine Descartes' texts more carefully, it becomes clear that it is not the concept of "subject" that is essential to him but the term "substance" in its new meaning as given by Descartes himself: the term "subject" is found neither among the extensional nor among thinking things but rather is a primordial concept of relation, namely the causal relationship between the finite (things) and the infinite (God). God is the ultimate cause and because all finite things (so-called substances) are caused by God, they are in a causal relationship between themselves. For Descartes, besides thinking and extensional substances, there is a "third substance", which is the unity of soul and body, that is the individual who becomes a "subject." As such, according to Descartes, the I has a dual status: the I is a substance which, on the one hand, is the subject of its accidents but on the other hand, is the subject of Divine sovereignty. The latter is implied by the ideal of the rule of God. Finite things can only be understood in their dependence, i.e. as subordinate to God. The Cartesian subject is still *subjectus*, which is another name for *subditus*, i.e. it is the individual, subjected to *ditio*, to the orders of an authority (God) who is sovereign. From the natural perspective, man is *subjectum*, but in relation to God, he is *subjectus*. In other words, in relation to extensional things, the individual is free and sovereign, like God, but in relation to the authority of God, he is a subjected/subordinate being. Hence the question "Is this not a contradiction within the concept?" To deal with this ambiguity, Kant invented the distinction between transcendental and empirical subjects. The transcendental subject, which by definition is in the third person, in impersonal neuter—"*das Subjekt*" (German) differs from the subject as an individual or a person who is subjected/subordinate to authority; his form is primarily political and his concept is legal. The question, "What is the subject?", "**What** is called a subject?"(*Subjectum*) differs from the question "**Who** is the subject"(*Subjectus*). [47] The former is the subject which is opposed to and distinct from the object or predicate, but is a carrier of properties while the latter is the subject to whom the commands are addressed. It is of the latter that Bossuet stipulated: "*All men are born subjects and paternal authority that accustoms them to obeying accustoms them at the*

---

[47] See the paper and its analysis which we employed: Ettienne Balibar. Citizen Subject. Eduardo Cadava, Peter Connor, Jean-Luc Nancy. *Who comes after the Subject?* Routledge, New York, 1991.

same time to having only one chief." Monotheism as a type of theology is based on this relationship between the One Lord-ship and his subordinates, and all philosophical theories, which perceive God as the original cause, creator, higher Being, etc., reproduced this metaphysical scheme as onto-theo-logy.

At the time of the Old Testament, Man was allowed to give names to things and animals so as to rule over them, but he enjoyed that right not just because of his own Reason but because God had so ordered. This meant that the subject was authorized to be *subjectum* (holder of rights), but only because and insofar as he was firstly *subjectus* (subordinate). Leap forward to the revolution of 1789 that claimed to mark the end of the era of obedience, it was declared that the citizen had to replace the subject (in the sense of "the subordinate"). Contrary to the thesis of Bossuet, it was proclaimed that people are not born subjects, i.e. subjects to the rule of power, but free and equal in rights. The point at which Kant created the transcendental subject coincided with the time when in political life the "king-subject" was beheaded so that citizens of the republic could prevail autonomously.

However, even Descartes faced the dilemma of how the absolute freedom of the individual, or rather his free will, the basis of judgments, could be considered as the likeness of God's will without questioning the will of God itself? On the one hand, it must be the image and likeness of God's sovereignty; on the other hand, it must be subordinated. According to Descartes, to have free will, in the sense of necessary freedom illuminated by true cognition, is consistent with the act by which God maintains the self in every moment of time. My obedience to God becomes the beginning of my reign over nature, i.e. absolute power over objects. Freedom (independence) can be determined herein only as the freedom of a subjected being, which leads to a contradiction in terms. In order to resolve this contradiction Kant's transcendental subject appeared. Therefore, in Kant's philosophy the "I think" uttered by the transcendental subject which is present in all my representations and concepts and is nothing but self-consciousness, guarantees unity of conditions of experience and enjoys freedom, unlike the empirical subject, that is, subject to the forces of natural existence. The transcendental subject himself (the independent, autonomous, rational being in each of us) prescribes to himself (but in his capacity as an empirical subject, that is, the heteronomically dependent being) how to act with the help of the categorical imperative. Even in Kant's theory and after it, the question of the subject is initially about the right and the regulatory principles of behaviour. The transcendental subject or citizen, that which is common in all of us, is not man *de facto*, subject to various internal and external forces and hence just an empirical subject, but man *de jure*, i.e. the normative, universal subject.

In the political history of Western Europe the era of subjects (subordinate to royal power) coincides with the reign of absolutism. Absolutism appears as a complete and unequivocal form of power founded on itself and reproduced by itself. Such power is the prerogative of a being that has no boundaries, i.e. whose authority is unquestionable and uncontrollable by definition. It is this kind of power that renders people as subjects, leading to their subjugation to another. The very existence of subjects coincided with obedience to a higher power. The claim of power to embody good and truth is fully valid in relation to the subject: the subject does not need to know, and even less to understand and think, because what he is being told or prescribed is vital for him. Where individuals are subjected to the power of a supreme sovereign, one who is markedly different from them, the question arises of how to proceed from absolutism to the idea of community, the basis for which is the organization of a group that forms a sovereign people in which they themselves set the laws, i.e. how do equal citizens as autonomous subjects in the totality of the State emerge?

Sociality and Justice: Toward Social Phenomenology 75

In Roman jurisdiction, there was a fundamental difference between dependent and independent individuals. Obedience existed in various forms: slaves, wives, children, relatives ... However, these individuals were not subject to a common regulated relationship with one another. It was the Empire that formed the prerequisite needed in order to transform them into subjects. Subjects were defined as such by their attitude towards the person of the emperor, to whom all subordinate citizens owe *officium* (office). The Empire was theologically justified and the power of the emperor was legitimized as granted by God and protected by him, when the Christianity was adopted. Insofar as subjects were dependent and subordinated, they were viewed as *subditi*, i.e. those who obligatorily turned to *sublimes* (the chosen to command) to hear the commands or laws. Obedience was not coercion, but rather obligation. As *subditi*, subjects felt obligated and wanted their own obedience. Such was the principle[48] ingrained through the entire hierarchy. The chain of hierarchy ultimately derived from a transcendent origin which transformed the subordinate into members of a single body or a single entity that is the Empire. Through this they were created and saved. Loyal is the subject who is voluntarily faithful and who actively and willingly subordinates and takes to heart his obligations and fulfils them, *abiding* by the law and carrying out the orders of the sovereign. As a Christian, he knows that all authority comes from God and by *abiding* by the law of the Ruler, he is obedient to God. The order to which he responds with his behaviour, comes from "beyond" and with his response as an individual, i.e. as an element of the entity of the Empire, he is constituted as a subject.

In the West, at least, that which is endowed with divine attributes is royal power and not the person of the king. Being an incarnation of God's

---

[48] Principle means both a beginning and a command. *Philosophie première et pensée principielle. Le révélateur néoplatocien. Le principe.* Vrin, Paris, 2006, p. 9

will, the King himself still could not claim to be God. Spiritual and secular authority were separated and even began to oppose each other claiming supreme sovereignty over the other. This antagonism required the passage from the divine right of kings to the requirement for direct election of the king. Thus, the corpus (personality) of the King is divided into the human and the divine as is the obedience of his subjects. Troughout antiquity obedience was situational, because man happened to be in it. Anyone could fall into slavery. The slave is to his master as the body is to intellect, i.e. a tool to be exploited. From this perspective, the notion of "free submission" is itself a contradiction in terms. To arrive at the idea of freedom as a foundation of obedience, it had to be shifted to the realm of the soul, which was not conceived as a natural phenomenon, but as a supernatural, supersensual part of the individual which hears the Divine voice in the command, that is, in the issued order. In antiquity, man became a slave when he became dependent on the Commander (*archon*) and was subject to the command (*arché*). To describe such dependence, analogies were employed, using such oppositions as part and whole, passivity and activity, body and mind. However, in Christian culture the soul of the believer is subjected to God and the Christian can never be an object as the slave was to his master—a tool to be used and thus abused. Christian submission fits the idea that could bring salvation. Furthermore, as *subditus-subjectus* was a situation differing from that of the slave, so the sovereignty of *sublimes* was distinguished from the despotism exercised by the master upon the slaves. Of course, the premise is maintained that the only and absolute sovereign is God. Then the free citizen, signified as subject is no longer a political/social animal, as in antiquity, because his soul is immortal and with his behaviour here on earth he participates in the drama of its salvation. His entire earthly life is nothing but a response to God's word. This is the point where another, older layer of the understanding of subjectness is revealed that was abandoned in favour of the modern understanding of the subject as an autonomic citizen. The modern secularized individual begins to perceive himself as emancipated from the prejudices of Christian humility whereas the true Christian does not seek to tear himself away from his relationship with God and even strives with his whole existence to respond to the appeal of God. Both Levinas and Heidegger resorted to the understanding of human existence as a responsibility, resurrecting the understanding that the human is a response to the appeal of the supreme sovereign—Being in Heidegger's understanding and the Other in Levinas'.

* * *

We have a habit of speaking uncritically of the Judeo-Christian culture as a culture of the Biblical word. This culture comes from the alloy of Judaism and Greek philosophy. Levinas thought that some very important meanings were abandoned when Hebrew beliefs were translated into Greek. Such is the case with the translation of the concept of the humanity of men. Levinas actually recovered the forgotten or devalued former meaning of the subject.

According to Judaism, *humanitas* of *homo humanus* is created by the Word. The first word understandable to men by whom it became word was the command: God's commandments. The Jewish people were chosen to respond to God's call. The first command is: "Thou shalt not kill."[49] Man is subject to God's Covenant and is responsible for the others and to others.

---

[49] One of the accusations by Levinas to Stalinism and Hitlerism is that this command was ignored when elevating the killing of innocent people to the status of government policy. He himself personally experienced this and his life was changed by the fateful arrival of these two regimes of power.

The Greek equivalent of the Hebrew word "order" is *kosmos* (the universe), where orderliness and regularity reign (e.g., the orbits of the planets). From this perspective, man is presented as a *mikro-kosmos*, or *microcosm*, where *logos* (reason, language, objective laws) is in power. Men are rational animals and as such—as rationally-constituted beings—they have their particular socio-political nature. In Christianity as it is also in Judaism, the Word creates humanity within man, but in Christianity the Word is incarnated. The initial order, the original command ("order" here is understood in the Greek sense as "initial regulation") is primarily understood as the incarnation of the Word as Creation. Christianity borrowed the terminology of the Greeks and Romans and converted it to assert itself as the core of Western culture. In the Greek language, as well as in Christian texts, humanity is understood as human **nature**. In his preface to the Old Testament Martin Luther discusses how Christians should perceive Moses: "Therefore, I preserved the commandments that Moses gave not because Moses is the one who gave them, but because they were invested in me **by nature** ... They are invested in each and everyone of us and inscribed in the heart of everyone."

The motive of being chosen is deeply rooted in Jewish culture wherein God speaks to everybody separately, in person, but is replaced in Christianity with the concept of equality of all children of God who form community. Moreover, the word of God does not come from the mouth of the prophets, but is embedded in the nature of every man. Modern Christian philosophy adopted the Christian inclination that shifts the place of God from "the outside to the inside", from transcendence into immanence, from exteriority to interiority. In Hegel's philosophy, this trend is taken to the extreme, because all exteriority is presented as interiority in the incarnation of the World Spirit, that is, in the world history.

From the Old Testament, however, we also learn that people become moral subjects, not through their response and obedience to God's commandments, but by violating them. Man became a moral being after eating the fruit from the tree of knowledge and began to distinguish good from evil. Since then, he began imitating God and wanted to become the master of human fate—to be free to take decisions for himself and for others. Levinas blames both Christianity and paganism for one and the same sin of idolatry. As paganism created its gods according to the norms of the time and began to pray to the forces of nature as gods, so Christianity created an image of God to befit human representations and began to pray in front of icons that replaced God or the Absolute Other. While in Christianity, man is the image and likeness of God and prayers begin with "My God", the Hebrew God retains his position of exteriority—God is the Absolute Other, God is Transcendence that even could not be named. Levinas insisted that Transcendence could not be contained within the ideas of it, nor could it be embodied. For Levinas true monotheism is not compatible with any belief in myths or with idolatry. God is present for us, precisely when he is absent, when he withdraws, such that, everything becomes dependent on us; it is up to us whether we will read His Word and follow His Trace. Our definitions, symbols and ideas reduce God to something we possess. However, Transcendence cannot be possessed. Western cultures create ideas about God in the conviction that as a result they know the Absolute Other. They tend to anthropomorphise God. With this confidence people begin to feel as free and autonomous beings because they understand themselves as God's images. On the one hand, Levinas praises Western culture for its development of the concept of personality and its inherent freedom; on the other hand, he is dissatisfied with this culture because it transports God from the exteriority into the interiority through ideas and a wilfull amnesia with regards to humanity's responsibility to follow God's commandment. In secularized, i.e. modern culture, freedom of the active subject borders on irresponsibility—everything that is not prohibited or does not meet the resistance of others is therefore permited. Levinas criticizes this type of culture.

Generally, efforts in Western philosophy were aimed at understanding human nature, the results of which are expressed by Ortega-y-Gasset in paradoxical form: people do not have nature—they have history. In the words of Sartre: only existence is given to men, but not their essence—being free to act, man makes from himself what he wants to in the concreteness of his historical situation. Levinas, however, was sceptical about these maxims:

> The concern of contemporary philosophy to free man from categories adapted solely to things, therefore, must not be content with the opposition between the static, inert, and the determined nature of things, on one hand, and dynamism, durée, transcendence or freedom as the essence of man on the other. It is not so much a matter of opposing one essence to another, or of saying what human nature is. It is primary a matter of our finding a vantage point from which man ceases to concern us in terms of the horizon of being, i.e., ceases to offer himself to our powers. The being as such (and not as an incarnation of universal being) can only be in a relation in which he is invoked.[50]

Furthermore:

> By relating to beings in the openness of being, understanding finds a meaning for them in terms of being. In this sense, understanding does not invoke them, but only names them.[51]

* * *

In a sense, Heidegger's philosophy is an attempt to restore the broken thread between the history of Being and the call of Being, between the openness and the appeal. Heidegger reverts to the old motive of the call and human existence as a response. Let us reiterate the question, raised

---

[50] Emmanuel Levinas. Is Ontology Fundamental? *Entre Nous: Thinking–of-the-Other*. Columbia University Press, New York, 1998, p. 8–9
[51] Ibid. p. 9

repeatedly not only by Heidegger, but since ancient times: Is man's humanity constituted in the fact that the human being is a rational animal? If the answer is yes, as it was for the Ancient Greek, then what does "rational" or "thinking" mean? What do we mean by thinking? What is Reason? Is the common way of thinking not just a way of reproducing the rubrics with which "*Das Man*" thinks? Heidegger believes that instrumental reason and passion for technologies triumph through these rubrics and their recurrence. Because of his efficiency due to such rubrics, *Das Man* is not aware of his own historicity, even when telling world history. *Das Man* is immersed in his everyday activities and has forgotten himself as a being-towards-death. Nonetheless, according to authentic ontology, thinking by its very nature is something very personal, coincidental to the facticity of temporal existence of *Dasein*. Thinking is done not as human control over the nature and world's circumstances, but in the understanding of *Dasein* as being thrown into the world and in a determination to accept his own fate. There is no difference between the understanding of *Dasein's* Being and the existence of *Dasein* in the world. According to Heidegger, the entirety of Western civilization is derived from the intelligibility of Being, even if it is oblivion of Being. For Heidegger, reason itself—whether theoretical or practical—is not just the ability to know and act; it is first listening carefully to Being. *Dasein* is the subject of cognition and labour; *Dasein* is the builder of this world and the creator of culture due to the preliminary attention to the silence of Being manifested in the language. The response to the silence of Being is the possibility of authentic existence of *Dasein* itself—a response that is possible and fulfilled as *Dasein's* own responsibility.

Levinas wrote his philosophy under Heidegger's strong influence (as already mentioned and as is well known, he first acquainted his French audience with the works of Husserl and Heidegger). However, Levinas sought another type of intelligibility that is *differentia specifica* of our humanness: he was looking for meaning "beyond Being"—a meaning that is not revealed in the terms of Being (existence) and one that precedes Being.

* * *

From the first wave of criticism of Hegel's philosophy the fight began against the elevation of totality to the rank of the highest value and the most reliable criterion for meaning. The first fight was waged by way of the demystification of the subject, identified with universal Reason. Nietzsche insisted that we must seek the "will to power" behind reason; Freud declared that our entire culture is not a product of reason, but is rather a sublimation of the libido, i.e. it is a rationalization of the unconscious impulses; Bergson called reason "enlightened instinct." This critical mood penetrated deeply into the intellectual atmosphere of Europe surrounding the two world wars. Modern optimism about the victorious progress of Reason in history began to disappear and was replaced with an era of suspicion where truth became suspect especially when it centred on the "reasonable" being. As is widely accepted, this suspicion was transformed into doubt about the existence of any reasonable subject. The subject was perceived as a rational being only insofar as it is a part of a supra-individual mechanism, supra-personal totality and a self-perpetuating structure of society. As a result, in the second half of the 20th century it was even proclaimed that the subject was dead, triggering an extensive and noisy debate which involved Gilles Deleuze, Maurice Blanchot, Michel Foucault, Jacques Derrida, Alain Badiou, Luce Irigaray, Jean-Luc Marion, Jean-François Lyotard and others. Postmodern philosophy attacked the main character in modern drama, namely the subject, identified with reason, yet without denying the individual's authority, because one who is still subjected to some social/political automatism is a part of a greater totality. Postmodernists sometimes openly (and sometimes more reticently) challenge all categories supporting the identification of humanity, sociality and rationality, going back to the earliest sources of such identification. Levinas joined the critics of Hegel's philosophy, but not in their attacks on the rationality of men. He was looking for another and more human form of intelligibility: non-intentional consciousness. Unlike the accusations made against society, which were grounded in the repressive function on the individual, which in turn fed modernity's individualism and egocentricity, Levinas proceeded with his philosophical interpretation, arguing that the sociality is constitutive of individuals and therefore public institutions are perceived positively as conditioning the freedom inside of the totality. Like many postmodern authors, Levinas delved into the roots of our culture and our widely accepted world-view. This enabled him to avoid dispute as to whether the totality or the individual took precedence over the other in explaining society. Furthermore, by basing his argument in the roots of Western Culture, Levinas avoided a philosophy that underminds trust in reason, in society and in the subject. Unlike the "philosophy of rebellion" (against oppression, nothingness, alienation, community, totality etc.), Levinas unlocked the possibility of a social phenomenology "of responsibility." We do not need revolutions, which always establish a new regime of oppression, nor should we fight against each other for more power. Instead we should strive for solidarity as caring for the Other's rights. Care or responsibility, however, goes far beyond simple equality and indifference of tolerance.

* * *

Levinas started from the phenomenological understanding of consciousness as intentionality, but did not believe that the conversation with someone, the attitude towards him, the meeting with someone, could be rationalized according to Husserl's concept of intentionality. Levinas sought to show the existence of another "intrigue", different from that described by Husserl's intersubjective relationship. Often when Levinas refers to the dialogical philosophy in his writings, we must take into account that, in accordance with his model, speech and conversation are not a reciprocal relation between equal partners, i.e. dialogue. Speech is not partnership, rather the Other is in the superior position: he or she is asking me and with this, questioning me by his/her presence, and then I am the one who is called to respond, i.e. the respons-ible one. However, that does not mean that I am in the position of slavish obedience, nor am I in the position of the subject of pastoral power (Foucault). The subject is the single responsible one whose whole existence is a response to the call—man is called being and not merely born to survive. This is investment of freedom in me upon the unspoken request by the Other and the expectation of an answer from me. As a moral subject I am summoned, authorized, empowered to respond to the Other, hence I feel chosen among others, unique, irreplaceable. I cannot escape from responsibility, because the lack of response on my part is in itself a response. If I try to hide and transfer responsibility onto someone else, this response would be immorality itself—a desire to ignore or escape morality. Furthermore, when as subject I respond and give of myself, I am no longer in the passive position of someone who asks "Does this concern me?" "Are you calling me?" "Is it expected of me?", but in the nominative case as "I"—I who answers and takes the blame and authorship; the initiator of actions on my part. The said then seemed to betray the saying and the moral subject is once again restored to the rights of an agent on the plane of the living world, where even conversation is considered a type of action.

The subject as an actor is "I" in its quality of identity and is the actual work of his own identification but my responsibility as a moral subject is a kind of identity removal. Identification as a process implies receiving continuous recognition from others. My decision is a response to the Other's appeal to me. It is to the Other who is in need and who is a vulnerable human being that I feel the moral obligation to give and to apologize for not being able to give more. Thus, the Other's exteriority and otherness are constitutive of morality. Only as a moral subject responding with "that is me" (as Abraham and Moses respond to God and not I am my Self as Here I am), does the Self transcend his egocentrism towards the Other. Because of the face-to-face encounter the Subject is freed from the condition of the anonymity that he accepted unconditionally where both the Other and his own persona were confined with their identity and their place in the rationally established order. This escape is inspired by the call of the Other. Even the mere presence of the Other is already urging my answer and my self-reflection. Called by the Other, I answer him, but I also distance myself from my own *Ego*. This is also the starting point for possible self-criticism, which is an ongoing process of the moral subject. The moral subject is never satisfied with himself: the more he gives, the more he is indebted; the more self-critical he becomes, the more guilty he feels; the better he is, the less satisfied he is with his own good deeds. It is important to emphasize here that the spiral of the endless penetration deeper into interiority as responsibility is provoked by the gravity of exteriority.

To acquire meaning, morality needs a subject that can carry the weight of the world on his shoulders: *sub-jectum*. He is responsible beyond any measure and standard, open to the difference, that is, to the otherness of the Other. Subject-ness therefore is the result of subjectivation: the Self, who in the encounter with the Other is transformed from "I" into "me". My self-identification is affected, challenged, questioned and turned upside down. Levinas describes the moral subject as having lost his place, unlocking his potential without any reservation for the Other. At the beginning, this happens through the sincerity of the Saying which is the model for every giving and openness. The moral subject is dedicated to the Other to such a degree that he maintains the Other's presence or his present time, which is in this moment transcending its own present. However, transcendence, as Levinas noted, is Infinity's life and although the Other will never be reached in this "never", we must look for the "ever" (i.e. eternity) of time itself. The Moral Subject supports the time of the Other, but this which supports, says Levinas, gives way to that which is supported. The moral subject is even responsible for the responsibility of the Other, whom the I can never grasp, or contain, or even anticipate, nor project. Morality of the subject is a dimension despite his own self; this dimension is his being chosen, his load of responsibilities or his inspiration, which the I owes firstly to the Other's unspoken call. Due to morality, the I acquires the uniqueness of the one who is signified, distinguished and chosen to respond.

1.4. Time and death

In *The Myth of Sisyphus*, Albert Camus says that in the life of any of us a moment comes when we have to take the burden of time on our own shoulders, whereas before this moment we were floating carefree upon its wings. Heidegger would have soberly corrected him by saying that *Dasein* as a being-towards-death bears the burden of his time from the very moment of birth. Levinas would have added in turn that the moral subject not only cares for his own time, but also undertakes to carry the load of the Other's time and because of this double burden, human existence is diachronic.

A long time ago we are accustomed to think of time as the synchronization of the moments through "I think", where "I think" becomes the foundation of "I can". However, Levinas' moral subject exists in diachrony, i.e. in double temporalization. My time does not and can not coincide with the time of the Other, although the moral subject spends his time maintaining[52] the time of the Other. In the frame of common time,

---

[52] With this wordplay Levinas uses the ambiguity of the word *maintenir*—support as foundation, hold someone, pay maintenance to someone, stand as stand in the adversity and carry someone like one carries a baby in one's arms and so on. But this kind of support always *maintains* the face to face relation.

the subject is in the nominative as "I" and the Other is just another "I" (Husserl's *Alter Ego*). In the appeal to the "I" by the Other, where the self is called (in vocative case) — from first hearing it and even before understanding it, the subject is in the accusative ("Are they calling **me?**", "Is someone summoning **me?**","Does she need **me?**"...). To avoid an answer which represents an action irrelevant to the question or an exercise of power[53], it is necessary to comply with the presence, desire, expectation, interest, situation, query, request made by the Other, even when silent. Thereafter the I speaks, not to express itself, although this inevitably happens, and not to show what the world is or what the world should be, although one of the indispensable functions of language is to indicate. Nor is the function of speech to seek the truth, although by speaking the I unavoidably points to it; the Self speaks, connecting with the Other — and connects to him/her, even when ignoring him/her.

a) Existential Time

As demonstrated in Heidegger's *Being and Time*, to be or not to be, i.e. the question of life and death is asked daily and hourly in existential time. It is the question of survival made possible due to the dialectic of being and nothingness (Hegel). In this struggle in which the whole is at stake and in this becoming, being the drama of aging (as added by Levinas), it is still Death that has the last word. Death makes ridiculous and irrelevant the free being with its determination to exist and its wish to be and to preserve itself. In a way, life maintains life, i.e. resists annihilation. We survive by engulfing the others in the identity of the Ego, that is, Ego's life, but for how long? Are not all attempts to escape death made in vain, and does "nothing" not triumph in the end over any effort to perpetuate the finite being? It does not make a difference if one is fighting "nothingness" with even the slightest advantage over others and with his face

---

[53] Because as we know — for example, from Roland Barthes — any speaking suggests that the speaker wants to identify with power and stand in the position of power.

turned toward the future since the future of any future is death; or if one is running, focused on an ever distancing past left in ruins by death, as the death catches one from behind to inflict its last stroke; or if one clings to the present, in the moment, which cannot be stopped, but disappears immediately into the abyss of nothingness. Whether heroic, nostalgic or calculating, in delaying the time of death, such postponement, within which the finite being lives its life, is the existential time. Levinas is fully aware of the fact that no one knows when death will come. The I cannot capture the moment of its own death which goes beyond the scope of one's possibilities. It is not, as Heidegger says, another possibility—the possibility of impossibility but vice versa, according to Levinas: the impossibility of all possibilities. Death seems to come from a power over which the I has no power. Death is the threat that approaches irrevocably. Time that separates the Ego from death, i.e. existential time, becomes increasingly thin in the course of life. Despite all the efforts and activities of the I, dedicated as they are to its own conservation, life dissipates into nothingness. In this resistance to transience, the I cannot make the last step, the last distance to the end, the last moment in which it is surprised by the bony hands of Death snatching him out of nowhere. In its surprise encounter with death, which comes as though with a leap, consciousness disappears. It is as if death approaches from an opposite direction in time such that the I is confused in its future project by death's absolute otherness. Fear of death is the fear of violence by the other, exercised over the I—fear of the absolutely inevitable. The individual has his own time due to the awareness of this constraint, compulsion, condemnation—of this tyranny. However,

Inevitability is at the same time threat and reprieve. It suppresses and liberates time. Timely being, that is, a being which is doomed to death, but still has some time is being towards death. But imminence is at the same time menace and postponement. It pushes on, and leaves time. To be temporal is both to be for death and to still have time, to be against death."[54]

Unlike Heidegger, who defines human being as being towards death, Levinas defines it as being against death. However, both know that death is not one moment only—the last moment in which the individual surrenders completely, but his way of existence in which "being" also means "being towards death".[55] Yet that last moment, the moment of Death, bears exclusivity because in it all resources to protect life have been exhausted and it marks the end of the power of the subject.

Nonetheless, the consciousness of time remaining, of time in which the I still may and in which he still has the energy, allows a postponement of violence. Resistance against the triumph of death—prediction, ambushing, cunning, and all tactics and strategies targeted at immortality—is possible only because of consciousness. Human freedom and human culture exist because of consciousness. Being a conscious, free being, according to Levinas, means to take into account the otherness, the future and death. It means that one has time to stave off one's own defeat—to know that one's freedom is in danger and to take measures to forestall the moment of inhumanity, to avoid it. But is this not utopian? How can one avoid the unavoidable?

Suffering (suffered life, endured life) is, of course, given in consciousness. Purely as a phenomenon, suffering is useless, meaningless and "for nothing"—it is the empty profundity of nonsense. It is not identical with the empirical situation of pain. But my suffering for the undue suffering of the Other opens up the moral dimension between human beings, where the Other has a meaning for me and is therefore the superior

---

[54] Emmanuel Levinas. *Totality and Infinity*. Duquesne University Press, 1992, Pittsburg, p. 235
[55] Emmanuel Levinas. *God, Death, and Time*. Stanford University Press, 2000, p. 43

one—the Other as such reveals the dimension of the superiority in life. The I can forget about itself because of the suffering of the Other. From this perspective, there is a radical difference between the suffering of the Other, which is unforgivable for me and calls me, and my suffering, my own experience of suffering. The uselessness of my suffuring acquires meaning because of being suffering due to someone else's suffering. In Levinas' conception, attention to the suffering of the Other (despite the atrocities of the century, because of them and in opposition to them) experienced as the very core of human subjectivity, is elevated to the level of the highest ethical imperative—the only imperative that cannot be questioned. Suffering because of the suffering of the Other is no longer "for nothing", nor useless, but "for the Other" and thus acquires immediate sense. Suffering is meaningless with regard to the experience of the Ego (the Self in the nominative is the beginning of the activity but suffering is passivity, enduration). It is however, meaningful for me, as suffering because of the suffering of the Other (the Self here is in the accusative "me" as enduring, remorseful, guiltful, called to take the blame and responsibility). Holiness, that is, suffering for the suffering of the Other, as the single ethical imperative cannot be questioned. It creates hope, inspires, promises, provokes expectations, lays the foundation of trust, communication, cooperation, and moreover, commands practical discipline in human groups.

b) Historical time

Consciousness as pure and mere thinking, even when thinking of itself, remains ineffective against the brutal force imposed on the single human being by sources much more powerful than it. The single human being resorts to unification and system—to the organization of nature and society, i.e. to order, which is meaningful and opposed to coercion as the source of all suffering. This order helps the fight for deferment of the supreme violence: the violence of death. Freedom of the individual with the fantasy of floating in the direction it wants, as the wind, is illusory. True freedom as realized in the world cannot survive except through the creation and maintenance of social and political institutions. This is the lesson Levinas learned from the German idealists.

Human will resists violence and suffering in their absurdity by cultivating arbitrariness into freedom. Freedom interferes with reality when decisions are carved in stone, in the written text of laws, technology and tools, in public institutions and facilities, in the entire organization of cohabitation. The techniques of politics, economics, law, etc. help postpone the last day. Conscious beings invest in public order to obtain insurance against death, albeit only with a temporary policy. The will trusts judgment according to universal laws, embodied in the system of institutions and human interactions, in order to seek protection in its resistance to death and in the hope of receiving an objective judgment of its meaning. Such a verdict is the verdict of history.

However, the verdict of history, says Levinas, is always pronounced in absentia. Free will is not present when the sentence is announced, i.e. it is present, but only in the third person—without being able to speak on its own behalf and without the right to defence. Man is judged by history with regard to his deeds, given the legacy he leaves behind. Judging the results of someone's performance as an actor, desecrates his humanity, alienates him from himself and objectifies him. The human being is thereby profanized. History shows disrespect and injustice towards the one judged as it deprives the individual of the right to defend himself and turns him into an object of a judgement. Man is reduced to his social role and is judged by society's terms: "He was a good father, a professional, a social activist ...", i.e. it is always man "in his capacity as...". People have meaning in terms of the personification of their historical roles, as performers in a drama, whose author is someone else. Man is, in effect, mummified in the tomb of wills, already dead and his sarcophagus is one among many. In the pantheon of historical memory, human beings are identified as from outside, exposed to a viewer who observes and assesses them from the position of the living, the survivor. Consequently, there is always some nostalgia for cynicism in history. From a bird's eye view historical events, reduced to facts, to something already past, become subject to investigation, certification, proof, and are then united by historical narrative. Courtesy of this narrative, history appears as a string of events with a beginning, middle and end with a reasonable course of development. Only from the narrator's perspective, filling the existential times into an historical whole and dividing it into periods according to times past, present and future—only from the perspective of an "objective observer" who speaks and judges from a supratemporal perspective, perceiving history as totality, can we speak of the meaning of historical becoming.

The ethical problem is meaning and not being
However, does the intelligibility of what has happened depend solely on testimony and proofs, on evidence and investigations? Is it only these factors that measure the meaning and significance of events and deeds? Should we not also take justice into account, which in contrast to historical justice does not deprive us of a defence? True respect for human rights requires the accused to be summoned and heard. He is the origin of the proceeding and the one bearing the most responsibility. He has responsibility, which cannot be transferred to someone else—to the Third, or to institutions, to the State, the collective, the circumstances, the case etc. The defendant is expected to vindicate himself. His position is fundamentally apologetic. Every court tests the arbitrariness, i.e. the question of the limits of freedom; hence freedom has to justify itself. My freedom, understood as the spontaneity of my decisions, my determination to be my Self, my assessment of things, employed by the all-permissive arbitrariness, are discouraged in the court hearing. In such a situation, the I is not alone but is questioned by others. The Court urges the

Self to respond on its own behalf, and the verdict is taken by the Self to the degree in which the others' enquiries are interiorized by the Self as its consciousness seeks the answers. Hence the question is not only to be or not to be, as in ontology and dialectic, but what is my right to be. Indeed, what is my right to be what I am? Or what I want to be? Or what I choose to be? This question, says Levinas, is against nature, against the normality of life where I am a creature among many peer creatures and it is a question to the evidence of my participation in mankind, where the I hides in the anonymity of interchangeable people. This question — Do I have the right to be? — is ethical and enquires about the meaning of "Da"[56] in *Dasein*, and not just "why there is *Dasein*, and not the opposite — nothing?", i.e. the ontological question.

The ethical question of the meaning of human existence, i.e. of the meaning of existential time, cannot be answered by referencing any natural or artificial expediency, that is, it cannot be responded to in any ontological, phenomenological, sociological, epistemological or any other logical terms. Any assessment in terms of participation in historical time sees individuals as cogs in a wheel of the Hegelian World Spirit and the very nuts and bolts in the mechanisms of society. History creates the illusion that we do not "speak the language, but it speaks us" (Heidegger). Questions about my right to be are similar to the conceptual questions in reflection (which are answered with concepts) only in that they destroy the spontaneity of my naive struggle to be. However, while reflection takes the Self back to itself, the ethical question that the I asks itself, is already a response to an inquiry from the Other. The ethical question is not prompted by the Self's desire for self-cognition but by the presence of the Other face to face with One-and-the-Same (the one identifying with himself in the process of his changing). This question is answered

---

[56] Heidegger's term *Dasein* could be translated "Here I am" and uses the nominative of the verb "to be" in Levinas' concept could be translated "That is me", where the grammatical first person is in the accusative.

by the individual I each time it utters "I do", "I think" or even simply, "I am." The responsibility of the I and its relationship with the Other are created simultaneously, i.e. the responsibility of the I is the fundamental relation with the Other.

The I exists in the process of its own identification, rediscovering its identity again and again and going through everything that happens in existential time. Heterogeneity of experience can be qualified as "I think" and is homogenized in *Jemeinigkeit*. This is the world of the imperialist and self-centred Self. The I being accommodated and being "here", on the Earth and under the sky, in the company of mortals and awaiting the gods (Heidegger), is the way it faces the otherness of the world. "Here" is not an empty receptacle but the place where the I is a subject, displaying its capabilities and depending on a reality that is different, but is already under-stood by the Self and totalized by him and presented as an entity. From now on everything in the world is "in its own place"— thanks to the nativeness and the place of the Self. The other here is the reality on which the Self depends and exists as a being maintained in its freedom. Each reality is correlated with the Self, everything belongs to it and is in-corporated thanks to its corp—everything is theoretically apprehended and practically controlled. The identification of this I, however, is so to speak, territorial. Its totalization is never complete and the being is forever open not due simply to the weakness, limitations, inability, finitude of the Self and his quivering when facing his destruction as a being; it is primarily due to the Other. The Other is the one that does not allow capture and enclosure in a system and does not become part of the world's entity. The Other is beyond. The Absolute Other eludes all attempts to be conceptualised, thematized, perceived and in this sense is transcendence and infinity. This is his way of being Other. This Transendence and Infinity is revealed for each of us by the otherness of the Face.

The essence of speech as interpreted by Levinas, is that it questions, calls and awakens responsibility. If a stranger (and we are all strangers on this earth, as is written in the Bible) asked me a question, I could choose whether or not to answer, but his very presence as the Stranger questions my right to be the native one, the usurper of this land. The Alien questions my inner spontaneous freedom to identify with this world, with the established order; he commands my freedom and looks for an answer, causing me to justify myself; he judges me and makes me see the truth about myself. However, the truth is not achieved from the distance of time as historical justice, something which Hegel would have probably maintained; true justice is to see in the Other, my master, my teacher and mentor, whose commands, orders, instructions and pledges are understood through being fulfilled before I have any knowledge of them. This first understanding in fulfilment of the command, executed before any awareness and cognition, makes the human a subject. This understanding in fulfilment is more ancient than consciousness, i.e. than the subject-object-relationship. The more just the I is, the more guilty he is. His obligations increase to the extent that they are fulfilled. In historical time, where the individual is a citizen of the State, a member of society and a participant in the community, his rights and obligations are balanced in the struggle for mutual recognition between various groups and individuals. In the immediacy of social relationships, i.e. in the face-to-face relation, the more the Self gives, the more indebted he is. Unlike human rights in general, as protected by a *Charter*, for example, which limits group or individual egoism, in ethics it is not my rights that are central but the rights of the Other. Being I, says Levinas, is to see beyond universal rights and laws into the insult inflicted by the verdict of history, which does not respect the uniqueness of the Other. What is not seen in historical time is the ignoring of the first person and its rights of defence, which no one else could perform for it. Being myself, and not just the embodiment of universal laws or dialectic movements of the

World Spirit, means to be responsible not only for one's own actions, as per the judgement of history and the laws of the State, but to answer first for the Other; to fear for the rights of the Other more than for one's own rights and to foresee my responsibility even before an action has been committed. This means managing to predict my own potential for moral lapse and fall into the arbitrariness of my liberty, not preceded by responsibility. That is to be afraid for the Other, more than the I is afraid of death and to take risks to avoid leaving the Other alone and without an answer, i.e. *to expend my time for the time of the Other*. Immediately when the I assumes that its duties to the Other have been fulfilled and stops feeling summoned to watch over the Other, non-indifference to the Other is replaced by in-difference and depersonalization. Being-for-the-Other is not achieving equality by escaping relations of domination and subordination that is at stake, but going beyond equality. The intrigue with the otherness of the Other, charity and love without fusion and unification, without lust, without flirting and self-interest is degraded in the struggle for recognition through the plotting, the calculation of gains and losses and in outplaying the Other. In the struggle for supremacy whether in war or in peace, the outcome is only a temporary truce until the next battle. However, the problem is not the peace compromise achieved on the battlefield as a result of temporary alliances and enmities but the messianic peace that is above history.

c) Eschatological Time

Levinas insists that Messianic peace does not reign after the epic of history has been concluded. On the contrary, in every "now" in history, the Other calls the I and urges him to speak. The difference between the existence of the individual in history without the right to raise his voice and his existence for the Other in the face-to-face relationship distinguishes historical from eschatological time. Eschatology is the end of history, when history is not the judge but is itself judged. It does not happen

Sociality and Justice: Toward Social Phenomenology 97

at a point external to history, but within history. Eschatological time masters the course of the One's existential time, which leads to death, directing it towards the time of the Other. It is as if the existential time of the I (where present, protention and retention are in play), comes out of phase and the power of the Self as subject creates the possibility of the time of the Other. It also overcomes depersonalization in the course of history. This transition, this prevalence originates as being for the Other—expending my time to create and maintain the time of the one who will be after me, even when I am not here. Eschatological time is produced as overcoming *conatus essendi* of the mortal being in the diaconate, in the vigil for the Other, in the selflessness of the apostle's work, in the service and lithurgy for him and for the others.

In eschatology the Ego has no hope for itself. Moses brings his people to the Promised Land without himself setting foot there. The transformation of the Self into a subject, responsible for everything that happens or does not happen in world history, opportunities taken or missed, puts him in the position of the Messiah. At any point in time, he judges history not only because of his own being-towards-death, where his own existence is a problem, but above all because of being-towards-death of the others. Hence eschatological time is diachronical and not synchronous as is biographical or historical time. Eschatological time is the relationship with the Other itself. This relation is not symmetrical, because the I is always weighed down with one more responsibility—it is always responsible not only for itself but also for the Other. The I is even responsible for the responsibility of the Other while the responsibility of the Other to me, says Levinas, is his business. Eschatological time is diachronic because my existential time is important not for me only, but also and primarily for the existential time of the Other (and hence for the historical time of the Third).

Time itself should not be confused with that which is not time, but is only temporal—as for instance historical time is regarded in the case of the becoming of being, community, State, etc. Historical becoming is represented by the change and preservation of beings that unite and separate, live and die, like atoms in the void. What is left after them is a temporary effect, which disappears quickly and melts in the resultant of history. But Levinas argues that there is a genuine and ineffaceable trace, manifested in the obligation of One to "be his brother's keeper" here and now, when the true mandating authority has already been withdrawn from the world; however, its absence flashes in the epiphany of the face. Transcendence, which is already passed, shines in the eyes and the face of the Other. But this light, this superiority, cannot be deduced from being, from "the here and now", neither by its disclosure nor by its invisibility. The trace is the inclusion of the immensity of the Other in time, i.e. in the present—the point where the world is directed to a past that is not the time of the world "here and now" but an irretrievable, irrevocable and invisible transcendence. "A trace is a presence of that which properly speaking has never been there, of what is always past."[57] Levinas argues that God who has passed us by is not the model for the Face: "To be in the image of God does not mean to be icon of God, but to find oneself in his trace."[58] To follow this trace is not to go towards God, but towards the others.

> The Other is the very locus of metaphysical truth, and is indispensable for my relation with God. He does not play the role of a mediator. The Other is not the incarnation of God, but precisely by his face, in which he is disincarnated, is the manifestation of the height in which God is revealed.[59]

The path to God passes through the responsibility for others. Perhaps, says Levinas, this transition is eternity. I seriously believe—he declares—

---

[57] Emmanuel Levinas. Meaning and Sense. *Collected Philosophical Papers*. Duquesne University Press, Pittsburgh, Pennsylvania, 1998, p. 106–107
[58] Ibid.
[59] Emmanuel Levinas. *Totality and Infinity*. Duquesne University Press, 1992, Pittsburg, p. 78–79

that this utopia affects history. Existential time cannot be just an interval in historical time, or mere survival as a result of problematizing our own existence and choosing ourselves with triumph and determination, so that the time of world history can be reduced to the moment of existence. Messianic time breaks down the progressive course of history and of existence, making each of them possible anew and defining their direction. Messianic or eschatological time is the sacred in the profane. It is time expended not for my salvation from death, but to save the otherness of the Other—that is my life for others: "… where the will is transported to a life against someone and for someone, death no longer touches the will."[60] In death biological movements lose all dependence on signification or expression. Death is destruction; it is in-expressiveness, lack of reply, response-less, and it is thus ir-responsibility. Death is an incurable void and vice versa: when someone lives and is himself, he is not indifferent to others and thereby expresses himself and replies to them, that is, he is responsible for them and takes the blame for them; he is a person, not a mask and does not allow human intimacy to be invaded by futility, nor slavery to be immortalized nor emptiness to reign.

* * *

Responsibility testifies that to be human is to live by meanings. Primary among these meanings is the Other. Meaning—any meaning—is born from speech, and speaking is first of all a conversation with the Other (before being a monologue reminiscent of what has been said, heard and indicated). Reason is constituted in conversation. However, Levinas argues that for people in the West, it is not approaching the Other through speech that matters; what is more important is communication of information—meaning is attained in what is reported. Signification is consid-

---

[60] Ibid., p. 240

ered a representation of being. Levinas, however, spoke of the importance of the relation One-for-the-Other, regardless of any content and any communication of content. At the ontological level, Levinas says, "for" has the meaning of a break-up with rationality, but on the level of ethics, where One calls the Other, "for" in the relation "one-for-the-other" is the primordial rationality.

The moral subject is constituted not by the pattern of action and reaction, where every action leads to a reaction (as Newton noticed in solid physical bodies), but by the model of speech and conversation. For Levinas, real conversation is both instructive and apologetic. The conversation presupposes greeting, attention, respect for the Other, and this represents the first manifestation of justice. Levinas insists that justice is not the result of the "normal" game of injustice, i.e. is not the result of politics, economics, law and, more generally, of any fundamental or regional ontology. Justice is done as a principle imposed from "beyond being." Justice is an understandable motive of behaviour only if the starting point is the authenticity of caring for the other, loving thy neighbour or, in other words, from the responsibility for others, from morality. Levinas reveals the intrigue and dramatic character of the human, first and foremost by reference to language, where the said betrays the saying.

1.5. In the beginning was the Word ... with the Other

Levinas insists that every true word is a commandment.[61]

Of course, this statement shocks today. Nowadays, it is believed that the true word is dialogue which is a kind of mutual exchange—a type of negotiation between partners, a discussion to achieve common understanding about what interests us. Hence a command or even a mentoring tone is unacceptable. It is believed that the decency at least presupposes

---

[61] Emmanuel Levinas. *Collected Philosophical Papers.* Translated by A. Lingis, Duquesne University Press, Pittsburgh, Pennsylvania, 1998, p. 23

tolerance to the rights of others to be able to express their opinions. It is thought that not only compulsion, but even the simplest impediment tends towards hindering communication rather than allowing it to happen. In true dialogue everyone should have equal opportunities to maintain an independent perspective and thus be an equal participant in the discussion. This means that everyone has the opportunity to contribute to the mutual agreement, to achieving general consent or a common solution. Discussion in dialogue is considered to be a reciprocal exchange of information, perspectives and assessments etc. Objectivity, which we could rise to in the dialogue, presupposes intersubjectivity, which is at least bilateral (potentially multilateral). Each discussion is a dialectics of questions and answers. What is spoken unites interlocutors and makes their relationship symmetrical because they are centred on the conversational topic. The conversational theme is therefore the common place, which allows for the achievement of a common language, i.e. the overcoming of particularity by delineation of a general horizon. Through understanding between participants, a common world is established.

Levinas would not disagree with any of the above, because he knows that language is a manifestation of *logos*. However, before being *logos*, it is an appeal; before being the articulation of things in the world, it is a call from the Other. Indeed, in the art of inference, the most important moment is to find the middle third, i.e. the middle term. Moreover, before establishing a symmetrical and reciprocal relationship between interlocutors who reference their perspectives to the third, the word addresses the Other.

> Language as an exchange of ideas about the world, with the mental reservations it involves, across the vicissitudes of sincerity and deceit it delineates, presupposes the originality of the face without which... it could not commence.[62]

---

[62] Emmanuel Levinas. *Totality and Infinity*. Translated by A. Lingis, Duquesne University Press, Pittsburgh, 1992, p. 202

So every conversation first presupposes a particular approach to the Other, and that is an asymmetrical and non-reciprocal relation in which it is the I that is called. In this orientation of One to the Other, the Other is the superior one. It is for him that the word is spoken and every effort made and every risk taken. He motivates the initiation of the conversation and sets the primordial intentionality of the speech that follows. The attitude of One to the Other further defines every "what", "how" and "why" of the meeting. The topical, interpretation and motivational relevance, which are united in *logos*, are preceded by the relevance of the Other.

Levinas insists, as already previously reiterated, that the Other has a transcendent dimension. The Other is the privileged one and is not on the same level with me as is the usual idea of dialogue. The path to him does not resemble a trajectory, connecting two points located on the same level. The inequality between the Other and I, though, is not that of master and slave, in which two finite beings are hierarchically positioned in the same finite world in certain social and political conditions set by power. The approach to the Other also differs in the interaction between two natural or social beings, equally active, that interact amongst themselves. The difference between the Other and I is similar to that between Infinity and finitude as far as the Other is always beyond the scope of my intentional field. In conversation he is not thematized, nor is he the object, as a set of visible properties. The Other supersedes the idea of the Other in me; at any moment he goes beyond the image that I create of him. The representation I have of him essentially depends on my choice of measure, on my abilities, interests, intentions, motivations etc., which impose outlines of him. But in the conversation, the Other always gives more than my expectations. The face of the Other expresses itself: firstly, because the face has meaning in itself; secondly, because I can always be surprised by his reactions, questions and answers; thirdly, because even before he says "yes" or "no" concerning the topic, all agreement and disagreement between us is in his hands; he is the condition for both the truth and the untruth, for good and evil, for justice and for abomination. Hence, according to Levinas, to approach the Other in conversation is to encounter his expression.

The face is independent of my initiative and my power. It calls into question my freedom to compose images and concepts, to make evaluations, to attach meanings to things and to others. It commands my ability to see, to understand, to judge. It itself judges me and makes me seek truth and justice, i.e. it makes me doubt my right to spontaneity. Therefore, I am being mentored and the face of the other "teaches me to apply reason" and questions my naive struggle to be and the glorious egocentrism (primitivism, narrowness) of my being. In the conversation I am being instructed, educated, shown the way. The true word is guiding and prescribing. It is not simply and only a description of the lunar landscapes with inert stones or of the deserts of quicksand, where you do not meet a living soul. It is not just a celebration of nature, as indifferent to men; nor is it only a prediction or a calculation of the results achieved in the production of goods or the creation of new wider horizons. It is not even a contract for exchange, made possible by comparing otherwise incomparable human beings. Every word is appropriate and "to the point" when carrying meaning, primordial in relation to anything uttered, i.e. the approach to the Other. Our orientation in the world depends on the orientation towards the Other. The Other, by his very presence and otherness sets the meaning preceding any signification: for him, the speaker puts signs into circulation.

Levinas believes that we always approach the transcendence of the external world with intentionality, as we are led by our own goals, needs and intentions. Transcendence of the Other, however, is something entirely different: this is not the transcendence of the beyond—in relation to my boundaries—but still something included along with me in the common world, which allows us to relate to each other; The Other is beyond in respect of my world, and me, in terms of the reality with which I identify as part of it (I naively perceive the Other as part of it too). If the objective world is produced by human activity, cognitive and practical, thus being an extrapolation of experience onto strangers and unoccupied territories, the Other is transcendent in relation to the world and to each territory with which my I identifies, practically and cognitively. The Other is both the condition and the ultimate sanction with respect to the correctness of the world. "The relationship with the Other is not produced outside of the world, but puts in question the world possessed."[63]

True experience is the encounter with the Other. Infinity shines in the face of the Other and speaks to me; the Face always goes beyond the transcendental image I have of him. The parameters of every thing in the world acquire meaning only through the pedestal on which I place the Other, opening myself to him. This is a dimension of depth and not of breadth. The depth of my world coincides with the height to which the Other is elevated.

* * *

After the death of God, his throne, his superior position was vacated, only to be occupied by something Third and impersonal, e.g. Reason, History, World, Revolution, Freedom, Society, State etc. in terms of which the positions of all "children of God" are equal. Hierarchical human relations or vertical arrangements were attacked as relations of unlawful and unjustified privilege. Early modern philosophers argued that people are born equal and free and that it is not only the primordial condition of human existence, but also the social ideal—the equality of rep-

---

[63] Emmanuel Levinas. *Totality and Infinity*. Duquesne University Press, Pittsburg, 1992, p. 173

resentatives of the human race. However, according to Levinas inequality is the primordial human relation and not equality: I always have one responsibility more than the Other; apart for myself, I am first of all responsible for the Other. Inequality is not necessarily domination and slavery, but responsibility for the Other, i.e. a calling, a mission, giving, support, assistance etc., including even the substitution of the One for the Other. If I try to escape responsibility by reference to the Third, e.g. someone else, institutions, values, society, etc., it means that I do not take personal responsibility for the Other. The most common excuse is that the fate of the Other is his own business which does not affect me and I should not therefore interfere. I must be as Cain when he asked himself: "Am I my brother's keeper?!" In modern society we usually say that there are institutions and departments responsible for the protection of the rights and responsibilities of others. Such discourse is typical of anonymous relations. Except the paradox is precisely in this, as Levinas repeatedly argues, that personal responsibility cannot be escaped, because even when I treat the Other with indifference and do not answer him, this is also a kind of answer, a kind of relation to him. As with Descartes, when I am doubtful of whether thinking exists, thinking cannot be denied, because doubt and denial are also a form of thinking. In Levinas' perspective, when I refuse to respond, this is also a kind of response: one cannot escape personal responsibility. Irresponsibility is the attempt to transfer my responsibility to someone else or to some impersonal agency (collective, the State, fate, curcumstances, etc.) and the abandonment of the Other without any support from me: "there is nothing more I can do for you". Accodingly, as Levinas argues, when the Other is left in God's omnipotent hands, one tries to avoid the responsibility for the Other and for the order of things in the world. In fact, God is present in human relations and in the human world when He is absent and does not interfere in them, leaving everything in the hands of people. "God is present in his absence" is a paradoxical phrase that can only be understood if one is familiar with Levinas' philosophy. Similarly, the phrase "Each step forward is actually a step backwards", is a paradoxical expression according to a common understanding of things, however it becomes understandable from a philosophical point of view when enrobed in Hegelian dialectics.

Levinas actually sees God's hand in the fate of human beings in a completely opposite direction, compared to traditional onto-theo-logical interpretations: as much as we try to turn our back and ignore our relationship with others, we can not succeed in this endeavour because, through the eyes of others, Transcendence is always watching us. Levinas sometimes uses the same phrase to say that with the eyes of the Other the Third is watching us.

Levinas is convinced that we are not able to destroy and annihilate sociality. We are not able to stop meeting each other. Here we can once again draw an analogy with Descartes. As we know, Descartes said that God put the spark of Reason in us and no matter how much we try to squash it and put it out, it does not go out. The human mind, according to Descartes, contains something divine, in which the first seeds of thought were sown, and even when we prevent them from their growth, they may grow crooked and sideways but still produce fruit that ripens by itself. In a similar way, Levinas thinks about sociality whereby human reason is manifested first. In the relation of One to the Other, something divine is contained which can not be destroyed and annihilated. We are created (by others) so that even if we play deaf and blind to the Other, he is still present, albeit as one ignored, unnoticed and overlooked. The Other is present, even in his absence. The relationship with him inevitably bears fruit by itself. As I cannot escape myself, no matter how hard I try, it is even more difficult to escape from the relationship with the Other. No man can break away from the gravity field that is created between the Other and the I. Freedom of my I is already invested by the otherness of the Other. The Other commands even without being aware of this because his very presence/absence makes me conform to him. The primordial consideration of the Other's existence and position, even implicitly, already takes a stance towards him. In this sense, Levinas argues that the relationship with the Other precedes my initiative. Not just because as Sartre says, the Other is not constituted—he is encountered, but also because the very existence of the Self is already in the answer "that is me!" to the imperative presence of the Other and the resulting heteronomy. We will reiterate that every "I think," "I do" and even just "I am" corresponds to the appeal from the Other to me. The behest of the Other is not pronounced, but we obey it before we have understood it. The direct relation between One and the Other is the saying which even at the moment it is uttered, freezes in what is said, i.e. in the relation mediated by words. The saying is positioning the One in relation to the Other prior to the establishment of a common space and world. Before crystallizing into equal and symmetrical relations or becoming a game with its own rules which the interlocutors follow and so unify, speaking implies difference. If the Other is like me and feels and sees things in the same perspective and assigns the same importance to them as I do, why speak? Everything would already be common and communicated. The One speaks to the Other, as they are different and the One has something to give or pass on to the Other. Furthermore, while the first speaks, the second listens. Word is necessary where I signify something for someone else.

The difference in level can never be overcome. The depth of the conversation is not visible to the Third. It can be understood by the Third one only indirectly. True conversation is the face to face encounter with the interlocutor. The essence of the conversation simultaneously asserts oneself and respects or even admires the Other. In some Eastern nations, even in present times, bowing is the usual form of greeting when one encounters the other. The interlocutors are not located on a common plane; the relationship between them is asymmetrical, as between a native and an alien. The alien going towards the local never has the same meaning as the response given by the local to the stranger knocking on his door. What is essential in this relationship is the welcome, hospitality, attention to words, awaiting the message of the newcomer. The real conversation suggests addressing the person carrying the message: it is only then that facts and events are elevated to the rank of facts and events which are fraught with meaning. Primordial meaning is derived from the face of the interlocutor. The Other is not just the one I understand, the one I capture in my imagination and thinking, or the one whose messages I read through his gestures and clothes or through his words and silences. This is only the Third one, who appears immediately together with the First one (the First one is the Stranger and the Second one is me). Approaching the Other in a conversation means to greet his expression, to break down any plastic forms, every smile or sadness fixed on his face, each mask and image included in the category of the "Third". Speaking to me even merely by his/her presence, the Other is deincarnated. The expression of the Other updates his alive presence before me. When one expresses oneself, one inevitably gives meanings to the things spoken about. The discourse forwards meaning from One to the Other. However, as Levinas stresses, what is forwarded is also the process of forwarding. Only through it can things and ideas be forwarded. The presence of the forwarder overcomes the anarchy of facts, events and information, by introducing the forward direction and thus outlines order thereby creating a common world, shared and established by what is said.

1.6. Heidegger and Levinas on the path to language

There would have been no common grounds to compare Heidegger and Levinas if both did not believe that in language we should seek the specifics of man. They were both convinced that man is himself only whereas he does not perceive himself as born to survive among other beings, but feels called—called to respond. Then his whole path is nothing but a response to the call. While in Heidegger's theory, it is the call of Being, in Levinas' it is the call of the Other. To understand both the call and the response, we need to address the metaphysical difference between these two thinkers.

a) Martin Heidegger

Heidegger stated that man could not exist without language.[64] Moreover, we do not just speak the language but inhabit it—it is our home. We depart from it to arrive anywhere and to get anything. The word is pronounced even through silence.

However, if starting from language, we need to get back to language, what kind of a path is it? This raises the question, is it not rather a pointless circular motion to take language as a starting point and follow its direction with the inescapable entanglement it inevitably leads to, especially given that the path and the place to which we are directed consists of nothing but language itself?

Heidegger does not think that this confusion and circularity can be avoided by classifying language as a common generic term—e.g., language as a kind of activity, or ability of the spirit, or as worldview, or expression, etc. When we try to put language in the grip of generic terms, it eludes us: to highlight its specifics, we need to obtain it as a difference

---

[64] Martin Heidegger. The Way to Language. *Basic Writings*. Trans. by David Krell, Harper Collins, San Francisco, 1993, p. 397.

in kind compared to other kinds of genus. Moreover, that is what is actually done, if language is perceived as a system of signs (system of signifying tools) in which representations are coordinated to guide us from one object to another. Thus language loses its specificity, namely to reveal, indicate and make something appear—either before our perception, or as a topic of discussion, or as the object of action. Then the relationship between indication (the original function of language) and the indicated can be converted into a conventional relation between the sign and the signified, changing the essence of truth. What is spoken is detached both from speaking and from the speaker—it no longer belongs to them and is comprehended according to a meaning, which is common, banal, worn out, trivialized and false. Language does not betray its function to reveal only when what is said is obtained from what is yet unsaid or what could not be said. What is unspoken, remains hidden—it is a secret, a mystery. The saying is the appearance of something from the concealment in order to be seen and heard. But when what is spoken is revealed, when it is shared, the secret is already disclosed to the public and is commonly accessible. The obvious needs no justification—it is out there. Reasoning about it, i.e. judging it as understandable to all is pronounced loudly and everyone is aware of what is being judged. From now on we can speak without saying anything, because the meaning of what is generally accepted has been proclaimed in advance. Conversely, someone may not speak but with silence can still say a great deal. Therefore, Heidegger stressed that speaking and talking are not identical.

However, does speaking not merely mean to say something to each other?Furthermore, to say something to each other should mean we can show something to each other, in order for us to have something to focus on? Accordingly, each of us turns towards that revealed, each in his/her own way. However, according to Heidegger, this simplifies things in terms of the requirement that the conversation between us is preceded by the appearance of things themselves. For Heidegger revelation through speech cannot be reduced to just people's activity. We do not just speak the language but we speak due to it, meaning that at any given moment we are listening to it. Speech is both speaking and listening. They are usually seen as oppositions: when One speaks, the Other listens and vice versa. For Heidegger speaking says something if speaking itself is also listening to the language we speak.

But what do we hear when listening to the language? What and how does language speak to us? Does the language speak itself in the sense that it is the language that speaks? This is precisely the disagreement between Levinas and Heidegger.

Heidegger argues that language speaks. It speaks to itself and is therefore lonely. We only listen to this monologue of language, a monologue which, however, cannot occur without human speech. It is listening to language that guides people's perception and understanding and allows something to be present or to disappear. The saying allows those who listen to it to appropriate what is said. Moreover, in appropriating what is said, we ourselves become part of a historical language, thereby belonging to the place illuminated by it. Owing to the light cast by language, the world discloses itself to human beings, such that, we try to adjust our language so that it is "in place", i.e. corresponds to what has already been said and to comply with what is revealed to us by listening to and understanding the message of the language itself. Human speech is therefore a response—a response articulated following the speech of language itself. We mortals speak with our human speech, inhabiting the region of openness reveiled to us by language. Humanity is a requirement for language to be able to speak and to follow its path. In this sense, language that is given to us, allows us to speak in the language itself and is fateful to us. Through speaking, we make our way to language so that it corresponds to the path that language has already cleared for us.

We can neither impose nor even invent arbitrary changes to language. Coining new words and phrases will not help us in the effort to modify language. Only when we change our attitude towards what is said in language, as determined by the way we are embraced in it and by the degree to which we have the use of it, can language itself change. What we say as a response is always correlative—it corresponds to the call of language. This relation is incomparable with other relationships that rest on it—all of them; this relation is co-relation, co-existence—a reference to being expressed by language itself. We do not speak the language, rather it speaks us. Speech is the greatest privilege that is given to us: to inhabit the region of language. Our word is obedient and its thinking is grateful for what is given to us by language.

For Heidegger the power of speech is in the condition of existence, of what is there. The oldest word for this power of language is *"Logos"*. *Logos* is the simultaneous appearance of the word and the object, of what is said and what exists. In the light of speech they become identical. Only in their division, in questioning speaking, which can no longer tell us anything new, do we hear the sound of silence. Only in this inquiry and division, the difference between Being and beings flashes as the most fundamental of all relations—the most radical of all differences.

Language is the place where Difference is revealed. This difference, however, was forgotten in the epoch of Western metaphysics. *Epochal* is not something accidental. The meaning of *epoch* here is not just as a period of time but the particular manner in which being is presented in existence; but being may also withdraw so that what was may not be there once the epoch is over. It is through different modes of presence and absence that history follows its course and is divided into different periods. In every *epoch* something is spoken, but something remains unspoken, something is thought, but something remains unthought. It is because of the limitations of what was said and thought that an epoch reaches its end and makes way for the next one and the possibility for renewal. In the gap between the epochs the unspoken, unthought and undisclosed takes the floor in order to appear as an historically existing world. Heidegger believed that Western onto-theo-logy, which was the epoch of oblivion of Being, would be followed by a new epoch—that of understanding Being as such.

b) Emmanuel Levinas

Levinas agrees that historical epochs and historically constituted languages can be interpreted as the ways in which Being reveals itself, i.e. as different ways of the appearance of truth. Subsequently, it could be argued that the communicative function of language is derived from the cognitive function with communication as such being reduced to the transmission of information. Furthermore, in the development of cognition, the many alternative perspectives come together to achieve a broader universality, as communication is subordinated to a kind of teleology or type of intentionality, that culminates in truth. Hegel describes this process as continuous progress performed thanks to the sublation of the stages already acquired[65] Levinas emphasizes, however, that being appears to be a theme, i.e. an object of discussion and understanding and hence truth or untruth, by virtue of its significance. It is important to note that without meaning constituted through communication, being could hardly assert its existence, i.e. to reveal itself to us. It is meaning defined trough speech that reveals being in truth. Consciousness is not a copy (though limited, subjective and particular) of what is presented to it as "in flesh and blood". What is given is perceived as such only because it is ranked and understood in a way that is endowed with the privilege or the importance to be considered a given.

From the phenomenological perspective, intuition perceives any given as "this" or "that." "*Understanding as* this or that..." is the source of consciousness. Each reflection suggests such an intuitive pre-reflexive

---

[65] In Heidegger's philosophy the respective concept is not sublation but recovering "the forgotten" and it has guite a different sense – it is also transformation, but not in the sense of progressive development, as this movement is described by the dialectic.

understanding of meaning. First, that which exists is named by declaring it as this or that; this kind of recognition is neither a form of perception nor a kind of imagination, but the work of identification—identifying the different cases of appearance of the same which is already known under this name. However, the *kerygmatic* essence of identification allows for the destruction of the idea of correspondence between words and things. Discrepancy is possible because words have sovereignty over what is given to knowledge, as well as conversation having sovereignty over practices. The same "given" takes on different meanings in different contexts, from different perspectives by different participants in the conversation and "the given to consciousness" is inseparable from the meaning. That is why we can therefore recognize the Difference in historically formed languages and systems of signs.

The appearance of something is inseparable from its identification, i.e. from its signification as this or that, but also from its designation for someone, i.e. from the *kerygmatic* intention. Language thus becomes subject to the search for truth (such as identification and thematization), but in it things appear according to their meaning, which is constituted for the speaker's relationship with others. It is not cognition that is a condition for communication but *vice-versa*; communication is the condition for cognition that henceforth becomes commonly shared and is reducible to the search for objective truth. Communication is not a mere addition to the organization of information done by thought in the system of language. If it is subordinated to the tasks of ontology, speech would be only important as a means of communicating the truth—it would be an exercise in the expression of thought, which would ultimately be de-personalized and universalized. The main question here is whether the Other is only a carrier of his own particular perspective in the search for a more common truth as well as whether he is an incarnation of the idea which I and/or others already have of him. Can the interlocutor to whom truth is announced and with whom it is shared be himself if he is reduced

Sociality and Justice: Toward Social Phenomenology 115

to the idea that we have created of him and can we grasp his true meaning through cognition?

Levinas emphasizes that the relationship with the interlocutor is not reducible to cognition. Here it is necessary to point out that the *kerygmatic* function of speech itself points us to the interlocutor and this is a different orientation of language compared with its orientation to the topic or object. This orientation of speech towards the Other is also his signification as Other — the Other with whom I form a human connection and who will later respond with "as for me ...". However, before his "as for me ..." is heard and understood, it is necessary to pay attention to him, to hear (paradoxically!) his way of seeing things. This paying of attention (or neglect respectively) itself demonstrates the importance (or insignificance) of the Other. Even the lack of response is already a response, hence silence is also a kind of communication. Addressing the Other is the original silent language, without which speech cannot begin. But addressing the Other is provoked by the Other himself. It is not about the Self extending his capabilities to grasp the world (and the other as part of it) through the figure of otherness (what the Other is); it is not about the I taking over an increasingly wider territory, enriching its current knowledge, learning something new from the difference with others; nor is it about adding a new particular interpretation of its environment to the already generalised one; it is about the opposite process — limiting the expansion of the Ego in approaching the Other, so that the Other is allowed to participate into the conversation. The Other is approached as another when I do not go towards him according to my own prejudices, but rather leave him in a position beyond my universe, urging him to be the judge as to its truth or untruth, justice or injustice, beauty or ugliness and so on. It is only later and only thanks to the subsequent conversation that we can establish a common world to which we both belong. The initial relation with the Other is equivalent to a relationship with an alien with whom we have no common homeland. This is the establishment of proximity, which is no longer *logos* but a relation of non-in-difference to a neighbour. The place of the first meeting with him is non-verbal language, which is based on an unarticulated and unthematized call—a relation of immediacy, which is not physical proximity but moral in nature. The language then is the connection which touches without the need of a tangent and without overstepping the border, without the need to put boundaries or to observe them. The pathway of language cannot be described as penetration or the conquest of foreign territories. The bridge from One to the Other erected by speech is committing through responsibility, i.e. it is ethics and not ontology or any other "scien-to-logy". Remember again that for Levinas the first philosophy is meta-physics, i.e. ethics and not ontology.

The I addressing the Other cannot be objectified—at least in the same moment as it happens; and yet somehow, though not in the way of objectification and reification, the call is stabilized. The response to the Other is respect and recognition of his meaning as a face. The contact in which I approach the Other is not getting to know him as Different according to the categories of my perception and thinking. The appeal by the Other which precedes each conversation and each understanding to which I answer, even before any willingness from my side, is the ethical event initiating the communication. This primordial event is fundamentally presupposed by any transmission of messages and the establishment of association in which words and sentences are spoken. This contact is not thematization but a signalling which precedes any signification of things in the world. This pre-original sign is a call from the Other and an addres to him as a face since the face is important in itself. The mission of the approach to the Other is not just to name things or to identify them or recognize them in order to indicate them to others, otherwise proximity would be reduced to the logical function of language and would again include communication in itself. The first word, although it is not uttered, expresses the very possibility of communicating meaning before any thought in which the being is seen, understood, constituted or reflected. The significance of anything as well as the need for signification is based on the importance of the interlocutor. The significance of the face is the condition for every speech and every constitution of the order; being is revealed by its signification for the interlocutor. Moreover, the face carries significance or importance in itself; it is always open because it cannot hide behind what is said, since the saying is always implicit and because the encounter with another has taken place even in the spoken lie.

Logos, i.e. coherent thought, understands the extravagance of the pre-original word, which is *an-archic* because it questions the established order in the universe that is my homeland. This initial word, says Levinas is *an-archic*, i.e. without a principle yet, without *arche*. The pre-original word, that we understand before it is heard and before we have understood the message of the subsequent conversation, battles the *logos* because it breaks any logical form and conceptual fixity, which has been turned into an anachronism. The *Logos* which is challenged recognizes the mystery of primary sociality, but can never state it exhaustively, no matter how it reformats it. At any point in the conversation, the presence of the Other transcends every image, idea, concept, statement or conclusion. However in the relation to the face, the very appearance of the Other becomes closeness—non-indifference. The separate being is then not seen through the prism of the general concept, *eidos*, in which the individual is understood through his belonging to a class, idea, essence etc., but is accepted for its uniqueness. Uniqueness is possible and revealed by speech. Closeness is not necessarily a basic determining feature of membership to a group or system and all the elements that entails; closeness is established even before forging a bridge from one bank to the other, but a bridge that can later be used to transmit logos from

One to the Other (and to the Third Party and every one, when the relation is institutionalized). Moral closeness is responsibility for the Other and is the basis for the authentic community.

Speech can be analyzed regardless of its consistency or inconsistency, or the truth or falsity of the information transmitted, to capture the event of closeness—a proximity that did not exist between the stranger knocking on my door and me, when I am settled in the place I feel is my home. Unselfishness of proximity is a disappearing event, swept away by the flow of knowledge and the messages presented as the condition of proximity, but actually presupposed by it. Closeness is not an event of intentionality. To approach the other person in speech, means "to touch him, without actually touching him"; to approach him independently of the "data" and "methods", crystallized in the distance of knowledge and reflection. Closeness is non-dimensional, the zero point of the coordinate system that represents both the start and end-point from which all distances (and not only between the I and the Other) are created and defended.

Addressing the face in the inevitable response that I give with my very existence is similar to an invitation from a generous host. Or to put it more clearly, it is similar to the caress. In endearment the hand of the One follows (or rather invents and creates) with love the shape of the Other. But if love means closeness, does not closeness imply distance and absence as well? Absence of what? According to Levinas, the absence of God, who has left us behind, leaving everything in the hands of people. God has gone before the start of the conversation between One and the Other, leaving an invisible trace in the face of my neighbour (and hence only through the nakedness of the face does he leave a mark in the moral framework of human relations). The I is obsessed without realizing it; it was obsessed before consciousness and understanding because this play had begun before the advent of decision-making that came with freedom of the Self. Man seems to be chosen to be responsible in that no one else could replace him. The I is left alone with the responsibility for the fate of his brother and that of the community. This relationship with the Other is there, even when the Ego turns its back on him. The I does not coincide with its freedom as arbitrarily understood and exercised, but is hostage to the freedom of the Other.

From here on the main question is how my freedom correlates with the freedom of the Other. There lies the problem of justice. According to Levinas, God is present for us, the people, in justice. Not because God with His presence and omnipotence resolves human problems, but through bypassing us and in His absence, He leaves the answer to me. The responsibility falls on the Self in the accusative as me. Freedom and justice are not just bound by the necessity of existence but by the responsibility for the neighbour. Responsibility or sociality is the most authentic unavoidable necessity.

c) Heidegger and/or Levinas

The dispute between Heidegger and Levinas has more than the mere understanding of language at its core. The discussion surrounding the most important questions of Western philosophy, with particular emphasis on the pathway of language, in addition to the emergence of new *aporia*, was put before us by two of the most renowned Husserlian scholars in their attempt to rethink tradition: Heidegger, because he was not satisfied with the onto-theo-logical truth, which is not true enough and never can be, and Levinas, because humanism of any onto-theo-logy is not sufficiently humane and can not be such.

Heidegger himself never expressed interest in this debate, although Levinas became a prominent name in philosophy almost a quarter of a century before Heidegger's death. However, in 1923 the then seventeen-year old Emmanuel Levinas, born in Lithuania to a Jewish family, went to France and enrolled as a student of philosophy at the University of

Strasbourg. He then spent the academic year 1928/1929 in Freiburg, Germany, listening to lectures by Husserl and Heidegger and helping in seminars. Heidegger thus had a very strong influence on his student. As Levinas himself acknowledged, reading *Being and Time*, printed in 1927, filled him with admiration and he returned to France already devoted to phenomenology. In 1930 Levinas received French citizenship and published his doctorate *Theory of Intuition in Husserl's Phenomenology*. In 1939 he was mobilized and in 1940 captured in the war. In fact he spent the war years in a German military prison for French officers. All of his family remaining in Lithuania were killed by the Nazis. In France, his daughter and his wife were able to hide and escape death. In 1949, several years after the liberation, his book *Discovering Existence with Husserl and Heidegger* was published, and played a very important role in the subsequent development of philosophy in France by introducing the themes and methods of phenomenology. By the end of his life, Levinas spoke of Heidegger as a great philosopher who proposed a new language, that gave us the opportunity to discuss the meaning of being. Of course, after existentialism this problematic has been 'banalized', but at the time it was unusually innovative. It suggested an unsuspected interpretation of the history of philosophy, European culture and the pathway of all mankind. According to Heidegger's understanding of human existence, although it looks like a purposeful activity, in fact it is animated all along by the ontological meaning of "nothingness". The latter is not derived from knowledge of human destiny, its causes and objectives; "nothing" is like the shadow of Being, a constant companion to existence, experienced in the metaphysical fear of death. In fact, Levinas with his philosophy points the way in which man overcomes himself as a creature, shivering before death and the concern for his own survival—this is the way, cleared to the Other in response to the appeal of his face, naked before death. The nothingness of death is the test for the capacity and dignity of humanity of the I in the face-to-face situation; but capacity and dignity do not belong merely to the order of cognition, being and truth but first of all are of nobility, morality and justice. Levinas developed a motive known long before him, that holiness is, in its hyperbol, to die for the Other. However, we would like to add "off the record" that there is a better way to define holiness—which is, not only to die for the Other, if necessary, but daily and hourly to live for the Other (others). For modern man with his rational and pragmatic attitudes, it sounds too pathetic, but in this rational and pragmatic spirit we actually ask ourselves is it not the *inspiration from the Other* that elevates, and animates us? Is it not the *inspiration* that sets the vertical dimension of human existence? The *inspiration* urges us to leave the here-and-now existing world for beyond it. Any thinking—even the most pragmatic—is already utopia. Not because it is possible by generalizations but first of all because it is conditioned by morality and it is the haven which is nowhere available. It is nowhere and perhaps is eternity of time itself.

Up to his last publications Levinas repeatedly acknowledged his tribute to Heidegger's existential analytic. However, he pointed out that he was shocked by Martin Heidegger assuming office as rector of Freiburg University, by his speech and by his position and work in the service of the Nazis. He could never forget the political commitments of his teacher and even less to exculpate him. His homage to Heidegger cooled. He found Heidegger's subsequent work on the theme of language and hermeneutics, if not unconvincing, at least not convincing enough. In reality, however, Levinas took up Heidegger's theme of language, giving it a completely new interpretation. This is really his eminently noble response, i.e. born from the good and ethics, to the "philosophy of power" as he described Heidegger's fundamental ontology.

Levinas emphasizes that human speech is important, not just with its information value in terms of the question of being, but also and rather with its orientation to the interlocutor. Despite his reservations regarding the problems and the approach of Heidegger's theory, Levinas never missed the opportunity to express his assessment of Heidegger's philosophy as "the greatest event of the twentieth century" and of *Being and Time* as one of the most magnificent books in the history of philosophy.[66] Nonetheless, he wrote *Otherwise than Being* — the book that after *Totality and Infinity* was his second major work, contributing most to his worldwide recognition. Levinas reiterated that everyone who engages with philosophy nowadays, cannot ignore Heidegger's ideas, even if he would like to escape from them — to philosophize without them would be "naive" as they indicate a new and direct way to converse with the philosophers of the past and search for the contemporary dimensions of the lessons of the great classics. Levinas was indeed aware that one must himself be directly involved in the dialogue, not to instrumentalize or update an already obsolete problematic, but to return to the unthought and unsaid, so that it became the thought and said. But thought and said for whom? In any case, not first and only because of truth, nor for the self-realization of the speaker, but above all for the other participants in the conversation.

Levinas said of Heidegger something which is true of himself: a return to the primordial philosophical themes does not stem from a pious choice of *philosophia perennis* (eternal philosophy) but from the attention to contemporary problems. The abstract problem of the meaning of being and the issues of the day join together and even coalesce.

---

[66] Amidst four others: Plato's *Phaedrus*, Kant's *Critique of Pure Reason*, Hegel's *Phenomenology of Spirit* and Bergson's *Time and Free Will*.

Chapter Two:
The Other and the Third One

2.1. The Third One

What Alexander Kojeve states at the beginning of his book *Introduction to the Reading of Hegel Lectures on the Phenomenology of Spirit* could serve as the motto of the entire philosophy of the twentieth century as nowadays nearly all modern philosophical trends and schools focus their attention on language and speech:

> To understand man by understanding his "beginning" means to understand the origin of the Self revealed by speech.[67]

Husserl's phenomenology concentrates itself entirely on the intentionality of consciousness and meanings. The intention itself, if we are to rely on Husserl's philosophy is "consciousness of...", "orientation towards ....". With Levinas, every consciousness and any intentionality is preceded by the orientation to the Other. Taking into account the Other and saying something for the Other (saying which is itself inspired by the Other), determines further any reasoning and every *logos*. Nonetheless, this pre-logical orientation to the Other is not itself intentionality, nor thematization and does not aim to achieve a result. Levinas is focused on moral, non-intentional consciousness, unlike Husserl whose phenomenology announced that every consciousness is intentional.

According to Levinas, my approach to the Other never reaches him — the Other always eludes my knowledge and my ideas of him; the I always reaches the Third one. The Third one is the Other but in the quality

---

[67] Alexander Kojeve. *Introduction to the Reading of Hegel Lectures on the Phenomenology of Spirit*, Basic Books, New York & London, p. 3.

of an entity; as something existing inside of a given territory, as a particular case of a certain typology, as what is visible before me, deriving its meaning from the horizons of the world but not from the height and beyond. Whether my overhearing the appeal of the Other and the answer I give him can be interpreted as a special kind of intentionality? We must immediately clarify that it is so insofar the Third is already looking at me with the eyes of the Other and so is all mankind. This Third Party is a creation of my constitutive abilities and is understandable in the *logos* of language. And the resource of my linguistic abilities is what generally could be shared with everyone speaking my language.

Levinas revised the concept of speech that reduced language to *logos*, stressing the primordial function of speech as an appeal. In *Otherwise than Being or beyond Essence*, he insists on a distinction between language as an appeal and language as logos by use of the respective terms "the saying" and "the said". It reminds us of Heidegger's distinction between "to be" and "being", but is not reducible to it nor should it be confused with it. This distinction between the act of "saying" as an appeal, on the one hand, and "the said", as the intelligent understanding and response of such an appeal, is essential for Levinas because it corresponds to the distinctions in his philosophy between the Other and the Third, ethics and ontology, morality and politics, sociality and justice, beyond-existence and existence, and so on.

* * *

In fact, the distinction between "the saying" and "the said" has a long history perhaps even being traced back to the distinction between revelation and reason which is valid in all monotheistic cultures.

Reason is the ability which helps us understand that which we encounter in the world. The question, then, is how the signs and words of revelation can be understood if they are not of this world and if they are not expressed by God in any of the historically constituted languages.

Sociality and Justice: Toward Social Phenomenology

The question is about the way in which Transcendence can be understood. By countering many contemporary philosophers, Levinas privileges not the narrative forms of speech but the command (and, in priority, the Commandments of God "Thou shalt not kill!"):

> It is the commandment rather than narration which marks the first step towards human understanding and is, therefore, the beginning of language.[68]

But when the message of revelation is delivered to humans, it is no longer in heaven but available to them on earth. Man is not just a recipient of God's word, but the one to whom the word was "said" or "given" ("fallen into the hands of," as Heidegger describes it). Revelation becomes revelation not because God himself makes accessible his infinity but because it was revealed to the understanding (the reason) of man. Through the human response this revelation was turned into Word. In the response that revelation receives from humans, the Word ceases to be an incomprehensible noise or meaningless silence, and obtain the status of words. The commandments become prescriptions of behaviour but only through their implementation. The multiplicity of people will create a diversity of meanings. Only then, through communication between humans, will the common, understandable, and shared significations crystallize and form a system of language, that is as Heidegger states, the home of Being.

But how could the commandment (the prescription, the order, or the call) addressed to different people, be protected from the arbitrariness of everyone's subjectivity? Could it be that revelation has its own authority and its own message is not just being left to the fantasies of subjectivity? Illusions and phantasms do not constitute the essence of subjectivity, although they may also occur in it. Subjectivity is subject-ness as taking the

---

[68] Emmanuel Levinas. Revelation in the Jewish tradition. *The Levinas' Reader*. Ed. by Sean Hang, Blackwell, Cambridge, USA, 1993, p. 204.

burden of responsibility for others. It is not just substantial unity or identity but it assumes otherness in all its weight. Levinas uses this seemingly incomprehensible wording: the-other-within-the-same. It is only due to human responsibility as substitution of the one for the other that there is such a thing as revelation. However, since no one can take my place and respond instead of me, nor can do what I do, then my responsibility is the core of my uniqueness. Every human life is the unique response through which the call of God's word is being answered. Transcendence shines in the face of the other human, but is not any more omnipotence of God, but weakness, vulnerability, being-towards-death of the Other and an appeal to me not to leave the other alone in his suffering (enduring, which is human life as ageing) and in his/her rebellion against the nothingness of death. The face coincides with the ethical requirement, as understood by Levinas' definition:

> ... that non-in-difference-for-the-other-in-me (or of my "me")—that is no doubt the very meaning of the face, its original speech. In it there can be heard the demand that keeps me in question and elicits my response or my responsibility. ...the face is meaning of the beyond. Not sign or symbol of the beyond; the later allows itself to be neither indicated nor symbolized without falling into the immanence of knowledge. The meaning of the face is not a species whose indication or symbolization would be the genus. The face is alone in translating transcendence. ...A Transcendence that is inseparable from the ethical circumstances of the responsibility for the other ...[69]

The only way to hear, realize and respond to Transcendence is the answer I give to the presence of the other human. Transcending, as an act of crossing the border, is equal to going beyond the ego-centrism of my own world in order to pay attention to the Other and do something for him. It is the only way for the other to be close to me and for my Self to not be a narrow-minded primitive egoism. Responsibility of the I is evoked as suffering due to the suffering of the other. However, closeness

---

[69] Emmanuel Levinas. De la signifiance du sens, *Hors Sujet*, Fata Morgana, 1987, p. 141–142.

can never eradicate the distance between the Other and me, for at the time of our meeting the neighbour becomes the Third.

* * *

Human being, according to the understanding of Aristotle and the entire Greek philosophy, is determined by the place of man in the Cosmos. One can never leave it: he is always a being-in-the-world; part of this cosmic order. The world, uncovered in its truth, is adequate to the totality of what is thinkable and human understanding is an ability that allows adequacy or correspondence between micro- and macro-cosmos. But in biblical culture, unlike paganism, the human being is no longer defined as *zoon politikon* and a reasoning alive being, but as being that has heard the Word of God. The human response to Transcendence is the very transcending of the world and being-in-the-world. The command "Thou shalt ..." is not derived from "You can ..." but is superior to the possible. Transcending, as a going beyond, is an establishment of relationship with the exteriority and infinity. According to Levinas, this transcendence means something for us because of our link with the other humans. Human intellect wants to assimilate the beyond and the otherness and to find a place for them in the whole of the world. However, in the repetition of the cycle specific to the cosmos, in the deployment of identity according to objective regularities, reason is not simply the comparability of the macrocosm and microcosm on the base of their sameness, but identity is instead awakened from its serenity by the otherness of the Other. Otherness is alarming. Levinas demonstrates that we should perceive revelation not as a form of given wisdom, but as an awakening to what is different. In common-sense and dialectics, however, this awakening is mortified by the return of the Subject to its sameness, being the ground of any identification and absorption of the other. Returning to oneself outlines a path of self-consciousness and self-reflection, where man, having been lost, rediscovers himself but already changed. In ethics, on the other hand, the subject does not return to itself as Ulysses returns to his homeland to rediscover himself after his travels to foreign lands. In the ethical relation, the otherness of the Other disturbs the complacency and self-sufficiency of the Self encapsulated within its own orbit. With regard the moral link the Other questions me and I become a subject of this questioning; even by his bare presence the Other breaks the circling of the Subject around itself and opens the subjectivity towards exteriority and beyond by opening towards the alterity of the Other.

Searching, asking, desiring, etc. are the modes of our openness to beyond. Beyond what? Beyond that which Heidegger named *Jemeinigkeit* (mineness). These modes of openness are incommensurable with my measures and are condemned to infinity—answers raise new questions, desires feed new desires, and the "search for..." leads to new strives because of the dissatisfaction with what has been achieved. When these modes of operation are not engaged in a pre-planned project, in reaching a strictly determined goal or arriving at the expected result (and we never know how far the results of what we did stretch), questions, searches, desires, dreams, utopias, etc. are aimed at something more than what is and what is possible. For them to remain modes of unconcealment, authenticity and sincerity of the saying, they are insatiable and move towards otherness as towards death—without knowing why, for how long and where. But the logic of this movement does not match the description of self-propulsion and self-reproduction of the first mover, which is the subject-for-itself, and is rather described as breaking with "this I hateful *for-itself"*. The question is, therefore, can we understand transcendence in our own answers without losing it when we confine it to our own immanence and our own present? The command from "beyond the world" is precisely the command not to lose sight of otherness; to devote attention to the different and not to remain in-different to the

Other; not to go to sleep, satisfied, innocent and with a good conscience in a problem-free "dogmatic slumber" content with the current degree of our understanding and our happy survival. Staying awake means to be alert and restlessly attentive to the otherness of Other. Only the I, sensitive to the vulnerability of its neighbour, can watch out for him. This means that I can not feel any more guilt-free—and not merely in respect of the actions imputed to *me* as my personal deeds, but in general as to what happens in this concrete meeting with others. As the "I" is not some kind of substance or a simple process of identification in the course of everything that happens to it, its uniqueness is not derived from its previous experience or some exceptional quality that it possesses. I am myself through serving others without satisfaction from what I have done. This is not the decisive individual who always chooses himself in the first person as a proud "I"; but the responding and responsive one in the accusative through the biblical, "that's me". This accusative "me" is taking the responsibility for what happens to others in the world as my problem and my guilt.

Reason itself, absorbed in its rightness and truthfulness, identifying itself with universality, is not easily called into question. "I do not care" about the otherness of the Other means that he "has no meaning for me". Actually even this "has no meaning" is, in itself, meaningful. The "I" as "that's me" cannot avoid being affected by otherness. The subject has no choice, but he himself is the chosen one and is already marked not to be enslaved and left with no choice but to receive inspiration to be himself by exercising his freedom "for the other." This inspiration is unrelated to the expectation of a job well done, but is my breath stopping before the loneliness and helplessness, before weakness and poverty, vulnerability and defencelessness of the other. The condition of the Other I assume as my problem as if it is a call to me not to remain indifferent, whatever this indifference costs me. This means exactly to bear the burden of responsibility for the other.

Levinas notes that to be *chosen* is not a privilege but a burden which has moral meaning. The chosen one is the first to hear the appeal. He was not chosen before the others as if he is elevated above them, as most often happens (regrettably) in political elections, but he is ordained to *serve*. But there and then immediately appears yet another deviation. The feeling of being chosen, as a feeling of distinction due to my unique responsibility, can turn into arrogance and selfishness: precisely the symptom of a moral crisis. As we are aware, freedom is possible because of truth. At the moment when truth is shining, all fences have fallen, all barriers have been raised and reason becomes reliant on itself and its own knowledge. Nothing is prescribed, nothing is forbidden. In this moment when man is so self-confident, trusting himself and his own understanding, as well as feeling as the sovereign master of his state, he can lapse or even collapse into crisis. Then only the prescription can protect him from evil, because evil also enjoys complete freedom and could even overlap with it, i.e. with arbitrariness.

In philosophy it is typically argued that the "I" or subject-ness (understood as "I can") is measured and controlled by observing what is visible and objectively valid for everyone. This seems the only way to avoid arbitrariness. However, if the subject is subordinate to predefined rules, then do we not mislay the central meaning of subject-ness, that is, to judge by itself and when it is necessary even to leave any universal order? Before abandoning the objective, that is, the universal framework, there are two possibilities:

1. Freedom, as taking responsibility and responding (in this case, the beginning is the Other);
2. Freedom as arbitrariness or, perhaps, as a game, which I can quit at any time, i.e. freedom of action without responsibility, decided by my will (in this case, the beginning is the I).

The I as a subject is usually at the crossroads between these two possibilities. The depth of subjectivity is created not through whim, nor by power for the sake of power, but by taking on the ever increasing weight of responsibilities with all their contradictions, amplified and sharpened in the process.

* * *

For Levinas, language was born by the appeal heard in the moral relation. He is not inclined to hypostasize language in itself but such hypostasizing is typical of many Heidegger's followers in their belief that by itself "language speaks". Opposing this point in Heidegger's theory Levinas looks for a way out of monologism and logocentrism. He searches and finds the first meaning in the pre-original, an-arch(e)-ic call of the Other. Facing the Other is the beginning of every communication and any foundation of oppositions, rules, structures, constitutive for the language itself. Levinas does not deny that the meaning of the said is already implied by the language system that exists before the meeting and the event of speaking. In the field of the said, all that exists is consistent with the meanings of a historical language understood as per various codes. But being the subject, the I has the resource of tradition, codification, symbolism and so on at its own disposal. This is its territory, its homeland: namely supported and rooted in the soil of its homeland, but ignorant of its conditioning by it, the I can see itself as the beginning — maintaining its presence, as freedom, coinciding with its own initiative, and in general, as an independent autochthonous being.

The proper origin, or rather pre-origin, of any communication is neither the language, nor the I, but the Other. The presence of the Other, which I feel as a call to me and to which I respond by "Here I am!" gives birth to the intrigue of human existence. Before expressing any thinking, feeling, and will and before the thematization and production of connotations, before any referential function, before being said, the Word is saying, i.e. an initial contact between the One and the Other. Words are addressed to someone else. Appealing to the addressee precedes and accompanies each sign and any meaning. Signification is made for the others; it is at work even when, as with written words, the author is the first reader of what is written but again the two roles—of the writer and the reader accordingly—do not coincide. Although the point of departure of each linguistic activity is our difference and our duality, language awakens in me and in the Other the common we possess and the shareable objectivity of everything mundane. Without this initial duality—of the addressee and the addressing party—speech would be impossible and pure nonsense. These two roles exist even in monologue—they are different, but the same actor performs both: monologue is internalized dialogue. Even when speech, as structuralists insist, occurs as violent language, we shall nevertheless admit that it's primordial duality remains, albeit in derivative forms and transfigured into monologue. The saying always presupposes not only content of the message, but also a potential or actual addressee, as well as an addressing party anticipating some understanding from the other. This other is not the language itself, as perhaps followers of Heidegger believe, for we speak but with the other humans.

When the One addresses the Other, he potentially speaks to every Third who, although not a direct participant in the conversation, can hear and interpret what is being said. The I and the Other are in a straightforward relation—they constitute the event of the encounter, while the Third has no direct access to the closeness established between the One and the Other as he is not involved face-to-face inside of it. The I and the Other are in the interior of their conversation but the Third is outside. The Third approaches their relation from the distance of a witness. It is from his perspective only that the conversation is embraced as an event or an entity and is applied within a certain horizon of world or history. Of course, this position of the Third could be taken also by each of the participants in the talk, but in that case they have escaped the direct contact and have placed themselves at a distance from the meeting and have objectified the situation. This is also the position of the judge, of the speaker of deliberations, of the contemplating one, of the reflecting one, of *Das Man*, of the scientist, the governor, the holder of the privileged perspective in the community, who is expressing what is common for all, the supervisor, the commentator, and so on. The Third is anyone who is not within the relation face-to-face and who through the notions, opinions, meanings and values, that is, through some rubrics, understands, describes, thinks, judges, evaluates, constructs and reconstructs what has happened between those who are in direct contact. From his point of view, what is happening is already a fact and he reflects on it as something already done but the truth is that namely he turns it into something already past and reflects on participants in it as "she", "he", or "they":

> The originality of the relation lies in the fact that it is not known from the outside but only by the I which realize the relation. The position of the I, therefore, is not interchangeable with that of the Thou....For if the self becomes an I in saying Thou..., my position as a self depends on that of my correlate and the relation is no longer any different from other relations: it is tantamount to a spectator speaking of the I and Thou in the third person.[70]

We are accustomed to thinking that the situation of speech can be represented dispassionately, objectively only from the perspective of the Third one, while inside the talk the participants experience it completely differently. The Third one observes the situation but what is observed and the act of observing presuppose an advanced enacted sense. Meaningfulness is not something added after the seeing, contemplating, feeling, perceiving, as if they by themselves are meaningless and would

---

[70] Emmanuel Levinas. Martin Buber and the Theory of Knowledge. *Proper Names*. Translated by Michael B. Smith, Stanford University Press, 1996, p. 32.

have to be modified in order to render them meaningful. Meaningfulness is first produced by the moral relation and consequently complies with the *a priori* categories of our thinking, i.e. of universal thinking, inherent in everyone. Placing the topic of the conversation between the One and the Other as a matter, accessible to everyone, i.e. for the Third one, conceals the preliminary effort of signification of speech between the interlocutors. Signification refers to the signified but to the signifier, too. Indeed, the signifier is not the only person; there are at least two signifiers: the addresser and the addressee. The speaker is speaking of the world, but in speaking he also expresses himself, thematising the world for the Other. Signs are given to the Other in order to be understood and interpreted. However, understanding of the significations is not derived out of the identity of the I as being the Same but of the necessity of addressing the Other. Willingly or not, each speech act includes in itself an instruction, a point of view that directs the others. In this way everyone gets the opportunity to confirm, doubt, ask, interpret, thematize, and, in a word, to have their own perspective.

"You" is not an unusual entity (e.g. a living, reasonable, conscious, animated, etc. being), in contrast to the habitualness of the rest of objects of cognition, and the movement that connects the I and You by the speech is not simply thematization with only topical relevance. Before all else, to speak to You means to allow a recognition of the otherness of the Other, since the You is constantly withdrawing itself from the Third. The I-You relation is not constitutive of knowledge and power,[71] but of morality. Within knowledge and power meanings are the result of constitutive activity of the Self, while in morality they are the answers given to others. The Other cannot be mastered by the I as object, i.e. according to its importance attributed by me to him; he cannot be absorbed, assimilated or reduced to his meaning for me or somebody else, nor can he be

---

[71] The power understood as despotism that treats the other as an object or instrument.

abandoned to himself as a pure thing, which is without any orientation-towards-nothingness (Heidegger). What is revealed in the face of the Other is his mortality, that is, his being towards the nothingness of death, as well as his command to me to not leave him alone. I respond not on my own initiative, but because, as Levinas metaphorically expressed it, the smooth surface of my skin is pierced, hurt by the Other without the latter even touching it. This means that I cannot experience the world as if I see it from the outside in the capacity of an objective bystander. Furthermore, the I also cannot place itself on the same level as the Other. The I cannot be in some kind of symmetrical relationship with him, for such commensurability and establishment of equivalent positions already implies the perspective of a Third. Levinas overturns our understanding of disinterestedness: it is no longer objectivity, impartiality, lack of sympathy and complicity; disinterestedness is not possible from the perspective of non-engaged coldness, but, vice versa, it is such unavoidable attentive care "for the Other" that it is rather an "obsession", "being hostage", "substitution" of the Other by the Self, wherein my Self is forgetting my selfhood and my own *persona*.

The I as a mortal being included in the world, but transcending it, one that exists "in the flesh", but elevates beyond the carnal and does not just respond to words, but is capable of giving its own skin and the last morsel from its mouth (as we say, not just giving my shirt off my back but my skin too). Responsibility is not only formulating responses with the help of words and signs—the words and signs themselves are understood by their relation to things and actions whose meanings they are. The saying is inseparable from the said, i.e. from the embodied, visible, materialized, objectified. Objectifying itself happens in words, signs, actions, structures, the systems and, certainly, in something accomplished where the saying is hypostasized in the said and descends to its fulfilment as spatiality. Then, it is understandable, heard and seen, potentially by everyone, i.e. by the third one or they.

But isn't then the Other as a *being* just similar to my being? Isn't he the same creature of flesh and blood like enormous multitude of others within the horizon of the world? Or is he a transcendence, escaping from my sight and perception? Levinas insists that the moral relation to the Other is different from the knowledge and activities of the subject, aimed at things in the world. The I could be portrayed as the beginning of knowledge and activity because they are both a kind of grasping things, by analogy with their grip within the hand. The moral relation is different from knowledge. I do not just think of the Other, I do not just grasp, perceive, imagine, remember him (i.e. accept him as an entity in my world), rather I turn to him. This means that I do not stop at conceiving his existence in general, existence as a general idea, i.e. an idea that is embodied in each and every one in a similar way; but at the same time I connect to this separate being, to whom I respond with my behaviour and who is different neither because of comparison with me, nor because of his particular situation, but in himself. In the face-to-face situation simultaneously with my understanding of him I demonstrate my attitude towards him:

> Man is the only being I cannot meet without my expressing this meeting itself to him. That is precisely what distinguished the meeting from knowledge. In every attitude toward the human being there is a greeting—even if it is the refusal of greeting. Here perception is not projected toward the horizon (the field of my freedom, my power, my property) in order to grasp the individual against this familiar background: it refers to the pure individual, to a being as such. And that signifies precisely, to put it in terms of "understanding", that my understanding of a being as such is already the expression I offer him or her of that understanding.[72]

Man is the only creature to whom I cannot speak without making the meeting common and without conveying the meanings I attribute to things, to myself and to the others. But in my address to another human

---

[72] Emmanuel Levinas. Is ontology fundamental? *Entre Nous. Thinking-of-the-Other*. Columbia University Press, 1998, p. 7.

being the nominative case is also vocative. I do not just consider the Other, I also call him by name. Of course, the I also has names for objects, but they themselves "have no idea" about it. Man recognizes himself by his name which he not only bears but through which he experiences himself as called upon: people refer to him by name.

> Human beings when we speak of them in the third person, "he", "she", "they", as well as my own private psychological states, belong to the sphere of the It. The I experiences these; but only explores their surface without committing its whole being, and its experiences do not extend beyond itself. The It is neutral. The neutral gender suggests, moreover, that in the It, individuals do not enter into the type of unifying relation in which their otherness is distinctive... To have an idea of something is appropriate to the I-It relation. What is important is not thinking about the other, even as an other, but of directly confronting it and saying Thou to it. Hence the real access to the otherness of the other does not consist in a perception but in thou-saying, and this is at once an immediate contact and an appeal which does not posit the object, but of which the object-relation is, in fact, a distortion.[73]

For Levinas, Martin Buber's contribution in the analysis of conversation is unforgettable. Levinas modestly says that he could not claim to improve the lessons of the great master, as he called Buber, but there were some points, on which he did not quite agree with Buber. Levinas does not agree that the I-You is a relationship of equality and reciprocity, as it is according to Buber's understanding of dialogue. The original novelty of Levinas' philosophy is that the intersubjective relationship is represented as a non-reciprocal and asymmetrical relation of inequality. Although this philosophy is devoted mainly to understanding of the subjectness of the Self, at the same time the figure of Other is privileged in it. Levinas asks if morality actually begins where I can place the Other higher than my Self. The Other's face is not reducible to the plastic forms of phenomenality and thematization; it is always expressive and its expression coincides with its humanity exposed to death. Because of its

---

[73] Emmanuel Levinas. Martin Buber and the Theory of Knowledge. *Proper Names*. Translated by Michael B. Smith, Stanford University Press, 1996, p. 26.

mortality the face of the Other has the meaning of an order to me not to leave it alone and in such a way to become an accomplice of this death. My responsibility for the Other cannot be calculated and measured according to the weight of accusation for some free actions on my side. It is not a consequence from the activity of my Self but is gratious responsibility which does not seek a recompensation and is similar to that of the hostige who takes the place of the Other without being linked in some way with him. There is substitution for another, expiation for another without any reciprocity or reparation:

> The ego is not an entity "capable" of expiating for the others: it is this original expiation. This expiation is not voluntary, for it is prior to the will's initiative (prior to the origin). It is as though the unity and uniqueness of the ego were already the hold on itself of the gravity of the other. In this sense the self is goodness, or under the exigency for the abandon of all having, of all one's own and all for oneself, to the point of substitution. Goodness is...the sole attribute which does not introduce multiplicity into One that subject is, for it is distinct from the One. If it is showed itself to the one, it would no longer be a goodness in it. [74]

Being good is not an ability that can be cultivated. Ethics as a kind of moralisation is always doubtful and can even be an expression of false morality. When people perceive it as a moral admonition, even in the most benevolent sense, they devalue it by reducing it to childish morality in which adults require children to be good. Goodness is also not the reflexive Hegelian morality but is always the inability of the I to escape 'problems that are not its own, but are of the others', yet accepted by the I as its own. The Self in the moral relationship is in the accusative, precisely because it is responsible (even when rejecting responsibility) for the freedom of the Other and even for the responsibility of the Other for others. The morality of which Levinas speaks, as he himself underlies, is for adults and not for children. He often quotes Dostoevsky, who in the

---

[74] Emmanuel Levinas. *Otherwise than Being or beyond Essence*. Translated by Alphonso Lingis, Duquesne University Press, 2000, p. 118.

novel *The Brothers Karamazov* expresses the deepest moral truth that "We are all guilty of everything and everyone, but I'm guiltier than anyone else."

In the pure moral relation the Other is recognized to the extent that I am myself his hostage, paying for the freedom of the Other. As Levinas notes, German idealism does not see that "I" is without reciprocity. The hostage and the free, although taken for interchangeable, are in fact irreducible to one another. We cannot say that we are Selves-in-the-world. The I is a unique presence in the world precisely because it is responsible for the Other without expecting the same from him. In the strict sense of the word, this is non-reciprocity of intersubjectivity. However, we do not see it as some extravagant novelty. Here we recall the moral position of Socrates who said that it is better to suffer injustice manifested towards him from others than to himself be the agent of injustice towards them. Or Christ, whose redemption of the guilt of all humankind was without himself having committed any evil.

> Freedom means, therefore, the hearing of a vocation which I am the only person able to answer—or even the power to answer right there, where I am called.[75]

It is only thus that freedom is not arbitrariness, but acquires meaning and form. My freedom is then a vocation—it is called to happen. My responsibility is my being chosen, my "birthright"—I am the first who can respond to the call of the Other in a given situation and I am thus unique and irreplaceable in it.

---

[75] Emmanuel Levinas. Revelation in the Jewish Tradition, *The Levinas' Reader*. Ed. By Sean Hand. Blackwell (Oxford, UK & Cambridge, USA: 1993), p. 210

> The formal meeting is a symmetrical relation and may therefore be read indifferently from either side. But in the case of the ethical relations, where the Other is at the same time higher than I and yet poorer than I, the I is distinguished from the Thou not by the presence of specific attributes, but by the dimension of height, thus implying a break with Buber's formalism. The primacy of the other, posterior to the act of relating, but directly qualifies otherness itself. Otherness is thus qualified, but not by any attribute.[76]

Levinas is aware that his definition of the Other is completely different from that of Buber. According to Buber, the I-You relationship is a relation of mutuality and equality, while Levinas sets out toward mutuality and equality from the moral inequality or asymmetry.

> The knot of subjectivity consists in going to the other without concerning oneself with his movement toward me. Or, more exactly, it consists in approaching in such a way that over and beyond all the reciprocal relations that do not fail to get set up between me and the neighbor, I have always taken one step more toward him... [77]

Namely because of the asymmetry of the moral relation, created by the I, because of all the responsibility falling on him, the freedom of the moral subject is "paradoxically, the only freedom released by the omnipresent shadow of dependence."[78]

In the truest sense of the word, freedom is not merely independence. "Freedom from..." does no coincide with "freedom for...". "Freedom for ..." is manifested in "taking responsibility for ...". Levinas reiterates that responsibility creates the closeness between people and their liberties. But when talking about closeness and liberty, we do not in any way mean physical space. We do not even yet consider social space, which is established only with the presence of the Third; we mean a relation of immediacy between the Other and me. When starting from this relation and to some extent through its abandonment because of the Third, we

---

[76] Emmanuel Levinas. Martin Buber and Theory of Knowledge. *The Levinas' Reader.* p. 72
[77] Emmanuel Levinas. Otherwise tan Being or beyond Essence, Translated by Alfonso Lingis, Duquesne University Press, Pittsburgh, 1998, p. 84.
[78] Zygmunt Bauman. *Postmodern Ethics.* Blackwell, 1995, p. 86.

Sociality and Justice: Toward Social Phenomenology 141

can then speak about social distance, of structure of social relations, of private and public space, of some territorial distinctions, and so on. Closeness, says Bauman, interpreting Levinas, is not a very small distance; it is not even overcoming, ignoring or denying the distance; rather, any distance starts with this immediate closeness of one-for-the-other as the zero point of the coordinate system, in which all other relationships and interactions are located. But this zero-point should not be understood as a "fusion" of the identities of the I and the Other; it is rather a substitution—the I is the hostage, whose time is spent as a guarantee for the freedom and existence of the Other.

> The neighbour concerns me before all assumption, all commitment consented to or refused. ... I am as it were ordred from the outside, traumatically commanded, without interiorizing by representation and concepts the authority that commands me. ...
> The face of the neighbour signifies for me an exceptional responsibility, preceding every free consent, every pact, every contract.[79]

But when in the encounter with the face inevitably the Third lurks behind the Other or rather within the face of the Other, then his appearance raises many new questions:

> It is inside such a "moral society", "the moral party of two", that my responsibility cannot be fathomed or satisfied, and feels unlimited; and it is under this condition that the command needs no argument to gain authority, nor the support of a threat to be a command; it feels like a command, and an unconditional command, all along.
> All this changes with the appearance of the Third. Now true society appears, and the naïve, un-ruled and unruly moral impulse—that both necessary and sufficient condition of the "moral party"—does not suffice any more.[80]

The appearance of the Third evokes the comparison that the I must make initially between the Second and the Third, and subsequently the Fourth, Fifth, and every Other. Who has the right to be first? And what are the relations between them? The I has to judge, to decide about their priority,

---

[79] Emmanuel Levinas. *Otherwise than Being or beyond Essence*. Translated by Alfonso Lingis, Duequesne University Press, Pittsburgh, 1998, p. 87–88.
[80] Zygmunt Bauman. *Postmodern Ethics*. Blackwell, 1995, p. 112.

to move from its relation of closeness to reflection, requiring distancing, measuring and calculating. The comparison of the Other to the others induces the need for objectivity and justice, for measure and principles according to which judgements should be made. Justice and objectivity extend even over myself and I am also subjected to them:

> ... my responsibility for all can and has to be manifest itself also in limiting itself. The Ego can, in the name of this unlimited responsibility, be called upon to concern itself also with itself. The fact that the other, my neighbor, is also a third party with respect to another, who is also a neighbor, is the birth of thought, consciousness, justice and philosophy. The unlimited initial responsibility which justifies this concern for justice, for oneself, and for philosophy can be forgotten. In this forgetting consciousness is a pure egoism. But egoism is neither first, nor last. ... That is because, from the start, the other affects us despite ourselves.[81]

My subordination to the Other is not seen as an attitude that accepts the Other's domination, but, on the contrary, as selfless service which in its exaggerated form is equivalent to the diaconate, to apostolic activity. But in the primordial moral relation there is no room for more than two. In this non-spatial space constituted between the Face and me, which is rather the point of beginning and departure of any further events, the relation is relieved of the determinants of context; it is despite all circumstances and obstacles, but above all despite the desire of the I to preserve itself and its tranquillity. Moral commitment seems to be against the pursuit of survival, against selfishness, against rational choice of objectives and means, of calculating the profits and losses, of the pursuit of pleasures; moreover, it seems to be in spite of power, economy, politics and established standards "for such cases" in society. In the context of the conflict between individual and group interests, where the I is "for" or "against" others, opposing them or cooperating with them, before or after them, the I starts from itself. Attention to the Other, which is morality

---

[81] Emmanuel Levinas. *Otherwise than Being or beyond Essence*. Translated by Alfonso Lingis, Duquesne University Press, Pittsburgh, 1998, p. 128.

itself, abandons the everyday rules and conventions and deprives participants of their everyday status, of group belonging, of community prejudices, of the pursuit of superiority, and so on. This primordial moral connectedness is, so to say, naked, pure sociality. It is my attitude toward the Other as an unique human. However, it is not easily noticed when each of us, according to our institutional roles, goes through his daily grind and everybody is a functionary in society. In everyday life, humanity has itself been transformed into an imperceptible, mundane relation and morality into reciprocal mediated bonds, channelled institutionally and arranged in the system. In other words, the commitment to the Other in its purity and selflessness in fact cannot be upheld because along with the Other immediately the Third appears. From the depth of moral connection with the Other the I surfaces, entering into a relationship with the other of the other, and with all others. This structures a new constellation of space in which conventionality, averaging and normalization have the effect of relieving of the burden of exclusive responsibility. According to Levinas, in the presence of the Third we depart from the command of morality, of love of thy neighbour, where the Other affects me, regardless of his position in the midst of the numerous other individuals and even regardless of the common essence we share as representatives of the kind of "Man."

In morality, the Other is the transcendent and unique one, but beyond the interpersonal relationship, beyond sensitivity to the otherness of the other, the vast land of decisions and interactions extends and in it the Third is not just inescapable, but he is inevitable and absolutely necessary. It is logical then to have a situation of comparing otherwise incomparable human beings, judging them, ranking them according to a measure, scale, preferences, etc. The comparison is already the first act of violence precisely because it is the abandonment of the responsibility of the I for the unique Other and including him in a line of repetitive cases. This is the first constraint exerted on the Other by reducing him to a standard or concept and ignoring his otherness. Can this type of violence exercised by framing of the Other be prevented?

When the Other and the I are both turned into the Third ones, they are already "free" (meant ironically) participants in Totality, parts of the whole of community, of the majority, of the multitude united from the privileged point of view. In a formal community or society, everyone's freedom appears to be limited by others. In Totality everyone is more or less affected by the coercion exercised over his free will (understood as unlimited power for being himself) and over his egocentric needs and desires. Levinas is hesitant but still concludes that *"totality can be constituted only by injustice."* [82]

Justice itself cannot avoid constraining of the individual within one or another conceptual system and confining him to classes and categories [i.e. transforming him into a Third (*Das Man*)], even when these are fully justified. Morality on the other hand, requires not to place constraints on the Other, but self-restraint of the I "to make room for the Other" and to free him from the classifications and subdivisions, which confine him within a description from outside. This means that when the I universalizes its own conceptual system, it is deaf and blind to the others, insensitive to them all. The first justice is allowing for the otherness of the Other to disturb me. Perhaps, the Other disagrees with the meaning assigned to him from outside which renders him the Third and potentially "every one". Of course, the I does not always notice the insult in the face of the Other. He or she can blame me for the actions I have performed, before I have realized the injustice I have done, before I have even thought of any possibility for restoring justice. But justice is not "part of the game of injustice" and is not forged in the fire of battles fought unrelentingly in history. This understanding of justice as a fight

---

[82] Emmanuel Levinas. The *I* and the Totality. *Entre Nous. On Thinking-of-the-Other*. Translated by Michael B. Smith and Barbara Harshav, Columbia University Press, New York, 1998, p. 27.

against injustice gives birth to theories which try to express the moral codes as conventions of one society or another, of one or another class or group. Justice does not come from God either, who is outside history, but solely as a judgment over history, pronounced by participants in it in the midst of historical events. Then Reason, seemingly driven away by the primary commencement of sociality, returns as the ability to judge according to a common criterion, amidst a multitude, panoramically united as a whole (by reason itself). However, according to the self-conscious rationality of knowledge, activity and interactions, the Other appears, as it was already stressed, only as an average other, i.e. the Third. The really Other is at best only a trace in the Third.

2.2. The Ethical and the Political. Justice and the State

It is a common conception that reason precedes language and makes it possible. However, maybe language is based on a relationship established even before thinking and knowledge (before reason as reduced to thinking and knowledge)? Levinas argues that the moral relation—between the Other and me—cannot be reduced to understanding (to reason or *logos*). In *Being and Time* Heidegger writes that in order to understand separate beings, we must go beyond or behind them towards the universal, i.e. Being as such. In this way, the tradition of privileging the universal, originating from Plato, is still continued. In the history of philosophy through the universal, we approach particular beings—either through Plato's ideas or through Hegelian concepts, through Husserl's horizon or Heidegger's Being: in all of them, as well as in all of European philosophy originating from Greek antiquity, we know and understand the different beings by reference to the universal context. However, Levinas does not agree that every relation with a particular being can be deductible from the universal ideas, nor that meanings depend entirely on a horizon or context, nor from the closeness to Being, or from its oblivion, as it is in Heidegger's version. Levinas insists that we do not approach a particular human being as we approach objects in the world, i.e. as a part belonging to the Whole. The perspective of the Whole implies a timeless observer, speaking on behalf of eternity or the system, or on behalf of the Third one, who frames the situation in accordance with his own horizon or with generally accepted meanings. However, the Other withdraws from the frame of the Whole and always retains his position of Exteriority. The Other should not be replaced with the ideas and concepts that have already been coined, nor should he be reduced to a partner, to a role defined within a system of mutual expectations. Of course, it can be argued that if the Other, similar to all other beings, is a being of the world, then the attitude displayed towards him depends on the understanding that we have of him and on his appearance within a horizon of the world. However, the uniqueness of my encounter with him is in that which prior to thematizing him, the Other is the one to whom I respond. The Other in the world is represented by his phenomenality, while in conversation, he is the interlocutor, from which things in the world receive their phenomenal meaning prior to being placed and understood in a common, objectively existing world. The world is not an isolated, solipsistically closed, exitless labyrinth of one's own ideas but is an incarnation of our shared ideas. However, as an independent interlocutor with his own point of view and understanding of the world, shaped by his radical separateness of Being, the Other retains his otherness, exteriority, unpredictability and elusiveness. In this way, the Other is beyond world.

However, how does this relation with the Other unfold in activity, in labour, in practice, in production? In German idealism man is reified through the products of his activity. They form the sphere of not-I. In this not-I created by the I, in which it is alienated, the I rediscovers itself to return to its Self. The widely spread ideology presents the human being as demanding its satisfaction. This being returns to itself with what it has produced to satisfy its needs. This kind of discourse does not usually distinguish between man as an individual and as human kind. It is not sensitive to uniqueness of a particular human destiny. However, the objects produced reveal their authors as they are presented in the significations of language established beyond labour and bearing the meanings of things constitutive of any meaningful activity. They are in advance generalized because these meanings are shared among many speaking a particular language. Moreover, the product of labour is not inalienable property belonging to its author but can be usurped by the others. Furthermore, objects of the labour of the One are usually, from the moment of their very contrivance, intended for the Other. Hence their meaning will be decrypted by the Other, most often in the absence of their author. Everything produced is laden with ambiguity, due to the different meanings assigned to it by the maker on one hand, and the consumer on the other hand, as well as in the various uses by others. Objects can be appropriated, exchanged and used for various purposes. They take on a life of their own, which is not necessarily shared by their producers. The producer is present in his work, when he is already absent. The name that signifies things endorses their sharing with others, but the meaning of will that creates things is lost in the object's utilization by others. The objectivity of things consists in their preservation as common sense through language; but their significance, their validity for all, understandable through language, is precisely a condition and temptation for their private use. This implies their alienation as property of the manufacturer and their potential utility for future owners and users. Their inclusion in economic life turns them into objects of exchange to the point of being taken for granted while their social origin is completely forgotten, as well as the rights of their authors or creators. When products become commodified, they signify impersonal relations. Consequently anonymity emerges and is facilitated significantly by the mediation of money.

> The fact that the will escapes itself, that the will does not contains itself, amounts to the possibility the others have of laying hold of the work, alienating, acquiring, buying, stealing it. The will itself thus takes on a meaning for the other, as though it were a thing. [83].

The economic success of the One would be a kind of violence against the Other because no will alone could defend itself from its own betrayal: the will retires from its right as the proprietor of the product of its labour, giving it to others. In a market economy, the best outcome is if it is purchased. In the exchange, it falls into another context and the will is powerless to guarantee its meaning. On one hand, the will is liberated from its attachment to it, but on the other hand, only the intervention of the Other over which the will has no power, renders this alienation irreversible. The will does not have the force and means to defend itself against the privatization of the product nor the reduction of its meaning as construed in the private sphere of the Other. The will needs social and political institutions, the economic and political regime of the country, so that it is not alone and helpless against alienation as a kind of violence against itself. In public order it receives a warranty of justice by the universality of the laws whose justice should benefit "everyone". The concept behind the state is that it guarantees the peace and equality of citizens within the totality, arranging the rights and obligations of the various roles or positions:

---

[83] Emmanuel Levinas. *Totality and Infinity*. Translated by Alfonso Lingis, Duquesne University Press, 1969, p. 228.

An equality to which the state aspires throughout history, and in which, through reason, human individuals, so differently endowed by nature, are promised the formal equality of individuals within a genus. Human individuals within the human genus offer themselves for judgement and lend themselves to the objectivity necessary for the exercise of justice which eventually re-establishes peace.[84]

Nonetheless, the state may transform from mother into a wicked stepmother and the will learns this through its economic and political existence. It becomes aware of another type of tyranny, namely that of the tyranny of the universal, impersonal, levelling of the bureaucracy and soullessness of the state. Levinas says that this is an order that is inhuman, although its tyranny is not brutal. Economic existence, which separates every one and renders the Self in opposition to the others in the market exchange and consumption results in an inevitable antagonism of wills. Then the Other corrupts the Self, provoking the I to meet the Other with the hostility of selfishness. In the world where we need to help and give, I shut myself out and keep my resources for myself and the voice coming from the other side remains unheard. In his defining moral misery, the Other seeks to dominate my will by hiding behind the masks, imposed on him by social roles. Being in his primordiality and authenticity "the stranger", "the widow" and "the orphan" (these are the names that Levinas gives to the Other), whom I am obliged to support, in the totality of political and economic relations the Other approaches me as a kidnapper and raider of my property. In the whole of the state I am I in my identification through ownership, essence, possession (even if only through given characteristics, etc.). Security, guaranteed by the order within the state, does not eliminate alienation and antagonism. Inside the whole of the state the I (together with all products in which it is reified, with the property, through which it identifies itself) acquires its importance by deducing it from the terms and rules, i.e. as an example

---

[84] Emmanuel Levinas. Uniqueness. *Entre Nous.Thinking-of-the-Other*. Translated by Michael B. Smith and Barbara Harshav, Columbia University Press, New York, 1998, p. 190

or as a private, empirical case of universal law, as the actor playing a role. In order to justify this state order where individuals, as rivals in the entity, must be reconciled, the political thought resorts to the theory of the social contract. State power is greater than the power of every individual and thus holds everybody in obedience, thereby overcoming the condition of general insecurity. Hobbes' state is derived from the need to end war, accepted as the natural condition. If I retain my natural right to a free will, the threat created by the antagonism of wills in the rivalry for the better position, where everyone wants to deprive the other of the freedom based on ownership and consumption, to turn him into an object (or slave), is always hanging over me; however, if I step back and all others do the same, this will cause a rearrangement of forces and the transformation of the natural condition into political order. In such a political order it seems that everyone would behave wisely and reason would dictate the relevant clauses of the peace agreement, to which people can consent. Hobbes relies on the prudence of reason, helping egoistic forces to organize themselves in the totality to avoid becoming victims of their own passions. Fear of death and the desire to organise a tolerable life entices people to the civil status, which would be different from the barbaric. In this self-limitation of everyone, however, we do not detect anything that is not connected to self-interest and the struggle for survival. It is because the natural condition in itself is self-destruction that a compromise is made in the name of the negotiating relations.

Levinas emphasizes that rationality of individuals, perceived in this manner, is nothing but prudence in view of personal benefit and well-understood interest in obeying the sovereign. Reason seems to be infected by the instinct for survival. Hence, the glorious spontaneity of life, ontologically understood as struggle, finds satisfaction in the peaceful calm which is always a temporary truce, merely a cease-fire until the next battle. For Levinas it is an illusion to think that only by prudence can we achieve and maintain peace. Hobbes argues that the unity of citizens is represented by a single person—the head of state; consequently, any limitation on the sovereign's prerogatives would be a limitation on the state, risking a reversion to violence and war. Thus the state becomes the monster Leviathan, receiving unlimited, absolute power.

At first glance it seems that in Levinas' philosophy egoism is replaced by altruism for the triumph of true, i.e. messianic peace that has little to do with the temporary calm before another storm. However, Levinas is opposed to egoism not altruism (i.e. inverted selfishness), but the rights of others. It is not a question of to be or not to be—it ceases to be important when the focus of my attention is not my own overblown or shrinking Self, but the Other.

Levinas' principle—responsibility or "the One for the Other"—does not support the theory of social contract because, according to him, the state itself grew not as "monopoly over legitimate violence", as per the famous definition of Max Weber. Even if we assume that the state originated as a guarantee against the exercise of violence in the battle of everyone against everyone, then from there on the very legitimacy of the state is determined by justice, and the egocentricity of citizens in public life acquires another meaning—a guarantee and support of morality as the foundation of state institutions. The essence of the state is not contradictory to morality. With its institutions, the state is the means through which morality can be protected. Moreover, we must ask ourselves whether the state was not initially invoked by morality.

Herein the nature of the state itself is at issue. There is no doubt that everything in the life of modern people bears the seal of the state. Do not the component parts acquire their meaning only by the principle of the whole and their positions in it? However, when state power is declared absolute, isn't the state then deified and thus turned into an object of idolatry? This question is possibly even more acute when asked not only in terms of the nation-state but of supranational unions, the European state and why not of the globalized world state. This is really a question about totality.

Today the dimensions of society have become global. Thanks to communications, means of transport and the scale of the global economy, one feels on one hand connected with humanity as a whole, but on the other hand, alone and lost in the midst of events. Through the media one can experience sympathy to what is happening in the most remote corners of the world and feel connected with the people there, but also can realize that he is only a spectator, who cannot participate in person. It is as if personal destiny, freedom or happiness, as well as relations with others, are dependent on forces of inhuman dimensions. The very progress of technologies that allow every possible contact with anyone and everyone, simultaneously only serves to make people anonymous, multiplied and distant. Anonymous forms of communication displace more immediate connections in a world that, thanks to technology, is becoming predictable, programmed and controlled. Of course, the context of the state and the nation is less abstract than the global context, but it is also of sufficiently large scale so that the face-to-face relation is replaced by relationships that are neutralized, regulated by law, technically multiplied and valid for "everyone". Perhaps many would seek a way out of this situation in the dream of a society in which participants will be closer and will know each other. In this sense, it would be a society reduced to a small "warm" community where people spend time being receptive to each other, together in meetings and in conversations with each other, supporting each other, feeling for each other and helping each other. However, the creation of such a marginal society, existing on the edge of the real one, is not a solution to the problem. Society, organized as state, even with its impersonal structure is preferable to occasional isolated communities, new tribalist unions or club associations. Modern society, with its cities, industry and crowds of people, is not the result of an arbitrarily and wrongly chosen path, but the very essence of modernity.

Political order of the state often claims to be non-relative in terms of moral issues, and preoccupied solely with the issues of the day. The political world is presented as a world of interests, benefits and a pragmatic attitude towards things. It demonstrates a capacity to manage reality and mistrusts any being that is content with dreams or utopia. However, the political world is also a place of corruption and coercion, of improper deals and violence and hence a condition of atrophy or hypertrophy, envious of the exercise of power. The state is transformed into an idol and deifies itself—power for the sake of power. This hypertrophied condition or state in atrophy pursues hegemonic and imperialist ambitions and could be called "totalitarian", i.e. a state of violence. Its domestic "peace" is achieved by the subordination of some people to others, regardless of the numerous ideologies offered by those who are at the helm. The cynicism of government consists in enforcing obedience in the name of liberation and demonstration of concern while abdicating from responsibilities. Even those who refuse to participate in politics and to cooperate with the authorities, who try to remain neutral in politics, are involved and unprotected, often finding themselves repressed by the authorities. Levinas is very critical of the totalitarian state. Today such criticism is commonplace for many political and social thinkers, but for Levinas it is inseparable from his philosophical critique of the very concept of "totality".

Levinas is aware that totality is not just some evil that must be removed and discarded, as certain superficial comments by pluralists and multiculturalists confidently claim. Integrity of experience and unity, according to concepts and principles, are inherent in every thought and every successful action, including any political action. From a dialectical speculative point of view, totality means multiplicity, united in synthesis and the reconciliation of opposites. However, totality is achieved by the intellectual operation of self-reflection that is itself aware of this synthesis. Reason through its dialectical logic undertakes the reconstruction and unification of the whole range of conditions even to the unconditional. Thinking is directed towards constructing a system according to a common perspective and to arranging all the most diverse and contradictory elements within this perspective. Reason seems to be universal and impersonal only by definition. In contemporary politics the perspective of reason or that of totality belongs to the extra-territorial elites, who are themselves untouchable and are not party to conflicts within the system. This is the viewpoint of the nomenclature peering from the tower of the Panopticon who hold the whole range of possibilities. Ideologies and practices both of unity and of pluralism can be used, openly or covertly, for the purposes of dictatorship. This is true today, as it appears that Synopticon forms rather than the Panopticon is the prevailing scheme of government.

Levinas chooses to examine the possibility of going beyond totality and restoring the rights of Exteriority. However, no longer by means of negation, as in Hegel, where through the negation of negation every otherness, denied as the opposing party in the conflict, rejoins the expanding system. Nowadays even the system itself creates its own opposition. Levinas believes that totality can never fully integrate in itself the otherness of the Other, who is in the position of Exteriority, even when this is prohibited by decree. It is due to this exteriority that there is pluralism but not one that resists homogenization. Darkness in the sky over totality is torn and illuminated thanks to the light of the Face. What Levinas called "the idea of infinity," suggests a logic different from the "Absolute Idea", i.e. integration and assimilation in totality. Infinity or exteriority is a category, irreducible to an opposition of totality; transcendence exists in itself, and only then is it found in the phenomena of immanence, but also retreats from them. In this sense, namely the "face of the Other" is the factor of indomitable resistance to totalization in the system of society and transcends it.

Unlike many other thinkers, especially in the field of social and political philosophy, Levinas is not satisfied with the opposition between the liberal and totalitarian state. He does not believe that the liberal state, in its inner logical course, will lead to the limitation of its power through the separation of powers—e.g. the legislative, judicial and executive, each of them controlling the other through its own effectiveness. According to Levinas, any government, regardless of its political orientation, carries an inherent tendency to turn into totalitarianism. This also applies to the liberal state. The state as an organization does not appear randomly in history nor is it a coincidence that in the course of its existence it is threatened, along with all its institutions, by degeneration. This happens when it turns into an apparatus for exercising repression of citizens. Levinas repeatedly states that even if we deny that morality establishes public order, it cannot be denied that morality constantly calls into question the justice of the state.

When discussing social and political order, however, it is evident that in Levinas' philosophy there is some volatility and inconsistency. Levinas sometimes takes up the view that historical states were born out of competition, limitations and conflicts. His position on morality, however, opens another possibility for interpretation—the possibility of the existence of the state and political order as derived from moral responsibility. Levinas does not fully develop this theoretical perspective, invented by himself, in which the moral condition is seen as the natural condition of human beings. He is critical of the state, because it can be closer or farther away from morality. Namely, it is the criterion for its justice, but he does not derive the very system of state out of the moral relation between the One and the Other, but rather from betraying this relation. The state appears then as the necessary evil—the avoidance of the war of everyone against everyone, by virtue of obedience to a master who is more powerful than the individual parties to the conflict. It is possible, however, to have another definition of politics, namely that the political could not be reduced to the unavoidable evil and violence, that the political action could be guided by a practical wisdom, which does not confirm only my Self and my calculated interest but responds to the questions that are not chosen by my party.[85]

* * *

Humanity seeks to acquire and exercise power over the world of objects. This is the eternal desire to dominate nature. Is human reason not then a means of domination over objects but also over people? Do we not transfer uncritically reason's function as a tool of imposing hegemony onto the Other? When considering him as part of the world, as a natural being, as an existent among other existents or as the performer of a role whose meaning is revealed only after the final curtain of the life dramaturgy, do we not strive to conquer him? Paradoxically, we are conditioned to respect reason, as far as it is the winner in this struggle of forces and personalities, and insofar it dominates their relations. We think that reason overcomes the resistance of the multitude of beings, in order to place everything in the world in its place within the all-embracing horizon, but only by retaining its position of the privileged observer. The most common perspective of the winner in the antagonism of forces becomes a privileged point of view, which receives recognition from the audience as the perspective of Reason. Winners are not judged. Their "reasoning" will become the measure of all things and events in history. The history itself is rewritten accordingly.

* * *

It must be reiterated that all seeing, i.e. understanding, performs an act of violence and negation—it is only partial negation, because in violence

---

[85] See Alain Finkielkraut. Le risque du politique. *Cahier de l'Herne. Emmanuel Lévinas.* Editions de l'Herne, Paris,1991, p. 570

beings do not disappear, but are under my power. Their independence is denied—they become mine: grasped through knowledge and accessible within my scope of action, placed under surveillance, subject to control by my hand and reduced to what suits my interests. Knowledge, as such, is power and is necessary to power, not only because it provides the technologies used by power, but because it supports the exercise of domination, transforming the other into mine. The Other, however, cannot in the same way be completely in the field of someone's freedom, because he does not appear to me simply as something among other things. As already stated, the face is invisible in the visible. Things have meanings not in themselves, but as belonging to the world, as parts of the totality of the world, given definitions insofar as they are included in human knowledge and practice (through instrumental interest). They are understandable in the light of Being as beings, having their place or meaning in the system or in the context. While the face has meaning in itself and I communicate or associate with precisely this being, existing in itself and significant in itself. This communication is the event of the birth of a community. However, seeing the face is no longer seeing, but hearing and speech. Levinas asks whether the original and true rationality is not in the suppression of the resistance of the Other, as the I crushes the resistance of objects, subjecting them to its goals. With respect to other human beings, the question is, does rationality manifest itself in their destruction or in the pacification of conflicts? Levinas answer is that reason is manifested truly in the response to the appeal, uttered even by the mere presence of the face before me.

Of course everything accessible in the Other as captured in concepts and ideas through common meanings is intelligible and understandable, e.g. his environment, history, habits and so on. However, what escapes is precisely his autochthonous being. He exists for himself and is relevant to himself. The Other is a self-conscious being. I can negate him only completely, not partially as I negate objects to deprive them of their independent existence and turn them into my ideas, my property, my possessions, my conquest and make them dependent on my activity and power. The Other can be physically destroyed, but my I is not able to rule over the meaning that the Other associates with his own existence. Although some manipulation of consciousness is possible and we try to influence it, the Other makes his own decisions. And then the Other is not numb but is the being that utters the first word. Indeed, his autochthonous being will be over, if I kill him, if I physically destroy him. However, this power over him is the complete opposite of real power: in the moment that I seem to have established complete power over the Other, he is not in my power anymore. In killing, I can attain my goal and kill him as I cut a tree or decapitate an animal (these are literally the words of Levinas for physical extermination of the Other), but thus the face is understood as the other beings-in-the-world-in-the-openness-of-being-in-general, as part of the world in which I am too, within the horizon. The real power that supports the Other in his otherness, which without clutching him in its grip, is moral and not physical. Consequently, we must ask: what is the relation between physical and moral power and is physical power not subordinate to moral?

Morality itself is not some kind of relation, dwelling in another world, somewhere above natural existence, on a meta-level or on an ethereal height as a second tier, purely human or, as is usually said, social tier of existence. As if sociality or morality are a kind of luxury above the rough texture of the foundation, of the basis which is the struggle for existence. Here, however, we argue the opposite, i.e. that our very natural being is conditioned by morality. Each of us is created by others and exists thanks to the peace with and care provided by others—which often goes unnoticed, especially when depersonalized and technologized through institutions. It is a trivial truth that no one could survive as a human being without others, but one which has been forgotten since, as Heidegger says, the closest seems most distant and has indeed acquired the status of the farthest.

If my subordination to the Other is not understandable in the coordinate system of relations according to the laws of nature, is it not then unnatural (i.e. against nature, against animal instincts, against *conatus essendi*) the very appearance of a moral relation to the Other? Is not the humanity of man already an expression of a crisis of existence (as natural evolution, as struggle of species, as struggle for survival)? The crucial question in social phenomenology is whether ethics is not more "ontological" than any ontology? Does morality not constitute the very nature of our existence, as opposed to the "natural condition" in Hobbes?

On the one hand, the presence of the face is everything that I see as part of the world—this nose, lips, shape and indeed everything that I can destroy, but on the other hand the face is precisely what remains invisible in the visible and is not within my control through physical domination. The face is ambiguous:

> The face is exposed, menaced, as if inviting us to an act of violence. At the same time, the face is what forbids us to kill.[86]

The face always appears vulnerable and naked in the possibility to be de-faced from the earth, yet at the same time expressing this non-physical and metaphysical impossibility to kill it. The meeting "face to face" is always, willy-nilly, a conversation. If it is not peace and conversation, the meeting turns into war, and human solidarity is destroyed by the primitivism of violence and murder, leaving behind only ruins.

---

[86] Emmanuel Levinas.The Face. *Ethics and Infinity*. Duquesne University Press, 2000, p. 86.

160 Maria Dimitrova

> The Bible says: Thou shalt not kill! It isn't always a matter of killing with a knife. Daily killing with a good conscience, innocent killing—there is that as well! Thou shalt love thy neighbor and thou shalt not kill—that's exactly the same. For me it's quite extraordinary that being as such is always a conatus essendi, a striving to be. And then the Bible comes along and says—so you must read it—to be human is to be responsible for the other. The other is really nothing for me. ... He is indifferent "to me"; he doesn't concern "me." This "indifferent-to-me" is the nonhuman. The human enters into being in order to say the ontological absurdity: the other doesn't concern me...[87]

Levinas is undoubtedly aware that history is inhumane, full of violence and bloodshed. It has been explained in terms of necessity, the compulsion of existence, as opposed to starting with the ethics of caring for the Other. However, Levinas stresses that humanity has not simply and only existed for centuries but has attested its opposition to *conatus essendi*, condemning the horrors and crimes, turning away from violence and glorifying holiness. Is holiness not really the most authentic necessity for humanity? Levinas says that the call to holiness precedes the concern of exiting—before wars the altars were erected.

For Levinas the moral relation is maintaining the Other. The verb "to maintain", which corresponds to the French verb "maintenir", has many meanings: maintaining as foundation or as bearing someone, or paying maintenance to someone, or carrying the burden or holding in the palm of your hand, or taking care so that something is in good condition and so on. However, suggesting these different nuances, depending on the differences of context, we can still single out two meanings that seem to be extremes, with symbolic value:

1. supporting something in an open palm;
2. holding, grasping something in a closed hand, depriving it of its independence, clutching it in one's fist.

These two values correspond to:

---

[87] Florian Rötzer. Emmanuel Levinas. *Conversations with French Philosophers*. Humanities Press Internationa. Inc., New Jersey, 1995, p. 59.

1. morality, which is caring for the Other;
2. the authority and power that politics needs to subjugate the Other to.

Human relations are located between them as between two demarcation lines: on one side morality and peace and on the other—violence and war. Politics is precisely the search for a middle ground between them. However, the middle is not as with the ancient Greeks virtue par excellence, but the deficiency of good. According to Levinas:

> The occidental ethics always proceeds from the fact that the other is a limitation for me. Hobbes says you can come directly to philosophy from this mutual hatred. Thus we could attain a better society without love for the other, in which the other is taken into account. That would be a politics that could lead to ethics. I believe, on the contrary, that politics must be controlled by ethics: the other concerns me.[88]

Emmanuel Levinas does not believe that peace and violence, as well as good and evil, truth and untruth, justice and injustice, etc. are equal. Violence is the absence of peace, evil is the absence of good, injustice is the failure to seek justice etc. Levinas' philosophy is oriented to the "Most High" and does not favour circularity, cycles, symmetry, levelling.

* * *

For Levinas the relation between morality and politics is no less important than the relationship between ethics and ontology. In a sense, these relations are correlative. At the beginning of *Totality and Infinity* the political and moral are opposed to each other:

> The state of war suspends morality, it divests the eternal institutions and obligations of their eternity... War is not only one of the ordeals—the greatest—of which morality lives; it renders morality derisory. The art of foreseeing war and of winning it by every means—politics—is henceforth enjoined as the very exercise of reason.[89]

---

[88] Ibid., p. 59.
[89] Emmanuel Levinas. Preface. *Totality and Infinity*. Duquesne University Press, 1969, p. 21.

Commonly morality is based on politics. The actual relation is just the opposite however, because as the political war destroys the relation between people, morality creates it. Only that which has been created can be destroyed. As evil is the negation of and hence is secondary to good, so violence is the negation of and secondary to morality. In the moral relation to the Other, it comes not from defining and dominating the Other in order to provide security and freedom for my own self, but from the opposite motive—to welcome, to support and protect the Other and maintain his right. This means questioning the limits of my own freedom as arbitrariness and tyranny. Such self-restraint is not enforced. Even the ancients defined freedom as the voluntary self-restraint of the free citizen of the state—he was not the master over others as they were also free citizens, but was his own master and to be the master of those who were not free, i.e. slaves, he had to be master of himself and his own passions: we must command ourselves in order to be free. This is the prototype of the Kantian conception of freedom as autonomy, however with the assumption that the theory of the social contract is the prerequisite for this viewpoint. Freedom, of course, must prevent its own decline into tyranny. This can be achieved by written laws and institutions, by organizing the various forces in society; in a word—with the establishment of the constitutional state. Institutionalization and legislation ensures freedom with political tools. Freedom is no longer invested by the face, but rather by the credentials, accredited to the agents acting on behalf of the institutions and constitution. The entire philosophical tradition, starting from Greek antiquity, puts freedom, and hence morality into dependence on institutions, on the universality of laws and on the participation of individuals in the totality of the polis. If a person is ostracized, he ceases to be a citizen and therefore ostracism was considered equivalent to a death sentence. Long before Hobbes philosophy tried to derive the moral from the political order of the city. Here, by contrast, it is argued that the political is derived from the moral. In the totality of the Hobbesian type of state the supreme ideal was equality of freedoms. Equality, however, is unthinkable without something Third, in respect of which it is established—Leviathan is needed to make the unequal citizens equal.

Levinas rarely discussed the political views of famous thinkers in the European philosophical tradition and almost always when referring to them, he examined their metaphysical conceptions. His criticism was particularly adequate in respect of thinkers such as Hobbes, Locke and Spinoza, who found justification for the social nature of man in *conatus essendi*, i.e. the stubbornness of man to survive. In the natural state, which, according to Hobbes, is the war of everyone against everyone, people live in constant fear, in danger of violent death. Human life is lonely, miserable, nasty, brutish and short. With the conclusion of the social contract, however, individuals give up their natural rights in the name of peace. Therefore politics is assigned the supreme task of promoting one's own interest by limiting it through the common one. Here lies Levinas' disagreement with theories relying on the social contract that they place morality in subjugation to politics.

We are taught to think that every living thing strives to survive and preserve its place under the sun, without taking into account the destruction "of the other of myself." From this instinct to preserve oneself, inherent in individual beings and identified with the right of every individual to freely defend their property, the theory of the social contract derives its most fundamental conception—the undeniable right of freedom. However, freedoms so understood seek expansion of their perimeters and come into conflict with each other, leading to violence. It is from the notion of violence as natural, but also as a self-destructive state, that social order is necessitated. For Hobbes, the state grew out of the state of war.

It seems that Roman thinkers were the first who ceased to accept violence as self-explanatory and tried to find a solution to the problem with arguments supporting the use of force in protection of property or in self-protection. Patristics continued to raise the problem, but casting the legal framework for permissible violence in a different light. Holy Fathers spoke of a moral duty in protection of the neighbour, opposing relations of power to peace. For them, the use of force in time of war was needed to defend "their own" from the attacks of barbarians, but in peacetime the use of force was also permissible to fend enemies off, strengthen one's home and protect the neighbour from thieves and robbers. It was believed that this was just coercion and the one who does not help others against attackers, when able to do so, is as guilty as the attackers. The Bible says that we need to protect the poor and the orphan, the unfortunate and the needy, to save them from evil and vice.

History knows another solution to the problem of violence, besides legitimate punishment and legitimate murder. Tolstoy in his pacifist attitude pronounced himself for absolute non-violence: one should not respond to evil with evil, and when you have to fight evil, it should be done not by force, but by love and sacrifice. Levinas was influenced by Tolstoy in his youth, but he also knew the Old Testament well and the message of the Jewish tradition that evil must be avenged. However, what would revenge bring us? It was also his fate as a Jew, persecuted and prosecuted both by Stalinism and Hitlerism, that made him think seriously about the problem of violence. Is it possible to reconcile violence with morality, which, according to Levinas, demands respect, protection and selfless attention to the Other? Does not the commandment "Thou shalt not kill! on the one hand, being the moral imperative and on the other hand, the law of just revenge "an eye for an eye, a tooth for a tooth" mutually exclude one another? The problem is further complicated when is considered the Third one. In proximity the I is responsible for the Other fully and unreservedly, but closeness, as already highlighted, becomes problematic with the appearance of the Third.

...to make possible a dis-interested responsibility for another excludes reciprocity. But should another be without devotion to the other? A third party is necessary there. ...in relationship with another I am always in relation with the third party. From this moment on, proximity becomes problematic: one must compare, weight, think; one must do justice... The word "justice" is in effect much more in its place, there, where equity is necessary ...[90]

At first glance it could be assumed that Levinas simply defends liberal principles of equal respect for everyone: if we want fair treatment, then it must be for all, both for our nearest ones and for those most distant. There must be power, a law applied to everyone to be respected by everyone and everyone ought to be allowed to participate in elections for government. However, Levinas' position is different and far more sophisticated. He is not against the state, but suggests that we should go "beyond" it.

Levinas does not allow for justice to be a degradation of the moral, described by him through "for-the-Other", that is, due to restrictions of responsibility to achieve equality "for everyone", or indeed some sort of reciprocity, similar to the limitation of everyone's freedom. On the contrary, true justice has as its eternal ideal the non-reciprocal gratuitous responsibility for the Other. Levinas never gives up the asymmetry of the relationship with the Other. Once he was asked by a Japanese student whether the SS officer also had a face. Levinas' answer was that the SS officer also had the right to defense and respect, although the SS officers refused this right to their victims. The absolute indebtedness of the I to the Other precedes any posterior inception of relations and accompanies them everywhere and at all levels and exceeds their every drama. It extends as far as the responsibility for the persecution to which I myself am subject and to the responsibility for the responsibility of the Other.

In the tradition of liberal discourse the One restricts his rights insofar as he is disturbed and pressed to do so by the Other. In one of his two

---

[90] Emmanuel Levinas. Questions and Answers. *Of God Who Comes To Mind.* Translated by Bettina Bergo, Stanford University Press, 1998, p. 82.

treatises on Government, Locke postulates that those who are criminals and from whom people need to be protected, must be put down as wild animals because besides threatening individuals, as well as security, reason, law and all legitimacy, they declare war on all mankind, even by killing just one person. For Levinas there is no doubt that violence calls for new violence in response, but he is convinced that we must stop this chain reaction. Violence in some cases is not just inevitable, rather we must admit that it is a direct obligation in the fight against evil, and provided that it ends the escalation of violence, coercion must indeed be utilised. In such cases, the struggle of forces is unavoidable. Therefore, Levinas believes that the doctrine of non-violence (Tolstoy) is ineffective against evil and even encourages evil, for the possibility of endless apology and forgiveness leaves open the way for its ceaseless repetition. We must act against evil, but how? The real problem is not to reject violence by aiming to make it impossible, but to ask how and by what means to lead the fight against it. The problem is not only in that violent people must be punished in a just manner, but especially in that we must not allow the innocent to suffer. For Levinas pacifism is not a solution to the problem when dealing with an aggressor.

Can we rely on the state to protect us against aggression? Can we define the state as a monopoly of legitimate violence?

The image of justice is usually depicted as blindfolded, to emphasize the requirement of impartiality in the process of judgment. The judge does not judge the Other as a face, but by comparing this Other to the remaining others; he judges "every One", regardless of which one he is — anyone who could take this place. It also means that everyone should be held accountable under universal principles and common laws. But then the first use of power in the process of judging is ignoring the uniqueness of the face. In this sense, justice is also violence from the very outset. Its institutional blindness should be corrected by rediscovering a path to the face in its uniqueness. The justice of sentences requires patience and mercy to mitigate the severity of penalties. Justice is revised by mercifulness: the latter precedes the former, but must be continued in it, and after it.

> Justice comes from love. That definitely doesn't mean to say that the rigor of justice can't be turned against love understood in terms of responsibility. Politics, left to itself, has its own determinism. Love must always watch over justice.[91]

However, are there not entire government regimes that have nothing to do with justice? All Hitlerites were loyal to the Führer and strictly followed the laws of the National Socialist state. However, what happens in such a society when laws themselves are unfair? Does justice coincide with legitimacy?

Here we raise the problem of evil against which we must fight. Is the "murderer" not the one that threatens, instigates violence and is no longer a face but a threatening force? When we raise the problem of evil, it is not about the threat against me but about the protection of others whereby in the name of justice, violence against the "murderer" is inevitable. However, it also means that judges are inevitable, along with institutions, government, civil society, where face-to-face relations do not exhaust all relations. We can speak of the legitimacy or illegitimacy of the state on condition that the criterion of justice in it is the relation to the other as a Face.

> ...it is in terms of the relation to the Face or of me before the other that we can speak of the legitimacy or illegitimacy of the state. A state in which the interpersonal relationship is impossible, in which it is directed in advance by the determinism proper to the state, is a totalitarian state. So there is a limit of the state. Whereas, in Hobbes's vision—in which the state emerges not from the limitation of charity, but from the limitation of violence—one cannot set a limit on state.[92]

---

[91] Emmanuel Levinas. Philosophy, Justice, and Love. *Entre Nous.Thinking-of-the-Other*. Translated by Michael B. Smith and Barbara Harshav, Columbia University Press, 1998, p. 108.
[92] Ibid., p. 105.

In a totalitarian state everything is deduced and administered from the "top" or the centre. Moreover, the administrative measures are imposed by dictatorship, violence and ideological propaganda. In a panoptical regime people are disciplined bodies. In a liberal state, as Levinas believes, morality and charity awaken justice to realize its own injustice. Not that charity repeals justice and protects it from perversions, from reaching extremes, even cruelty. True justice is concerned about its own possible injustice or insufficient justice, i.e. one that can accommodate mercy. Justice, like morality and knowledge, cannot rest on the laurels of what has already been achieved. Dogma, complacency and turning away from otherness are exactly the opposite of what we call morality, knowledge and justice. Abolition of the death sentence is an example of the reconciliation of justice and charity, of politics and morality. Abolition of the death penalty is respect for the face and is consistent with the supremacy of the commandment "Thou shalt not kill." Murder under any circumstances, including as a legitimate death penalty, cannot be applied to the field of justice, and even less to morality. The escalation of violence cannot stop the killing—causing the death of the other cannot be allowed under any circumstances and cannot have any moral justification.

Although Levinas does not accept the theory of non-violence, he does not renounce the centrality of love in the pacifist doctrine. For him security of peace, amity within the state, is achieved not by power, which always targets and uses the weakness of the other, but by love: *To love is to fear for another, to come to the assistance of his fragility.*[93]

Love herein is not meant as love in general, as love to humanity, to the common good and so on. As is known from the time of Pascal, who was one of the first critics of the theory of the social contract, love for the sake of the common good is in its essence a concealed form of hatred.

---

[93] Emmanuel Levinas. *Totality and Infinity*. Translated by Alfonso Lingis, Duquesne University, 1969, p. 256

Levinas insists that politics should be at the service of morality as a means which serves the purpose. Morality is the single criterion of justice and politics, which is why there are good and bad policies.

* * *

Levinas does not agree with the political theory and practice of the West, because violence is considered the beginning and the driving force of its entire history. The question is whether violence or, conversely, solidarity between people is the true foundation of history. Is fighting (overt or covert)—war, fierce competition, rivalry, lack of recognition, not a challenge to the rights of others etc. restrained in its escalation thanks to the indestructibility of morality? Is not aggression, if not restrained, at least neutralized by the respect for the other? Levinas, like Kant, who relies on eternal peace, also thinks that violence is overcome only in peace, though not as reconciliation, established by "the cunningness of Reason in nature," (Hegel) but as a messianic peace. The latter always begins with speech, although if understood simply as the use of significations, speech is never enough. Speech is true when it is a relation to others and when understood, not simply with the help of new words, but by deeds. We must break with the totality of wars and empires in which people do not speak and are treated as forces without faces in the determinism of actions and counteractions—treated as existents governed by the laws of mechanics. The anarchy of good or morality precedes and goes beyond the rules of the political game between antagonistic forces. Politics is a *game* of life and death, but morality is itself the *seriousness* of life and death. There is no such thing as "bare life", reduced to purely biological survival—life, deprived of the sociality of humans. "Bare life", as it is understood by theorists of bio-politics, is an ideological concept which conceals political relations, presenting them as natural. However, actually, this is the naturalization of the social.

In his essay *On uniqueness*, the main question Levinas examines is the distinction between "moral" and "formal", or between the ethical and legal. Laws and institutions of the state should not be seen as bodies of repression and legitimized violence but as a framework enabled and conducted by morality. However, state enforced justice most often betrays its origin, i.e. morality as responsibility for others. State power is always tempted to centralize and monopolize resources and to establish totalitarian control over the civil society. While, conversely, in order to be government and not just coercion, it should constantly monitor itself in the light of morality, i.e. in the light of concerns for the freedoms of the citizens. Levinas concludes that, like good, justice means incessant self-criticism of the state and a requirement to do more than what has been achieved towards attaining human rights. Such a thing as complacent morality or complacent justice is a contradiction in terms. First, the requirement to "do more" is self-referential and not just discontent by others and a requirement on their part. This applies to both the state and individuals.

The liberal state, a proponent of which Levinas was by his own account, is based on the principle of the protection of human rights. However, it carries in itself a contradiction, because while rights are understood as protecting "my rights", they provoke antagonism, struggle and do not necessarily care about the Other or give attention to "his right". It is believed that the protection of human rights is not a function of government but of non-governmental organizations. One of their tasks is to appeal on behalf of the citizens to the state to improve the existing legislation, which in some sense has trampled on humanity, i.e. on human rights:

Sociality and Justice: Toward Social Phenomenology 171

> But justice itself cannot make us forget the origin of the right or the uniqueness of the other ... It cannot abandon that uniqueness to political history, which is engaged in the determinism of powers, reasons of state, totalitarian temptations and complacencies. It awaits the voices that will recall, to the judgements of the judges and statesmen, the human face dissimilated beneath the identities of citizens. Perhaps these are the "prophetic voices." ...But prophetic voices...are sometimes heard in the cries that rise up from the interstices of politics and that, independently of official authority, defend the "rights of man"; sometimes in the songs of the poets; sometimes in the press or in the public forum of the liberal states, in which freedom of expression is ranked as the first freedom and justice is always a revision of justice and the expectation of a better justice.[94]

For the state with its legislative measures, however—and this is true for any state—the pursuit of justice is forever an elusive task, because justice treats citizens by typecasting and categorizing them. The search for "more just justice" has as its ideal the respect for everyone's uniqueness. The political world—the world of the citizens, of the Third one and the multitude of others—is always simultaneously the product of morality and disregard for morality (or an attempt at destruction of morality, one could say). If the memory of the uniqueness of the Face is not stored in the individual and collective memory, the idea of objective, i.e. impersonal, justice would have never occurred. Of course, "impersonal" means the denial of the personal. The latter, however, can and should be maintained starting with the morality of interpersonal relations and throughout the totality of the state.

In *Dialogue on Thinking of the Other* the interviewer asked Levinas a question that is often at the tip of the tongue of many of his readers:

---

[94] Emmanuel Levinas. Uniqueness. *Entre Nous. Thinking-of-the-Other.* Translated by Michael B. Smith and Barbara Harshav, Columbia University Press, 1998, p. 196

The I as ethical subject is responsible to everyone for everything; his responsibility is infinite.Doesn't that mean that the situation is intolerable for the subject himself, and for the other whom I risk terrorizing by my ethical voluntarism? So isn't there an impotence of ethics in its will to do good?[95]

And Levinas replied:

I don't know if this situation is intolerable. It is not what you would call agreeable, surely; it is not pleasant, but it is the good. What is very important ... is the man who understands holiness as the ultimate value, as unassailable value.[96]

It is this value that makes it possible to awaken the sense of justice, and to utilize the capacity to judge all deeds, by subsuming them under universal codes and subjecting them to the jurisdiction of the state. Of course, this universalization is not enough from the perspective of holiness. Morality is not derived from the state. Moral authority does not always go hand in hand with the state power that legislates and enforces laws. It precedes the state and is the only source of the state's true legitimacy, the true judge of its policies. It might even be said that the state (respectively justice and institutions) is justified only as a means for effective implementation of moral responsibility.

2.3. Kant and Levinas on the Categorical Imperative

In modern European philosophy the undisputed authority on the subject of "moral law within us" is Immanuel Kant. All philosophical schools after Kant consider, deliberate and reflect on what is said by him. Hence it is useful to compare the positions of Kant and Levinas, particularly with regard to the central theme in the work of both of them, namely the moral imperative.

---

[95] Emmanuel Levinas. Dialogue on Thinking-of-the-Other. *Entre Nous. Thinking-of-the-Other.* Translated by Michael B. Smith and Barbara Harshav, Columbia University Press, 1998, p. 203
[96] Ibid.

The philosophical systems of Emmanuel Levinas and Immanuel Kant represent two different concepts of morality emblematic of two different epochs. Kant presented the rising ideology of modern times, animated by the ideals of freedom and social contract while Levinas lived in a society, which—according to his own assessment—lost the live contact with its true ideal of freedom and accepted forms that had degenerated. In the 20th century, trust in the "sovereign freedom of reason" was undermined and so the very foundations of community led by emancipatory spirit and the idea of the progress of civilization. It appears, however, that with the first steps of the discourse of Modern time, glorifying universal reason, with the postulates and budding practices of the ideal of civility, in the very core of the subsequent development, something was missing, which was the significance of the face of the Other and the uniqueness of the I revealed in its responsibility. According to Levinas the reason for all subsequent troubles, despite the initial good intentions, was the effect of raising freedom to the rank of the highest value, i.e. freedom put before and ranked above responsibility. Only after the act is done, responsibility falls on the perpetrator. This belated responsibility is determined by reflection and judges the results of actions, while we need to think before acting and think responsibly.

Levinas believed that the crisis that was said to put under question the philosophy associated with the fate of Europe, should be taken seriously. He deemed this philosophy privileged the Whole, the Unity, the Principle, the Totality. It stems from ancient Greece and was revived by German idealism. Is Man in European history really and truly a purpose in itself or is he reduced to a simple means in economy, politics, in the mechanism of the State, in the exercising of power? And what would come out of a society made up of "autonomous purposes"? Doesn't Kantian humanism sound hollow and is it not an illusion debunked by the events of history? Isn't the discourse which uses the categories "purpose" and "means" insufficient when we think the *humanitas* of *homo humanus*?

How is it historically possible that society, guided by the humanism of idealistic philosophy could arrive at contemporary barbarism with its wars, concentration camps, poverty, marginalization, genocide, injustice, and all modern forms of violence in general? Levinas is faced with the question that persistently hounded his generation: how to philosophize after Auschwitz, after the horrors of Nazism, anti-Semitism and totalitarianism, after Hitler and Stalin and every dictatorship? Is there a supra-historical locus where history can be judged? For Levinas such a place is morality, but not as subsuming human behaviour under universal law, but as my personal responsibility for the fate of my neighbour and then for everybody and for everything that is happening or not happening in the world.

Violence, as defined by Levinas, starts with the depersonalisation of the face. Modern barbarism as any barbarism consists in the ignoring of the face of the Other. Idealist philosophy has underestimated being but being must be taken into account in all its weight and in all its influence on Reason. The idealistic hopes contain the main strive of European civilization: in its initial inspiration any idealism seeks ways of overcoming being. A civilization which accepts one's own being as a highest value, brings hopelessness, justifies committing crimes and deserves to be named barbarism.

One of the postulates in German idealist philosophy is that the individual has to overcome his own particularity and his own limitations, his own needy and disadvantaged being and orient his own behaviour towards what unites him with others in the name of an universal interest, such as the progress of civilization. Kant believed that the pleasure or displeasure we experience when obeying laws, and the degree of satisfaction related to the content of the laws does not alter the imperative nature of the very form of the law. For him, the pleasure or displeasure, happiness or unhappiness, etc. are all things based on self-love and cannot be universal in nature, because the feeling of satisfaction or suffering is not directed to the same objects for all people, while the nature of the law is such that it contains the same common fundament of all wills. Reason is the ability that can place the individual case under the general law, valid for all. Individuals should follow reason or universal regulation of behaviour, which is its equivalent. According to Kant's idealism, man is free, following the law of pure practical reason. Freedom of will is in the possibility for man to disobey laws outside him, except those which he recognizes and accepts with his reasoning. Will is autonomous because it obeys a law set by itself as a governing principle for itself. Categorical imperative requires that the personal will of everyone is reconciled with the universal constitution of man as a rational and free being: act only according to such a maxim which you think could become an universal law.

However, maybe the path outlined by idealist philosophy is circular and the subject who wants to escape from his own particularity, from self-love and the limitations of his own empirical being, returns to himself and his own enchained being. Nobody can fully and forever escape from themselves. To strive for the "common good" means to strive for universalization of one's own interest, which implies the danger of imposing on others one's own system of values, disregarding their personal values. Furthermore, fleeing from natural determinism, the individual falls under the dictate of social determinism.

According to Kant, respect for man is guaranteed by equality before the law—"*liberté, égalité, fraternité*" for all. We know that the call of the French Revolution was directed against the arbitrariness of the monarch, against the privileges and inequality of individuals and estates. The postulate for universalization of man, for his liberation from class, cultural, religious and other prejudices and limitations, is consistent with the unification ambitions of the modern, internally consolidated and centralized nation-state. Kant declared the need for constitutional rights and fair law. However, he distinguished between the actions carried out in compliance with the law from actions performed for the sake of the law itself. In the first case, the goal of the action is to achieve a result by legal means and hence it is legal; and in the second case, the goal of the action is the law itself and then it is moral.

In *Critique of Practical Reason* we read:

> The notion of duty, therefore, requires in the action, objectively, agreement with the law, and subjectively in its maxim, that respect for the law shall be the sole mode in which the will is determined thereby. And on this rests the distinction between the consciousness of having acted according to the duty and from duty, that is, from respect for the law. The form (legality) is possible even if inclinations have been the determining principles of the will; but the latter (morality), moral worth, can be placed only in this, that the action is done from duty, that is, simply for the sake of the law.[97]

Kant declared as moral only those actions not dictated by the inclinations, effects, needs and so on, but only by the understanding and respect of legitimacy as such. It is not difficult to predict the tendency of man and law to start competing for attaining the status of the supreme and ultimate purpose. Levinas is very sensitive about the possible substitution of the Other by the Law:

> But, according to the wisdom of the Western tradition and the Western thought, individuals overcome the exclusionary violence of their conatus essendi and of their opposition to others in a peace established by knowledge, the truth of which is assured by reason. Human individuals, on this view, are human through consciousness. The various I's come to an agreement in the rational truth they obey without constraint, without givind up their freedom. The private will of the individual is raised to the autonomy of the person in which the nomos, the universal law, constrains the conscious and reasonable ego without constraining it. The will is practical reason. Persons, be they strangers to one another or just others, assimilate. The free assembly of particular individuals around ideal truths, especially the Law, is achieved—or at least sought.[98]

---

[97] *Kant's Critique of Practical Reason*. Translated by Thomas Kingsmill Abbot, Longmans, Green and Co., 1898, p. 43

[98] Emmanuel Levinas. Uniqueness. *Entre Nous. Thinking-of-the-Other*. Translated by Michael B. Smith and Barbara Harshav, Columbia University Press, 1998, p. 190

From the perspective of idealism, civilized man is guided in his conduct by reason, which is the true human essence and implies the restraining of the wilder instincts and affects of human nature. Reason dictates peace. The ideal of reason is eternal peace—balancing the freedoms and rights, overcoming prejudices and limitations; a contract for both boundaries and mutual obligations.

But Levinas notes that such peace still rests on coercion. For him, Kant's perpetual peace is nothing more than an endless postponement of war, which is a permanent, irrevocable threat, always possible due to breach of contract. In Kant's epoch, society was perceived as an organism in which individuals and institutions were parts of the body, each with its function and belonging to the system. Social order was considered to be the embodiment of the logic of the functioning of various forces and their balance in the whole. Disorganization of the system and the abandonment of its general principle would be a state of war—the return to primordial barbarism, i.e. to the state prior to the conclusion of the social contract in which one freedom opposes another without reasonable restrictions. The purpose of military action is to destroy the enemy horde, to force the enemy to withdraw. In war, the Other, Levinas notes, has no face—he is an enemy, mass, strength, a barbarian. Not that freedom of the opponent does not exist, but rather it is irrational, savage, barbaric. He must either die or be civilized. This is how modernity interprets the logic of war.

Levinas pointed out the connection between universalizing reason that depersonalizes man and coercion, which in its most extreme form is the violence of war. He noted that reason itself seems to have been infected by the animal in man, by his stubbornness to be. According to Levinas, in this union between reason and *conatus essendi* of every living human being there is autonomy of will. And for Levinas the human in man is exactly the ability to break the circle of being around the I and to transcend caring for one's own survival in the care for the Other, to direct love for yourself towards love of the neighbour. Levinas called the impulse towards the Other, "autrement qu'être" (beyond being). This is a breakthrough from the self-centeredness and self-sufficiency of the individual; it is the metaphysical (ethical) striving to respond to the Other. Eventually it coincides, according to Levinas, with the categorical imperative, although not exactly in the Kantian understanding of it. Within Levinas' conception it is the fact that one man can have a meaning for another man. Not just man as genus, man in general or reason in man, but man as a specific individual—"man of flesh and blood," who is presented in his meeting with me as a face.

The primary formulation of the categorical imperative, according to Levinas is "Thou shalt not kill!" If one does not follow this order, he closes any openness to others and infinity. In the face of the other, which is precisely the finite, temporal, mortal creature, shines exteriority, transcendence and infinity. Kant speaks of the dignity of man as a rational and free being—it is the eternal purpose in itself, towards which all humankind as a subject of world history must strive. Levinas insists, however, that this is not enough for the respect for humanity. Man ought to be respected in all his mortality, poverty, and helplessness—both close to and alienated from everything on this earth. According to Levinas, the dignity of man is in his ability to overcome his "existence-towards-death", by devoting his efforts to the "existence-against-the-death-of-the-other."

Levinas stresses Kant's huge merit for the defence of the primacy of practical over theoretical reason. Both Kant and Levinas agree that morality has nothing to do with the enjoyment of life. Neither of them accepts hedonistic, eudemonistic, utilitarian moral doctrines. Morality does not depend on values accepted in society but vice versa, values depend on morality. According to Kant, moral action is necessary in itself and has no connection with any other interest. That is why, moral law is not derived from positions relating to empirical situations—social, historical, psychological, political, etc.—and cannot be justified by needs and inclinations. For Levinas, initially the question isn't between the law and me but is between the Other and me. The moral question is not how much I need the Other and what can I gain from meeting him, including exploring his difference in comparison to me and the joy of diversity I experience, but how much the Other needs me and what I can do for him.

Categorical imperative is a prime "fact" in that it is not deduced or justified as all evidence, understanding, value, reasoning, and justification originate from it. As a fact, it is obvious, immediate and universal. For Levinas, however, the primal fact is not man's constitution, as a rational being, but the encounter with the face. The face—this is the fact that the Other affects me not in the indicative but in the imperative.

Levinas insists that there is a commandment of God written on the human face, marked by mortality and it is "Thou shalt not kill!" The impossibility to kill is not real but metaphysical, i.e. ethical. Let us remember that for Levinas, God is present among us when absent and when He has left everything in the hands of people, hence the life of the Other is in our hands or more precisely, in my hands. Encountering the face is the primal fact, as every other meaning is derived from it; only the face has a meaning in itself.

There is one crucial difference between Kant's and Levinas' concepts as to how man responds to the categorical imperative. In Kant's perception, reason dictates to the individual—"let Reason be our only legislator"—as to what human actions should be. Thus morality is an expression of freedom, understood as autonomy. Conversely, we are inclined to think that for Levinas any autonomy, before being a free decision, is preceded by heteronomy, i.e. by the appeal of the Other. The "I" hears it before it has been formulated as a requirement. My response, regardless whether I acknowledge this appeal or ignore it, is my autonomy's business and is preceded by a face-to-face encounter and by the light in the eyes in front of me—light, illuminating all around.

Like Hegel, Levinas does not agree with Kant's formalism but for entirely different reasons than Hegel's. For Hegel, the Other is always, like me, part of the self-developing entity of the community and in this sense they are entirely situated within the historical course of totality. The main issue for Hegel is that these two parts of the whole—the Other and I—rise to the universality of reason, and therefore to the shape of the law without abandoning their own interests, desires and goals, i.e. through the particularity of their experiences and therefore through their content added to the historical development. For Levinas, however, the face always remains as exteriority and always has the dimension of transcendence. At the moment the face is interiorized, it becomes an image of mine, my idea, a construction of my intentionality. But being my ideas and constructions of my intentionality is the doom of objects.

If the Other is a force similar to the forces of the world, if he is an object among other objects, his otherness would have been no more exterior to me than the exteriority of nature, i.e. of the world of perceptions, which, as Kant proclaims, is ultimately constructed by me. The relationship with the Other is not knowledge or struggle, nor overcoming resistance. In the struggle and in cognition, the I is confined to its own objectives, interests and intentionality. Knowledge and struggle are dealing with phenomena, forms, appearance, and the face is beyond the phenomenal play of concealing and revealing; rather the opposite, it breaks any form and escapes any frozen image and every idea. Its separation is the condition for any phenomenality. In the absolute nakedness of the face we read its misery, strangeness, weakness, vulnerability (let us remember that for Levinas human life is in itself the pointless putting up with what is happening and it receives meaning only because it is for the others) and at the same time a disarming authority which commands

"Thou shalt not kill!" (because only in peace there is a chance to heal this pointlessness by constituting meaning in the suffering endured for the Other). In both Kant's and Levinas' philosophy it is a prohibition which further on provides the positivity of connections (in Kant: "Do not act as if the other is just a means!", and in Levinas: "Thou shalt not kill!"). This "not", this ban, this taboo, this order is unconditional, which is the further condition for anything and everything that happens in the human world.

For both Kant and Levinas, the fact of humanity is inevitable. Kant says that man himself is not holy, but his personality is.

> Man is indeed unholy enough but he must regard humanity in his own personality as holy... By virtue of the autonomy of his freedom he is the subject of the moral law, which is holy...[99]

For Levinas meeting the face of the Other is inevitable and it is in this meeting that the face is holy. By the face of the other human the God's holy imperative "Thou shall not kill!" is heard by me. To declare myself a saint would be a gesture of immorality. The holiness of the face of the Other questions my own personality—the selflessness with which I try to respond, transferring my own personal responsibility to somebody else, therefore, puts my humanity to the test. Moreover, if the I and the Other are in reciprocal relations, if we are equal and commensurate from the perspective of Reason and the Law, if the I imposes on the Other a responsibility which is reversible, seeking revenge and instigating mercantilization and the measurement of merit, this for Levinas is also a fall of morality. Morality is rather the selflessness of love—love without voluptuousness, without calculating pleasure and suffering, without balancing income and expenditure. Can one really seek compensation for love!?

---

[99] *Kant's Critique of Practical Reason*. Translated by Thomas Kingsmill Abbot, Longmans, Green and Co., 1898, p. 46

Ethical responsibility is infinite because the moment I turn my back on the Other and he ceases to interest me; when I pass him by with indifference and he has ceased to affect me; in that moment when I do not care for him anymore or I have confined him to a role or image, shutting my ears and eyes; the moment I stop questioning my own usefulness and humanity satisfied with what I have already done: this is the end of morality. Levinas insists that morality is where the more innocent I am, the more I blame myself and the more guilty I feel. That is why responsibility as morality, before becoming justice, is infinite.

Love is present as if two beings were alone in the world. I get from You justification, i.e. the meaning of my existence. Isn't this a subtle game in which the "I" returns to itself in the contentment of a good deed done? Is then the intersubjective relation not the beginning of society but rather its negation? This type of discourse is possible only when I and You are perceived as autonomous and ego-centred beings and love is understood as a fusion into a new autonomy of centred on itself whole—a family, a group, a community, a nation, a society, etc. According to Levinas love is not a fusion, nor identification with the Other but care for his otherness. This is not about a part-whole relationship on the basis of the similarity of the parts, but about understanding another type of relationship in which the I becomes itself, maintaining the otherness of the Other, even though the I has to oppose itself for the sake of the Other.

The presence of the Other is sufficient for the moral community of two in which the Other occupies first position, i.e. the Other is always more important than myself. I am always responsible for what happens to him, whatever his behaviour is. I am responsible, even because I may not have been caring enough. This may seem the community of an isolated couple, as a couple in love who have turned their backs on the world and who do not want to allow anyone to deprive their relationship of the uniqueness and exclusivity with which they themselves endow it.

It is doubtful whether this community resisting generalization and universalization is a moral one. This is love for your close one that can lead to neglect and even to insult others; lack of attention and hurting of others. The loved-one is privileged above all others. But love without justice is blind because it is all-forgiving. Sometimes it does not see or even turns a blind eye to undeniable evil. It tries to ignore the Third who is lurking immediately peeking behind the one and only important Other. However, neither in the sublime moments of love, nor in our everyday routine and generally not in any circumstances can we act as if we are dealing with a single person in the world. Levinas mentions the anonymous recipient of almost all of our daily activities: the shoemaker makes shoes without asking his client where he will go in them, the doctor has taken the oath of Hippocrates and treats every patient who visits him, the priest comforts the soul of anyone who asks for help, and so on. The daily life we inhabit is an orientation to the anonymous fellow man, who is the Third. The You is actually not separated from the others—with his eyes and his voice the Third is already looking at me and speaking to me as well as is all of mankind; language already implies generality and generalization. The talk of love is not the only conversation and not even the real conversation, but rather "sweet bill and coo". However, the language of what it has already said elevates things to the level of publicity, evaluation and justice. Speech has a privileged role in the establishment of public life and just order. Therefore, freedom of speech is one of the most respected values in political life.

Justice as well as reason and freedom cannot be guaranteed by the imperative only. The matter is that it cannot only be subjectively distorted but that we need to ensure its external, public action. Kant and Hegel were aware of the necessity to establish political order to prevent citizenship falling into the clutch of despotism, tyranny or violence. Kant opposed paternalistic government, qualifying it as despotism and as impediment to the fundamental freedoms of citizens, to a type of government creating the conditions for everyone to seek their own fortune in their preferred way. Kant regarded the republic as the eternal norm of every political constitution—it corresponds to the natural rights of members of the civil society presuming that those who obey the laws, unite into a single body called the state. Freedom, says Levinas ironically, seeks haven in the just state. But the measures that will/reason takes against its own fall, though originating from free will, become alienated from it and turn into a new tyranny. Impersonal reason in the social forms it adopts—the institutions and laws of the state—can hardly be understood as a kind of "collective will". Levinas not only objects the existence of impersonal Reason, but believes that reason is not an *a priori* attribute of the subject. According to him, reason is born where everything human has its birth bosom—the encounter face-to-face. We will say that true rationality is the incarnation of responsibility towards the Other. Freedom of the I is invested by the Face of the Other with the silent command to respond, to talk to the Other and not to kill him.

Levinas underlines that responsibility comes before freedom. He insists that social order, economy, politics, institutions, social roles and the world of ideas in general, constitute an alienated world, which is to a lesser or greater degree a deformation of the primordial imperative. But we need to realize that good is only abandoned in order to be protected and that freedom is restricted in order to be guaranteed and that the face is replaced by the personality (i.e. by the third in Levinas'terms) to be judged fairly (and the court is inevitable). If morality is earthly, sound, embodied and not an empty ideal, then we must accept this paradox, which arises again and again:

Sociality and Justice: Toward Social Phenomenology 185

> An extraordinary ambiguity of the I: at once the very point at which being and the effort to be contract and congeal into a oneself, into an ipseity twisted bsck upon itself, primordial and autarchic, and the point at which the strange abolition or suspension of this urgency of existing and an abnegation in the concern for the "affairs" of the other are possible: as if they "regarded" me and were entrusted to me, as if the other person were above all the face. There, the otherness-of-the-individual-in-the genus has come out of its formality and logical banality in which this relation...went simultaneously or indifferently from me to the other and from the other to me. As if consciousness here lost its symmetry...[100]

A hospitable welcome to the Other as a face is the peace with him. Peace is a requirement of any justice. As love of the neighbour comes before duty, so peace comes before justice. But responsibility or morality (love the neighbour) is also what remains after duty is fulfilled. Justice is reason itself, between the law and the face. But before and after that is face-to-face. Justice itself must be seen from the perspective of morality or care for the neighbour as the Other, i.e. in light of the face and the categorical imperative. Peace is the condition for justice, but only through justice can it be further preserved.

2.4. Paul Ricoeur on justice—virtue and institution. Revision from Levinas' perspective.

Paul Ricoeur is one of the famous names on the European philosophical scene of the past century. As such it is a challenge to view his conception as a version of Kantian practical philosophy. Although still maintaining the ego-logical position of the independent subject and his ability to judge, Ricoeur draws attention to the essential role played by language in the process of judgement.

To judge is to bring a particular case under a general rule and Ricoeur follows this Kantian definition of the capacity to judge. According to

---

[100] Emmanuel Levinas. Uniqueness. *Entre Nous. Thinking-of-the-Other*. Translated by Michael B. Smith and Barbara Harshav, Columbia University Press, 1998, p. 193.

Kant, this capacity is rationality as opposed to non-rationality or stupidity. Therefore, non-rationality would be the inability to find a rule, when moving from the particular to the general, or vice versa—when you know the general rule and do not apply it to a particular example. Here we see that *universality* and *particularity* are the categories which, according to Ricoeur, apply equally to objects, situations and people.

All of this terminology and the logic of scientism it has instigated in us, undoubtedly represents an articulation of humanness, translated into objectivist and positivist terms relating to the measurable parameters of reified human relations. Men are thought of in the same way as objects, stones and trees, being parts of the whole and units of totality. From the perspective contained within Levinas' philosophy, in any generalizing and typifying judgment (but are not all judgments typifying?) we abandon the immediacy of the relationship with the Other.

From the perspectives of both Levinas and Ricoeur, bringing somebody under norms and standards is always judging the Third—for example, in historical science, in politics, in jurisprudence, in medicine (those are listed by Ricoeur). For Ricoeur judgment is virtue

> as a legal act but also as exercising of capability of judgment which is on a very wide scale, very global, the capability to subsume the singular case under the rules and to invent, to create something in transition from the rule of the general cognition to this practical knowledge of the particular examples as people also are. [101]

This ability to move from the general knowledge toward a practical wisdom in the Greek, Medieval and Modern sense is a distinction. It is a virtue, according to Ricoeur. But according to Levinas, precisely the ability to bring the individual case under a general rule coincides with the exercise of reason, which is impersonal and universal by definition,

---

[101] Paul Ricoeur. La Justice, vertu et institution. *La sagesse pratique. Autour de l'oeuvre de Paul Ricoeur.* Sous la direction de Jeffrey Andrew Barash et de Mireille Delbraccio. L'academie d'Amiens, Amiens, 1998, p. 11

while the question is not about rationality and my virtue but about my responsibility for the other.

When we talk about justice as a virtue we refer to fair people. For Ricoeur their actions are preceded by justice as an institution and he considers that there are not one, but more institutions of "justice", listing three: 1) the legislature, which makes the laws or general rules; 2) jurisdiction, where law is perceived systematically; 3) magistrates who administer it. Ricoeur assumes that there is always a conflict between people and institutions. It is from this perspective that he sees the place of the Third party, performing the role of serving justice. He is needed in a situation of conflict in which, of course, one of the parties to the conflict feels outraged by *the injustice* done by the other party. Firstly, there is emotion and it has a moral meaning, namely that what is unacceptable, cannot be maintained. Where things are said or done in the heat of passion one may be inclined to seek his own justice as revenge. Hence the need for distance from the feeling of indignation and from parties to the conflict; such that it may be necessary to find a mediator and for the situation to be brought before an independent judge. Such an independent body Ricoeur calls the Third one. This for Ricoeur is the state, for example, or its loyal public servants acting in the bureaucratic machine. This is the power that in rising above individuals, holds the monopoly over public violence (according to Max Weber's definition of the State which arguably borders on cynicism). The figure of the Third also includes written laws restricting arbitrariness. However here we can also find the courts as places of sentencing and judges. Ricoeur underlines, that they themselves are neither angels, nor gods, but rather are people who judge people. In this category of the Third party Ricoeur includes everybody related to the exercise of judgment.

According to Ricoeur, the most important feature of the process of judgment is that it is carried out within speech. Justice is a dispute but as long as it is grounded in speech it also has the function of separating us from violence—separation not only from the violent act that led to the conflict, but also from the violence which would be exercised in vengeance by the parties taking the law into their own hands. In the process of legal justice we seek a law which is applicable to a particular situation. Ricoeur sees as a given both the particular situation and the relevant clause of jurisdiction as the form under which the situation is classified.

But then the question is who has the say in this conversation which moves us away from violence. Who exchanges lines, arguments and evidence and with whom? With what justification? According to what rules and under what circumstances? In response to these questions Ricoeur insists that we must justify, legitimize and protect formalism, because it provides for the freedom of individuals and their equality before the law. Thanks to the codification of cases, similar cases can be treated in a similar way—this formalism regulates the development of the legal process as an exchange of arguments. Formalism stems from the identification of people and incidents as carriers of general form through which they are codified and ascribed to the whole as repetitive cases or specimens of the typology.

Ricoeur insured himself against Levinasian criticism. He seemed to anticipate that it is not about mechanical deduction of the particular from the general as there exists invention and novelty, because the outcome of each case is unpredictable and knowledge of the rules does not remove uncertainty; we never know who will win. He added that the logical side of things is known and is based on rules, but the game aspect and the unpredictable elements, the creative moments occur with the possibilities of interpretation. The end result of the legal process is obtained as a balance between possible interpretations—between seriousness in following the rules and the game aspect in their implementation. The game aspect comes from the fact that we could refer the case to various codifications, according to the arrangement of the data, depending on different requirements for proof of the facts and their very constitution as facts in the case, etc. Each case should be closed by issuing a verdict that separates the culprit of the crime from the victim.

Ricoeur stipulates that the concept of responsibility, used by him, is well fixed in its classical legal use: in civil law it is the obligation to repair the damage caused by someone's fault while in penal law cases—the obligation is to serve the prescribed sentence. According to Ricoeur the idea of responsibility implies two different processes: 1) attribution of an action to an individual, identifying him as the legal perpetrator of this action; this allows us to proceed from the general to the individualization of the sentence; 2) moral determination of someone as guilty—the moral qualification subsumes someone under the universality of the law by going from the individual to the common. In the field of morality to be guilty means to be the responsible one.

Of course, there is an abyss between revenge and punishment. With regard to revenge, violence escalates on the basis that if one has caused any damage or suffering to another, he in turn must also suffer no less than the former. In punishment, the suffering of the first one must be recompensed to the extent of rectifying the harm caused and at the same time limiting further violent action. Moreover, in terms of revenge the offended party decides on the appropriate retribution for the insult or harm inflicted. Consequently, punishment requires the Third as the judge who holds a position independent of the parties to the conflict. This is institutionalized authority, which prevents the spread of violence and provides that the sentence becomes part of the order of justice—"an eye for an eye, and not two eyes for one." Punishment alleviates the suffering of the affected to deter further acrimony against the guilty party. It is only possible by determining the general rule of subsequent suffering/redemption, which must be endured by the perpetrator of evil. The universality of the law is acknowledged as we judge, not according to the characteristics of the parties to the conflict nor according to their private relations, but by the criteria of justice. However, Levinas believed that such judgements are problematic—in this kind of dispassionate dispensing of justice, as presented by Ricoeur, in formalism and a formal attitude to the case, justice could itself result in injustice. For example, if a certain sum of money is determined to compensate for a violation, it would be significant for the poor and insignificant for the rich, who would not feel equity in the "grief of redemption." So, according to Levinas, justice should not give up the ancient principle of "an eye for an eye, tooth for a tooth", because otherwise it could lead to complete incommensurability between the gravity of the committed crime and the severity of the sentence, issued in response to it. Retribution cannot rely on rules only. This is also highlighted by Ricoeur, however, Levinas relates it, not to the space of creativity, play and interpretation, but rather to the inability to redeem guilt in relation to the Other through any reparations whatsoever. For him, true justice is the primordial relation to the Other—respect for the Other and his freedom. Equality between individuals means nothing in itself. It is only an economic expression and implies money, and rests on justice, starting from the appeal of the Other. It is recognition of his privilege to be Other. Justice is always delayed, because the Other is irremediably denied his otherness by a crime. Punishment is evidence that a situation has already occurred where the One and the Other are in conflict and true justice does not wait to fulfil its mission after evil has already been committed.

Ricoeur, however, borrows the meaning of imputability from the Kantian analysis: to the degree that a subject is free, his actions depend on the decisions made by his free will and the consequences of these actions are entirely his fault. He is responsible before the law, and only if he breaks the law, then is he guilty before the other; thus the law has the first and last say in the determination of guilt. The relationship between the perpetrator and the victim of the crime is always mediated by the

Sociality and Justice: Toward Social Phenomenology 191

law to such an extent that it is as if such mediation is individualised, according to which it is judged whether an act constitutes a crime and what the subsequent damages are. In Levinas' theory the relationship between One and the Other is immediate and the law as a general rule is not presupposed, so the law is not the only determinant of the situation nor of the guilt. Levinas would say without hesitation that the abused is not the law, but the other person; the law must serve the rights of the Other and not just criminalize the act. Formal law must be in the service of people and not treat them according to the clauses and paragraphs as individual cases on which those clauses and paragraphs are imposed and applied. In Levinas' theory the motion is from the affected to the culprit and then to the law; in Ricoeur's theory, however, it is formally determined whether someone is affected and to what extent someone is guilty, hence the law is elevated above the parties to the conflict. The legal system is therefore often criticized for not serving people, but the interests of bureaucrats, nomenclature, and in general the power that may be used as a tool of oppression. In consequence of which, not only jurisprudence, prosecutors, courts or lawyers, but all the other institutions in society are not doing their job for which they were created, instead becoming a self-serving bureaucracy of formalization and paperwork. They cease to promote fair relations between people (justice, regarding the face is never enough because one always seeks, as Levinas says, a more just justice) and by abdicating from its responsibilities are translated into an empty framework and even into an obstacle to justice.

For Ricoeur infinite responsibility (including infinite responsibility from the perspective of justice) would make it impossible to act. Human will is not heroic—on this Levinas agrees. The subject should always be held responsible for the results of his actions, which he could have foreseen and which are predictable. This is not only Ricoeur's conclusion—before him it is also found in Hegel's philosophy of law. Levinas, without denying this type of responsibility that is only sought after the action has taken place, insists on responsibility that precedes freedom and is moral before it is fixed in legal codes.

Ricoeur rightly points out that in each court trial the goal is to end violence and resolve conflicts through speech, to maintain the legal order of the state and to distinguish between the parties in the case (i.e. the culprit from the victim). He rightly concludes that these are specific goals, subordinated to the main goal—the maintenance of social peace. This primary goal is seemingly opposite to the objectives of the individual parties. What interests Ricoeur are those options for possible interpretation which are provided for by case law/legal written codes in reaching a verdict and delivering/dispensing punishment. For Levinas, of course, peace is a very important value and purpose, but something else is more important and should be added to the recovery of truth, peace and justice as well as mutual recognition—that "something else" is respect for the face. If Ricoeur is interested mainly in the law and the opportunities found in its interpretation, Levinas is interested in the face and the possibilities for justice, which he believes is first between the Other and me and then between the law and the individual. After the verdict is issued, the responsibility for the Other must remain, even to the extent of responsibility for his responsibility. Any violator of the law "has the right" to be treated as a human being and to be loved. Without love of the neighbour justice would become injustice and even cruelty. Justice implies mercy both to the victim and to the one who has caused the damage.

2.5. Jean-François Lyotard: prescription, description and norm.

While agreeing that speech has an exceptional place in the discussion of justice, Lyotard insists on a distinction, which is fundamental: prescriptive statements are incommensurable with descriptive ones.

Sociality and Justice: Toward Social Phenomenology 193

The prescriptive statement, which generally expresses the will of the one who prescribes, has as its addressee the other who must act after the prescription. Each order or request, advice or obligation is usually grammatically in the second person, i.e. this is a message directed towards the Other as "you"—e.g. "Write!", "Go!", "Hurry up!" and so on. It tells the addressee that s/he must act in order to fulfil the prescription, but by appealing to that other immediately in second grammatical person. The understanding of the imperative statements is verified by their execution, in contrast to the indicative sentences, where what matters is the plausibility of the information and where the interlocutor is invited to agree with or refute what has been said. However, the imperative cannot be inferred from another proposition and also cannot be evaluated as true or untrue. „What must be" is not deduced from "what is", but always transcends it.

According to Lyotard, to speak of justice means to talk about prescriptions. However, in fact not the message itself tells "You must!" but the addresser. Many well-known names in French philosophy (e.g. Foucault, Blanchot and others) assume that the prescriptions are never based on anything other than authority or power of the one who prescribes. From a Levinasian point of view, the proper imperativeness of any prescription is obtained from "You shalt not kill!" pronounced even without words by the powerlessness of the Other's face.

In monotheistic religions and cultures it is always thought that we are the addressees of the prescriptions, as they have a transcendent source. Lyotard thinks the same (although on different grounds), defining himself as a supporter of paganism.[102] He states that the culture of the so-called savage tribes reproduces itself with each new generation through narration. The question is how the narrative form of speech is connected

---

[102] Jean-Francois Lyotard, Jean-Loup Thebaud. *Au juste (conversations)*. Christian Bourgois Editeur, Paris, 1993. Lyotard's stance is represented here by following what he says in the book himself.

with the prescriptive. Within the tribes none of the speakers are autonomous, as before they speak, they have already been the addressees; before articulating the prescription, one has received it from others. The narrator does not present himself as the author. He is a former listener before he takes up the role of the speaker. As a narrator he is similar to a mime who animates the narrative and is a good actor, if he creates new episodes, adds to the story, composes etc. The narrative repeats itself but is never the same, because instead we are seeing different variations of the same theme. The most important is perhaps that at the beginning of this long sequence of narrators there is not a man, after all, but some kind of superhuman agency, a transcendent power overwhelming and even incommensurable with the human. The narrative is only the vehicle—the vehicle for conveying and passing along the prescription. It is animated by motion, coming to the next participant in the tribe, who in turn must pass it on to the next one. This passage presupposes not autonomy, but heteronomy. If one of the ancients refuses to speak and participate in the rituals, this is unforgiveable and he will be punished—the revenge of fate, gods etc. will fall upon him. Therefore there is a difference between the prescription to take up the narrative and the very execution of that prescription, such as narration. In the narration one has some degree of freedom, even if limited—he can create, add, interpret, compose etc., but has no freedom whatsoever in regard to accepting and passing on the narrative. Speaking is a pure act of obligation—when one is spoken to, this obliges him.

In paganism people are not the authors of what they narrate and therefore, of what they do. The meaning of their existence is never the result of their autonomous desires. They are in a constant interplay with the destiny they have been given and which is foretold in the narrative. There is an ordering of things according to their meaning included in the story. This ordering can be foretold—through dreams, oracles etc. Then

Sociality and Justice: Toward Social Phenomenology 195

the actions of the tribesmen are a reaction to what they have been destined to. In heteronomy the will is not free, but itself is based on obligation. It is ancient, primordial, anonymous and not an act of legislation—a law can be abided by or not, while a prescription offers no possibility for escape.

However, in Greece things changed radically. Fate exists, but it guides the actions of neither legislators, nor citizens of the polis. In *Rhetoric* and *Nicomachean Ethics* Aristotle states that a judge, who deserves to be called so, does not need a model for real justice to guide his judgement. To judge, punish or award means that he prescribes what must be done. Aristotle calls this virtue *practical wisdom*—to exercise justice without any prior criteria. This means that *theoria* cannot help here, because prescriptions are not within its domain. But what can help is dialectics—dialectics in its capacity as questioning. Science and dialectics are two different types of discourse and Lyotard interprets this situation in the sense that there is no common denominator between them or any common measure whatsoever. For Aristotle dialectics does not aim to create a model of the social whole, in which what happens in the polis is judged according to ideas, as Plato before him thought. Dialectics just allows one to judge step-by-step for each individual case and because each situation is unique, the judge finds himself among opinions and not in the domain of truth. He must judge on what is reported to him and has no other criterion than opinions. They are not of the eternal idea type and their weight depends on their frequency among people. According to Aristotle, there is no scientific discourse that can justify political decisions. But there is no authority beyond men, which stipulates unconditionally what exactly must be done.

However, Plato and Aristotle still don't ask the question which is very important for a political life. This question appears only in modernity and asks "who is the subject of the spoken statement?" First in Rousseau we find the notion of what generally is called will and which is *capacité enonciative*. Who is the one who prescribes? How is he empowered to do that?

The expression "capacity for judgment" is introduced initially by Kant. In Kant this topic is discussed in *Critique of Practical Reason*. But in Kant's philosophy the subject is at the same time the addressor and the addressee, i.e. the speaker and the executor are two instances of the same person. Thus, according to Kant, people are free and simultaneously obliged. Will is autonomous, when the one who articulates the law, i.e. the author of the prescription, is at the same time the one who executes it and therefore who obeys it. Autonomy is self-determination[103]. Understood in this manner—as autonomy, as law, which the Self prescribes to itself and abides by in its actions—freedom becomes the main character of modern politics and social theory.

Politics is always about challenging the status quo—whether it should be preserved, changed or removed. This means that each policy presupposes a prescription of some sort of action. Here is precisely the essence of prescription: it articulates what it seeks to induce in the recipient, namely an activity which creates, transforms or preserves reality or the context. But this is the reality or context during the act of speaking.

According to most philosophers, the beginning of the process of political change is reality, which is declared untrue or, in the words of Marx, is reversed. It is believed, however, that if this reality is demystified and truth is revealed to the public, then, from this point onward, decisions for action will be made in the name of another—just—reality. The transition from the true to the just sets a condition—"if..., then...": "if the king is a philosopher", "if laws are adhered to by everyone", "if the revolution succeeds" and so on. But to realize this transition from theory to practice, it is required at first that the recipient, before he fulfils the prescription, puts himself in the place of the one that knows and reports

---

[103] This applies to individuals and groups alike.

the truth, to verify the legitimacy of the prescription and the order prescribed. Therefore, it is necessary that the addressee sees things through the eyes of the addressor of the message. Kant's autonomous subject must be enlightened in advance and the problem is also how to make the transition from the theoretical to the regulative use of reason. However, Kant forsook such a deduction. It's not about what makes experience possible, but what regulates our reasoning. "You must" transcends the whole domain of experience. Kant forsakes using some theoretical, conceptual system as a fundament or criterion in the field of morality, while in the political discourse from Plato to Marx usually the topic is how to make this transition from the true to the just. This means to extract the political, i.e. the prescription, from the theoretical, i.e. the description. If a theoretical model of the just society is offered, then, from that point on, the question is how it can be implemented in reality. For Plato such a model is the ideal state, where the king-sage rules and where each participant in the totality of the polis performs his prescribed functions. For Marx the model of justice is the communist society with the principle "from each according to his abilities, to each according to his needs". For him the question is how to arrive to the scientific theory of society from the utopian view and how to establish a new type of manufacturing and social organization in order to achieve socialization of private capitalist property. In Marxism, science must lead to a revolution, prescribing a behavior which, however, is legitimized by the respective theory. Each concept of freedom also presupposes a certain notion of the human being, humanity, the individual, etc. defined as a part of the whole of society by the discourse legitimizing it. All this manner of thinking, which tries to deduce the imperative statements from the indicative, is based on a presupposition "if". It is an effort to deduce the laws of the state from the reasonable truth. It is expected that justice will be pre-contemplated and legitimized through truth. In this way, the prescription is deduced from the exposed truth.

In Kant's philosophy there is a very precise difference between hypothetical and imperative propositions. Kant does not accept that prescriptions can have a hypothetical nature in the form of "If A, then B". Hypothetical statements are characteristic of science. They are always derivative, deduced and deductible from the hypothesis, regardless of whether some experimental position, principle or norm is assumed to be such a presupposition. If the imperative is based on experience, it would be a hypothetical statement in which its incompleteness is taken into account. However, Kant deems the categorical imperative a fact of the mind. That the imperative or the prescription itself is a fact and not an inferred conclusion means that it is the starting point for all subsequent statements and actions. For Kant it is precisely in this fact that the pure reason is presented as practical to us. The fact of prescription is far away from the empirical facts of experience because it cannot be subsumed under this notion or be deduced from it. The moral experience is not actually in the true meaning of the word "experience". "You must" is not in the domain of the perceivable, not a fact of the sensory, but of the extrasensory nature. This means it is seen, but as an ideal. The categorical imperative is a *Faktum-Idee* and this means that "reason itself through ideas is an effective ground in the field of experience" and that in the form of prescription it constitutes the ideal, the domain of extrasensory nature. If reason is used theoretically, this would mean to ask ourselves how an object causes another and whether it, and not another one, is the cause for the particular consequence. Regarding the prescriptions, however, it is about how to create a condition of things, which is not pre-given and whose creation is yet to happen. For instance, in the order "Close the door!" what matters is to close the door—to achieve a condition which is not present as such. The prescription must become the reason for the desired future condition. It does not receive its legitimacy as such from referencing to some objective condition, i.e. from experience, but from some transcendent source, i.e. freedom, as per Kant. Freedom is nothing else but the pure reason itself, acting as a regulation in the practical domain. Thus Kant believes he has emancipated will from experience. Reason within each of us is the prescribing instance, but who does Kant regard as the addressee? Is Reason itself the addressee, if it merely understands the norm?

As is well known, the fundamental law of practical reason is formulated thus: "Act in such a way that the maxim of your will could always be also valid as a principle of general law!" This definition of the moral prescription is applicable to all beings that act, i.e. all reasonable beings, which must execute this prescription. The imperative prescribes activity as execution of any act: "Act!", "You must!", "You are obliged to!"

However, here it must be stressed again that a certain expression becomes a prescription when taken for a prescription and not given as such, i.e. it can be regarded as a prescription by the addressee and only through his response can it achieve a prescription status. It is namely the addressee who demonstrates through his behavior that the message, directed towards him, is not indicative, but prescriptive. Whether a given condition will be taken for prescriptive, depends on the response it receives. Whether the recipient will comply or not comply through his actions with the order that a prescription contains and how he will comply or reject it is his own business. But it is regarded as an obligation, prescribed to the one who receives it and, as Levinas hyperbolizes—to the indebted, even if he has done nothing yet. Each prescription contains an order "Obey!", but it is implicit and with no content from the perspective of the particularity of the action. It is not understood in the sense that it's related to the object, but to the one that must hear it. As Kant puts it, this is a truly pure form—independent from the content. However, Kant argues that it is obliging because it is universal.

There is actually no room for juxtaposition between these two stances—of the speaking and the prescribing one, on one hand, and of the listening and executing one, on the other. Strictly put, only the first position can be related to freedom. But in Kant they are not only unable to be juxtaposed, but match completely, because in the autonomy the prescription is self-referencing. In paganism no one speaking is autonomous. Before he speaks, he is an addressee. Before he articulates the prescription, he has already received it. The law of his narrative is the law that has already been told implicitly to him. Each narrator is presented not as autonomous person, but as an addressee subjugated to heteronomy, not as an author, speaking on his behalf, but as anonymous—he conveys and passes on the meaning. The notion which occupies a central place in Kant's practical philosophy, however, is authorship, freedom as autonomy, self-regulation, universality, emancipation from the shackles of tradition, legends and experiences, the conjunction of regulator and regulated. What is the guarantee then that the imperative is understood, i.e. that it is accepted as an imperative and adhered to unconditionally? Only the fact that reason is the same in all human beings. It is not some kind of external authority, but governs from the inside, from the internal constitution of man.

Lyotard is fully aware that the categorical imperative is understood in a different manner in Levinas. In Levinas prescription is mandatory, because it's external and not just a matter of my own choice. It does not need legitimation or decision on my part whether to comply, but only how to comply. The encounter with the Other is unavoidable and the command of the face does not presuppose my power. Meeting the face cannot be refused, even when I try to refuse him my hospitality. The command to meet, to give shelter and food to the stranger instead of killing him, as any other commandment, does not appeal to the host to provide a commentary as response, but to act. This action is an execution of the order and shows my responsibility. Even if I refuse to comply with the order, it has been heard and the refusal to act is already a response.

"Close the door!" is also a sentence, which is understood in the very execution of the prescribed action. But there is also another type of understanding—the understanding in the sense of commentary to the prescription and usually in the sense of counter-speech, challenging the already pronounced speech. Then the order is not met by the action, but the inaction of the addressee. For example, "He said I must close the door" presupposes the reflection and accordingly the distance. Or "I don't remember, did I have to close the door?" further increases the distance. As the listener enters the role of a commentator, the recipient of the commandment himself takes the position of a speaker. Understanding the discourse, he starts speaking in a metalanguage, which has the first one as his reference. Meanwhile, the true addressee of the commandment is its executor, who does not try to take the position of the addressing one in turn. All prescribing statements are like this, because of their perlocutionary power. They become prescriptive because of the situation, recognized as perlocutionary, i.e. in which one prescribes while the other obeys, regarding the commandment as executable. Such is the case with all imperatives and they are executable as long as one can reference the message of the imperative to some particular, existing here and now, singular situation in which to act. The one that hears the commandment references it to himself as the one in the role of the actor in it. Furthermore, "Close the door!" refers to not only this door here and now, but also to the still non-existent condition of the door. Thus only the actor can create the still non-existent condition "in his mind". The prescribing statements cannot be executed if the existing condition is their reference, if there is accordance and they are evaluated from the point of view of truth as correspondence between thought and reality— we cannot close an already closed door. They predict and command the achievement of some future state of things. The propositional logic of Aristotle does not allow us to judge on the authenticity or inauthenticity of the prescriptions and on their meaningfulness or meaninglessness.

Levinas wants to preserve the specifics of the prescribing discourse, namely its imperative nature. It seems he stands very close to Kant on this issue, as the latter strives to show in his second *Critique* that the imperative of the practical reason is independent from the principles of the theoretical, i.e. that the inference of prescription from truth is impossible. However, the command and obedience, as Levinas sees them, are not produced by the autonomy of the will. Kant deems the moral law "a miracle" because, while not being derived from facts of the empirical experience, in the moral experience it yields results, which are the very actions that correspond to it. From here Kant draws the conclusion that reason itself is an active cause in the field of experience through ideas and that its use transforms the transcendental idea into the immanent experience, because it causes the events in it. In the form of prescriptions reason constitutes the ideal, which is an extrasensory reality. For Kant this extraordinary force consists in freedom, which is nothing else but pure reason itself, acting as a practically efficient cause and regulation. In turning the direction of causality, which is not anymore from experience to the universal categorization and regulation but, vice versa, from regulation to experience, he sees the way of action of noumenal freedom. The result here is not a consequence of a phenomenological, conditional cause, but of an unconditional cause. Thus Kant implies that one and the same notion, namely causality, is used first in cognition and second in willing (or duty). The first use provides an opportunity to connect two phenomena as participating in a causal relationship, while the second connects the actor and the action, but again under the category of causality. Nevertheless, what happens in Kant's philosophy is the framing of the commandment into a sentence, proclaiming this commandment as a norm. Then the obligation, stipulated by the imperative, is granted the status of a norm and the addressee of the commandment, instead of executing the obligation it articulates, takes it as a reference to his discourse and thus moves into the position of the one that verbalizes another condition, namely the position of the commentator (philosopher, legislator etc.). The addressee of this newly created descriptive and not prescriptive sentence is required to reflect and not act. What the reader of Kant's critiques finds is not the commandment, but the declaration that the imperative "Act in such a way that..." is the norm. Something similar occurs in the philosophy of Levinas where the command "You shalt not kill!" is also described and explained in his works. But he makes a reference to the Greek language of Western philosophy and justifies his own position by the impossibility to escape it. In each philosophy whose roots are Greek the obligatory power of the command is neutralized and the author and the listener are both in the role of the possible commentators. Kantian law is not an instruction to act, but indicates the form that each instruction should have in order to be moral—for Kant this is universality of norm. However, in Levinas' philosophy we are dealing not with norm, but with order, which creates consequently the obligatory nature of each prescription. This is an order of all orders and is not a hollow form, but has content, which creates the urgency of responsibility—a response and not obedience. Then, the responsibility is inherent in other instructions and orders. We aren't dealing with a norm that can be discussed, but with a sacred commandment, whose reception is unavoidable. In this situation the one who orders and the one who executes the order are incommensurable. The ordering one (in the philosophy of Levinas this is the Other) is the free one, while the second one (i.e. the Self, which is the recipient of the commandment) is the hostage. The ethical and political issues never start with the freedom, exercised by the Self, but rather with the obligation. They start, as Lyotard puts it: "not with the power to announce ..., but with the other power, which in the West is regarded as a powerlessness—that of being bound to ..."[104]

---

[104] Jean-François Lyotard. "Levinas' Logic". *Face to Face with Levinas*. Ed. by Richard Cohen, State University of New York Press, 1986, p. 152

According to Lyotard, Levinas gives a new perusal to the relationship between God and the Jewish people and particularly between God and Moses, to whom God tells that the Jews must obey him. But He does not say why they must obey. Through the prescription God puts them in a situation of obligation to listen to what is said to them not because it describes or explains something, but because it prescribes action and this prescription is their rescue. The prescription itself is the first meaning. In Levinas' philosophy the Face is a prescription. Without it humanity will be meaningless and also it will be impossible as the being and non-being depend on meaning and not the opposite.

The common ground between Kant and Levinas consists in the refusal of both to deduce the good from the true: if we know what's good, it doesn't necessarily follow that we will do good deeds. Under Levinas' scheme, however, in contrast to Kant's the recipient of the prescription is not the same as the one that issues it, but is always Other. The place of the speaker, i.e. Transcendence itself, Illeity, who commands through the face of the Other, cannot be occupied by me. The deontological statements immediately create a situation of obligation, which "precedes" the understanding of their content. Levinas says that in Jewish religion God commands, but indirectly through the Other's face without using of any particular human language. He, Illeity, requires responsibility. Most importantly, the addressee of the commandment cannot say who or what God is and shouldn't even pronounce the word "God", saying "There is an order" instead. This order, which is, so to say, a meta-law, defines all other laws. It is not discussed, but outlines a space of lawfulness and from there on each must decide whether and how to abide by them. But this means that one must—constantly and in each particular case— choose, judge and reflect whether what is happening is just, because the execution of the order is always a different and a unique event.

According to Lyotar, this is why each community is directed through the prescription to a future time, to what must be done. What the *logos* or the ontology says is not of paramount importance, because, as in the pagan societies, it's about the very operation of passing the prescription on from generation to generation. This prescription does not depend on the context, but is an instruction which is valid under any circumstances. This instruction is the central point of everything that is being passed on. Only in this sense does Lyotard agree with Kant and Levinas that the imperative is not deducible from any ontology, but precedes it. According to Levinas' paradigm, in the simple fact that "the face is looking at me" or "the face is concerning me", the Self is open to the Transcendence. *Illeity* is looking at me from the face of the Other and this is an appeal that can never be justified and does not need such a justification. Due to this fact—the connection with the face of the Other—each Self is aware of its mortality, finiteness, temporality, etc. How will it think and act from here on, depends on the Self. However, before becoming a Self, each of us is "me", that is, an addressee.

The whole discourse, which tries to find justification for a particular social order through the description of the just society and the just distribution of goods or through the formulation of some codes and norms is, according to Lyotard, futile. Morality cannot play that role of a "grounding reason"—neither in Kant, nor in Levinas. An order is not legitimized. If it is, then it has become a norm and can be questioned. Unlike Kant, Levinas does not think that the meaning of what's happening between people can be understood through universal reason, since the reason itself is manifested as based on the "call" of the face of the Other:

> To recognize with philosophy—or to recognize philosophically—that the real is rational and that the rational is alone real, and not to be able to smother or cover over the cry of those who, the morrow of this recognition, mean to transform the world, is already to move in a domain of meaning which the inclusion cannot comprehend and among reasons that the "reason" does not know, and which have not begun in philosophy...There is meaning testified to in interjections and outcries before being disclosed in propositions, a meaning that signifies as a command, like an order that one signifies. Its manifestation in a theme already devolves from its signifying as ordering; ethical signification signifies not for a consciousness which thematizes, but to a subjectivity,

206   Maria Dimitrova

> wholly an obedience ... that precedes understanding... In this signification the ethical moment is not founded on any preliminary structure of theoretical thought ... Transcendence as signification, and signification as the signification of an order given to subjectivity before any statement, is the pure one-for-the-other.[105]

One of the serious problems in understanding the philosophy of Levinas consists precisely in his requirement that all modes of the prescribing language—the address, commandment, order, appeal etc.—are interpreted not according to the usual, for modern culture, meanings of dominance. For the modern man, for example, it is unacceptable to put himself in the role of the servant to the Other, immediately associating this relationship with serfdom, which has been imposed onto him by the Other as if by a dictator. We all require legitimization of authority, respectively of obedience and usually this requirement is addressed precisely from the perspective of such values as autonomy, freedom, equality, mutual respect, tolerance etc. Modern people have won their independence from the Old regime by blood and sweat. In pre-modern times, power and governance were not faceless relationships of the organization and regulation, but were through and through personal responsibilities. However, modern people seem subdued to orders, which are no one's, anonymous, general. Or, to put it differently, they think that the subject, which commands, is the same as the one that obeys, without any immediate coincidence between them; the relationship between them is mediated by something third—the transcendental subject, represented by some neutral agency, for example by the state bureaucracy, which is *par excellence* neutrality and facelessness, or by the market, or by the law etc.

If we look more carefully at the inclination of modern people to think that they must obey the power of the market, instead of the personality

---

[105] Emmanuel Levinas. God and Philosophy. *Collected Philosophical Papers*. Duquesne University Press, Pittsburg, 1998, p. 172 -173.

of a despot, it is so, because they regard it as a neutral, natural and faceless force. It is known that the market has its own laws, but none of human beings who meet there—neither the seller, nor the buyer—has personal power over the market regulations or has the right of personal power over the other. As if everything happens according to the objective rules of the commodity relationships. And if individuals participate in the market, as well as in the other relationships in the state, they are led by the conviction that in principle everyone can be a representative of the power or a represented by the power and that everyone obeys after he has personally agreed to that. The objective indicators that help us judge what's happening are not dependent on the desire or will of the individual, nor on some kind of monopoly over power, but on the combination of the actions of the multitude of individuals, which are reciprocal to each other—in terms of the result, of the whole, of the positions occupied or at least of the possibility of changing places. The activity of each one presupposes the activity of the other and vice versa. The only thing they need is the objective standard, the neutrality of the norm, the universality of the law. The absurd arises with the fact that neutrality as such has become the ultimate authority, that law has taken the vacant place of the highest power. From the perspective of the Levinasian philosophy this means that injustice being committed towards others—neutrality, indifference, reciprocity, interchangeability and anonymity etc.—instead of being declared a deficiency in our relations, is being elevated to the rank of the highest achievement and is even sacralized.

But realizing this, shouldn't we ask ourselves why the struggle of the oppressed receives meaning and understanding as struggle against the autocracy of the monarch, but is not understandable as a struggle against the "procedural power of those that make decisions on behalf of everyone"? Isn't the faceless power even more oppressive, because it's concealed?

If the moral problem with the responsibility for the other can be substituted by the political problem of the coercion over the other and if the political problem can be concealed behind the neutrality of the seemingly impartial agency or reciprocal actions, this happens only by means of the mediating and faceless power of the norm and law—the law as a legitimized coercion. The norm seeks to mitigate the sharpness of coercion and to bind the participants by the help of the Third. Such surrogate is possible, because depending on who gives out the order and who complies with it, this relation is either immediate or mediate, either moral or political. However, with the appearance of the Third there is always the question of justice—of limiting violence and of the limitlessness of responsibility.

Chapter Three:
From the Command to the Norm

3.1. Replacing the prescription (the command, the order, the appeal) with the norm

It seems that nowadays only retrograde moralists call upon morality while the majority of people believe that morality has been "nullified"; "nullified" in the sense of being reduced to zero, to nothing, no longer possible, cancelled, thrown out of the agenda of what is forthcoming. But if these are the facts, what is their interpretation? How should we understand them? What explanation can we give?

We may not notice morality or pretend not to notice it. It is possible to feel its presence, but to turn one's back on it. It is possible, like with drowning, to feel torment us and weight upon us like a stone on our neck as we try to get rid of it. However, it is possible to get rid not of morality as such, but only of the false moral principles to which we are accustomed. It is possible that we are living in the epoch of the sunrise and not the sunset of morality. Perhaps there is a way to renew our search for an authentic moral code, valid for all of us at once and at the same time for each one individually?

Zygmunt Bauman's intellectual forthrightness makes him respond to this type of question by disclosing disorderly, indecent and unholy truth that we seem to sense, but do not dare to express aloud: moral codes are now finished. The chant of an universal moral law as well the particular has long been sung. It can no longer inspire us, not because of its universality or particularity, not because it is sung in a choir or solo, but rather because such a concept as a "moral code" is a contradiction in terms—as wooden iron, round square and others of this kind.

Morality is supra-historical, supra-theoretical, supra-political, supra-ontological, i.e. meta-physical, but most concrete closeness in the communication with the Other, which is responsibility and care for that Other. Only from the height of its holiness is it possible to make judgements about what is occurring in the fields of history and politics, of the state and institutions, of theory and practice and so on.

Everything in human relations starts from the face-to-face meeting. Attention to the Other (or the lack thereof) commands the whole constellation of human relationships. Morality is omnipresent, indelible, indestructible, even when we do not know what to think about it or what to say. Morality is present—even when we do not know why we need it at all and try various ways of nullify it, leaving the Other with no response. The very indifference to the Other is already a kind of response. Therefore, morality should not be confused with the law (neither natural nor that of social life) or with some *a priori* constitution of man in general; it is not reduced either to the laws and norms accepted in society, or to principles even when they are strictly personal. It is the other way round: laws, values, principles, projects, programs, deliberations, assessments, judgments, behaviour, thinking and all the institutions of our common life follow morality and are authorized by it to serve us (whether they admit or deny it reactively, whether they emphasize it or try to ignore it). Very often the situation is just the opposite—instead of values and norms being dependent on us, we begin to depend on them; this reversal, relieves us of the obligation to be "for-the-Other". Such 'relief' however, is not wholly unacceptable, if reliant on fair institutions of society whose justice itself is attuned to morality. Moral behaviour is the first scene, unpreceded by any other origin and in the words of Levinas, it is an-arch-ic, i.e. devoid of beginning, inception of the plot—meeting between the characters, from where all other relationships in the drama of human life develop. If the planet is void of morality, there is no way at all for sociality and social life to be present on it and vice versa—if people continue to exist as people, there is no way that morality or primary social connection could have evaporated between them. The sociality and humanity of the human creature coincide with its meta-physical or moral dimension.

Perhaps we need to reflect on morality, interpreted as it has been for centuries as the normative regulation of human co-existence, which nowadays seems to have become completely ineffectual. In early modernity, when morality was viewed as the "unwritten law", i.e. a type of legislation or moral code, it was part of the arsenal of weapons with which people fought to seize new territories or to rule over those already conquered. In postmodernity or late modernity, however, morality appears in a rather misty atmosphere in which its contours and meaning are difficult or almost impossible to outline or grasp. This makes us look for support in the most ancient of sources and accordingly, rethink our knowledge based on the volumes of texts handed down throughout the centuries.

Bauman reminds us of the two biblical narratives that have become a framework in which the views of morality associated with the Judeo-Christian tradition are housed. One of them refers to the Fall, and the other—the receiving of the commandments of God by Moses. According to Bauman's comments, the first story suggests that being moral means choosing between good and evil, while the second suggests that being moral means to follow the commandments strictly, obeying unconditionally, while never deviating from the prescribed—neither in one's deeds, nor in one's thoughts. At first glance, these two versions of morality are mutually exclusive: you either have free will or you are obliged to follow blindly without question. But a closer look at the issues raised, shows that they can be reconciled and are even required to reconcile, which means that following the prescription itself implies and requires reflection, judgment and autonomous decision on how it will be executed. Autonomy is evoked by heteronomy.

***

In pre-modern times, it was believed that societies themselves were not created by people, but by some transcendent power prescriptive of morality—deities, spirits, predecessors, heroes, God, etc. People believed that prescription was salvation for those that obeyed, while those who ignored it would be overtook by misfortune, misery, natural disasters or divine punishment. Later on, in the autocratic regimes of governance, the emperor, king or other ruler issued orders which were binding for the subjects. However when secular power was separated from the church and the absolute monarch was not any more guaranteed by God's protection, it became imperative to legitimize obedience. Consequently, subject was motivated to act not because of the personality of the ruler, but because of the order this ruler imposed and the legitimacy these commands contained. The first step towards societal autonomy was the transformation of prescriptions, i.e. of commandments into norms. Norms are not any more imposed by a master or dominant, but are in the power of the people who comply with them and therefore are justified.

It seems that in our cultural tradition largely inherited from Ancient Greece, the fate of the polis as decided by an Assembly of the people first occurred in the classical period. It was there that free citizens had to be won over for one cause or another to adopt the laws thereafter requiring obedience from all within the polis. However, any proposed legislation was deliberated on. Disputes required skilful use of rhetorical tools and reflection was present along the entire process from raising the issue to the final decision. Instead of commands (orders) the supreme power began to issue laws. This changed things radically—while the command was not justified but was uttered and consequently should be executed, then, conversely, the laws (rules) could be discussed and disputed. They

Sociality and Justice: Toward Social Phenomenology 213

could then be modified, i.e. otherwise formulated, supplemented, improved, expanded or narrowed, replaced with others and so on. This opened up the perspective of choice. What happened in Ancient Greece can be summarized as follows: 1) prescription was replaced by rules enacted by the people themselves, not by a transcendent power; 2) norm was a matter of argumentation, debate, choice, voting, decision-making; 3) to implement the decision, appropriate order and institutions were established; 4) deviations from law were penalized as provided by the law itself 5) the assumption of responsibility was premeditated.

Bauman, however, points out that this kind of societal autonomy was replaced in modernity by the society of autonomous individuals. What in ancient Greece was in the realm of the polis, in modern societies is in the realm of the individual as such. The autonomous individual is the one whose behaviour is not determined by a prescription from an external body—he is self-determination; he has no ready identity but identifies himself in the endless process of self-creation. In the conditions of modern individualism any prescription from outside and every heteronomous order are perceived as repression on the person. It is believed that each of us knows best what one needs and how to make out of oneself what s/he wants—any external intervention is seen as a form of violence exerted on individual autonomy. Autonomy is precisely the postulation of the law which the individual himself sets as a measure for his own behaviour. Nonetheless, when autonomy is declared a norm, as in Kantianism, the individual seems to find himself in the paradoxical situation of being independent, while being simultaneously dependent; being free to choose and yet forced to choose, free to take decisions and at the same time coerced to take them. Bauman, along with many other critics of modern society, concludes that the only real obligation remaining in a society of choosers, the only repetitive behaviour, forgetting about all the other choices or being blind for them, is the obligation to choose. Today, freedom understood as autonomy is paradoxically imposed on everyone.

Liberalism and communitarianism, two major trends in social and political philosophy today, rely on autonomy as a self-evident premise. Liberalism gave up the idea of a law imposed "from above"—in the name of God, of the King, of eternal ideas or a universal good. Before being subject to any legislation or of any opinion of itself and the whole of society, or of any other authority, this weak animal called a human being must survive, fight for his life. This is its natural right. In liberalism, it is a pre-predicate belief that the animal struggle for survival is the foundation of all other human needs and desires, of all human achievements and ingenious inventions. Everyone's right to life is inseparable from the right to freedom; i.e. of the choice of the means for their survival. It is secured by the right of ownership. Security of ownership, however, cannot be guaranteed by each one individually, but requires the establishment of liberal institutions of society. They must pass laws which regulate the relationship between citizens, for the free coexistence of all. Nonetheless, this requires the consent of each citizen to obey them— these laws are voted for by all individuals or their representatives.

Liberalism starts with the statement that people are by nature free individuals and this is their only difference from animals. When they establish an association or society, only the relations based on the free will of each individual can be accepted because they are consciously established by the individuals themselves. Only the will of everyone can invest in the partnership and consent to the nature of moral obligation. Laws are based on the free will of individuals involved in the formation of a collective will. Conversely, to demand from common will the sum of all individual wills which always and everywhere be achieved by unanimity would make it an impossible task. Therefore, it becomes necessary for the common will to recognize only those characteristics of the multitude of individual wills which are crucial for their alliance. It also means that henceforth, individual wills should recognize as most important only those features that are found in every member of the collective unity. This is the first step to ignoring otherness and elevating on a pedestal similarity, repetitiveness, the average, the mass, the universal.

Unanimity is the true legitimizing principle of the liberal doctrine, but it has been replaced by the majority principle, provided, however, that it has the function of representing not just itself, but all members of society. Unanimity of wills is replaced by the will of the majority for reasons which are conventional and economical. They arise from demands for greater efficiency in discourse, to provide for decision-making and defend the decisions made. Recently we see that even the principle of the majority cannot be successfully maintained and hence we have liberal government on behalf of the minority. The most important criticism of the liberal doctrine is aimed at just this type of replacement—once elected, representatives of all, whether they are representing everybody, the majority or a minority, speak and make decisions on behalf of the whole group.

In liberal ideology, society is presented as a collection of individuals with their individual rights, but subject to common laws. Once the laws have been adopted and have become the norm of any action, from then on anyone who is not satisfied with them or with the representation associated with them, is in danger of being seen as subversive, not towards one or another individual, nor towards one or another political faction, but towards the whole of society, while those empowered enter dialogue, make decisions and act on behalf of the totality. This dissuades people from thought and hopefulness that they as individuals can exercise their right to freedom. We ought to be reminded that the individual right of freedom was the premise from which the creation of the liberal model started, yet that same premise is now being destroyed. If one opposes the authority of another individual or group of individuals, the forces are comparable, but if one opposes the authority of the State, the collective will, etc, s/he cannot rely on support when all others identify themselves with this highest instance. What is unacceptable in such cases is the fact that the replacement is hidden—behind the apparent neutrality of the State and its institutions, while there are, in fact, individuals with their own private interests, but in their capacity of expressing the universal interest.

The law does not care about differences of opinion or culture—all these can be tolerated, as long as members of the public do not use them as arguments in the violation of civil laws or the rights of their fellow citizens as they are defined by those laws. The danger of functionaries of the State or of the law to use its universality to pursue their own private goals is not just a theoretical possibility. Unfortunately, this is not the strongest criticism against liberalism. The deadly arrow against classical liberalism is the accusation that by ignoring empirically existing differences between people, labelling them as unfair or unimportant, fails to consider the possibilities for reforming institutions in light of these differences. As universal norms are discredited by the private use of public services, by representation which does not represent anyone, by the selfish abuse of unselfishness, by the dominance of "the few elected representatives of the people" over the vast majority and by many more countless forms of pious, self-righteous and officially legitimized hypocrisy, liberalism most often resorts to the only "norm" remaining at its disposal—competition. After the destruction of the social State, in favour of competition, liberalism again exercises influence, and is thereby transformed into neoliberalism. Competition seems to have remained the only candidate to take the place vacated by the central authority in social regulation, which has abdicated from caring for the citizens and has become a self-serving power—power that does not empower anyone other than itself. Central power itself requires deregulation and liberalization. However, with competition, gaining global scope, the war of everyone against everyone has returned and threatens to make life nasty, brutish and short, as Hobbes characterized it. A new barbarism is on the horizon and this time *The Leviathan* will perhaps have planetary dominion. In contrast to Hobbes and liberal doctrine, one can turn to John Rawls and his attempts to respond to the challenges presented by his neo-liberal theory of justice as fairness.

Today's revival of liberalism is significant not only in the field of theory but also in practical life. Most often economic and political measures taken to address state of affairs follow the liberal paradigm of thinking and various liberal schemes of government or abdication of it. Liberalism provides the concepts and networks in which these concepts are included. This liberalist revival means that both Americans and Europeans are likewise striving to grasp and formulate the problems of individual societies increasingly headed towards a world state order.

Still, from Kant's conception of autonomy another branch of today's social and political philosophy came to life as a challenge to the solutions proposed by the liberal tradition. The resulting communitarian paradigm is believed to have been inherited from classical German idealism. Generally speaking, the communitarian outlook opposes the liberal and is primarily occupied with revisionist criticism against it. Communitarians remind us that democracy is not just a procedure but rather, a mode of governance and a way of life for individuals, situated in a certain society. A particular aspect of this demystification of liberal short-sidedness towards society and the individual is apparent in the work of Michael Sandel under the ironic title "The Procedural Republic and the Unencumbered Self". In this work, he accuses liberals of giving priority to the legal and not the good, which he sees as the primary reason for the other disadvantages associated with their position:

As bearers of rights, where rights are trumps, we think of ourselves as freely choosing, individual selves, unbound by obligations antecedent to rights, or to agreements we made. And yet, as citizens of the procedural republic that secures these rights, we find ourselves implicated willy-nilly in a formidable array of dependencies and expectations we did not choose and increasingly reject.[106]

Both liberals and communitarians recognize that conceptions of justice are inseparably linked by respective views about the way of association of human beings. If justice precedes good, it follows that we must keep away from the particular conditions of our experience—as unencumbered individuals according to the interpretation of Rawls, who believes this is the only way we will not be tools of the very goals we pursue. Freed from the dictates of natural necessity and from the sanctioning enforced by social roles, each individual is encouraged to feel like a sovereign. Being a participant in the constitution of the original position, the individual is free to determine principles without complying with any preliminary values, traditions, social status, customs etc. Everyone is a "self-organizing principle of valid claims." In the view of Sandel this is the famous figure of the self-defining subject of the Enlightenment. Unlike the unencumbered Self of the liberal doctrine, Sandel insists that the individual, as a participant in the community, is already bound by moral obligations that precede his decisions. Relations of the Self with the Other are not only relations of cooperation but are constitutive of one's very personality. However, Sandel notes with regret, that we are increasingly drawn by chance into public life, instead of being associated closely with it and today, more than ever, we want to feel free from commitments. It looks like the unencumbered Self is approaching the self-fulfilling prophecy and from liberal illusion is becoming reality. However, with the liberal mode of governance, disappointingly for Sandel, instead

---

[106] Michael Sandel. The Procedural Republic and the Unencumbered Self. *Contemporary Political Philosophy. An Anthology.* Ed. By Robert E. Goodin and Phillip Pettit, Blackwell (Oxford: 1997), p. 254

Sociality and Justice: Toward Social Phenomenology 219

of being freer, we are in fact less powerful, included in a network of dependencies that are not the result of our will—we can not define ourselves in them in order for them to become meaningful and bearable. As social and political organization becomes less dense and fluid, the less we find within it some form of collective identity or a firm structure—rather we find only a fragmented environment around us. The forms of political life are devoid of the common values and objectives that initially supported them. Sandel, like most communitarians, is nostalgic for the social State.

* * *

From an existential phenomenological outlook that embraces neither liberalism, nor communitarianism, we must emphasize that it is not the universal, in the sense of the sovereignty, of the whole, of the group or the individual that is the foothold of morality. The moral subject is not defined by any moral qualities or by a general moral essence which he owns, but by his actions in response to the Other. In society, responsibility is always limited. Everyone is responsible for what he promises or through his actions, however the responsibility, as such, is not confined to the assumption of authorship or of guilt, but is seen and tested in the importance of the work done for others and its importance for them. The subject owes his uniqueness to his personal performance upon the appeal by the Other, even when the very appeal itself is not articulated. Some experts in the field of moral philosophy even argue that it remains unarticulated as a rule[107]. It is responsibility that individualizes but it is not just the task of the solitary subject. The ethical subject is not individualized in isolation, but is rather called to be individualized when the Other makes an appeal from which there is no retreat. No one else can

---

[107] See Knud Løgstrup. *The Ethical Demand*. Introduction by Hans Fink and Alasdair MacIntire, University of Notre Dame Pres, Notre Dame, 1997.

answer instead of me in the concreteness of the situation, i.e. to act from the place where I stand. However, in terms of the social order, which individual can claim to be indispensable? Here comes the difference that Levinas emphasizes between "me" and "every one", i.e. between the exclusive addressee, as one experiences in the face-to-face relationship, the Self in the accusative as "me," on the one hand and, on the other hand, my Self, that is, the conceptualised I as the everyone in this place. Also an 'I' himself as the Third is the universalized I and not an answer to an appeal, but compliance with the norm. Universalization implies distancing from oneself, as if going out of my own skin and looking at myself from the outside; in turn, this presupposes consideration of ones' decisions, negotiations with others and with oneself. It also means that to find the resources to respond, one can become somehow disengaged in reflection, escape the immediate identification with oneself as well as overcome the passivity of his own sensitivity and the provocation from the Other.

The Other as a moral challenge is singularity and uniqueness through the simple fact that he is present in front of me even before I can remember his history and before I was aware of him as a stranger, before I identify him according to his status, role, habits, behaviour and so on. He is the being whose existence is merely his own. He is the "abstract individual" clothed in flesh by the eyes of the I who fixes him intentionally and objectifies him. From the moral perspective, neither the I nor the Other are assigned to an ordered formation as specimens embodying the norm (the common, the law, the universal, the repetitive, the valid for everyone). The Other is otherness, uniqueness, only because of his ability to prescribe and to command in the singularity of the actual situation; but when the prescription is heard and understood through the norm, the Other is already the Third—he, she, they, "everyone". According to the norm, I also appear in the grammatical third person: "myself" subjected to it as everyone else. Hereafter, the intrigue of human communication

Sociality and Justice: Toward Social Phenomenology 221

and interaction can be described within the generalized means of expression of language. However, we shall remember that universality is revealed starting from the singularity of the face.

Kantian autonomy acquires a new meaning, if we start from the urgency to meet the face as a singularity. The interpretation of the Kantian imperative, in which the individual itself is the beginning and end, is unacceptable from the perspective of Levinas' conception of morality and sociality. The presence of the Third in the relationship actually means that justice is the central category. Coercion exercised by the Third, i.e. the norm, that applies to everyone, suspends the omnipresent possibility for total violence towards the Other. "Thou shalt not kill!" prohibits the greatest injustice. Justice draws division lines between "the initial couple of the Other and me" and also between others and between those most distant. Justice achieves and establishes a balance by limiting one and restoring the rights of the affected, by encouraging and sanctioning, by showing loyalty to the obligation to judge. Judging is an operation of thinking, but in society it means a reference point for individuals as set against laws and regulations, as part of the objectivity of particular institutions. Thus, between the two levels of social connection—interpersonal and institutional—a tension is created which cannot rely for resolution on some kind of arithmetic equation. This tension repeatedly raises the question of justice, i.e. of the justification of the norm.

In the dispute between the parties seeking justice, lasting peace cannot be achieved without the unselfishness of love of the neighbour, which has nothing to do with schemes of reciprocity and compensation. The point is that people cannot achieve reconciliation, recognition and peace either by imposing authority or by the eschatology of love. Justice is always ambivalent, because the retreat from the asymmetry of the moral relation is a requirement of morality itself—morality is "for all" and so it implies equality (always in relation to something third). Morality itself cannot be preserved in sublime purity but is "degraded" to search for justice. The point is that justice would in turn degrade if it did not bear or keep the traces of morality.

"To each their own" is a moral imperative. To judge justly is not simply to make decisions on the distribution of wealth and recognition — firstly, each and everyone must be admitted; everyone's right to participate must be recognized. The right of the Other is my business. Justice, however, is neither a sublation of morality into norms and laws, nor a synthesis between them, but the core of the conflict between persons and norms. It is not only respect for the law, i.e. recognition of the social order, but the taking into account of the lawfulness of responsibility to individuals. Attention to the order means that it acquires force and weight (or is assuaged and becomes volatile) in the light of the face. Justice is not a utopia; it is not served in any world beyond nor is it an attempt to postpone the conflict for some future time, for example during the history that follows and will issue the *post factum* sentence. The I decides in the present on the future of the Other and hence, potentially, of any subsequent one. Justice "is served" in the urgency of the present.

3.2. The neo-liberal notion of justice

Rawls believes that his conception of justice avoids any philosophical and metaphysical claims. He wants it to be independent of any religious and philosophical doctrines, which always challenge each other.

Of course, assuming that this conception builds on the basic intuitive ideas forming the core of the political conception of justice in a constitutional democracy, it is on the condition that some of the old controversial metaphysical and theological ideas have become intuitively "undisputed", establishing themselves in a struggle with their adversaries. These adversaries were by contrast pushed to the periphery or simply forgotten and acquired the status of "impossibilities". As we will see fur-

Sociality and Justice: Toward Social Phenomenology 223

ther on, Rawls' conception, firmly connected with the history of the liberal doctrine, is opposed by communitarians. They rely not on the atomized idea of the individual and society, but on the intersubjective connection of individuals within communities and traditions, i.e. on their common values platform that supports the understanding between them. In particular, we will consider the position of Axel Honneth, who used other "undisputed ideas" that have become intuitively self-explanatory and from whose perspective the theory of Rawls is criticized.

Rawls himself was not a philosopher and did not want to be one; through his work, he argues that his conception of justice as fairness is neutral and that it is intended as political, not metaphysical. Indeed, when it comes to making decisions, the most important factor is political — metaphysical truths are important in the build up, maintenance and transformation of the institutional order of society, but only if supported or rejected by the political forces. Rawls himself says he aims to avoid the question as to whether his conception of justice could be extended to a common political or moral outlook on the different types of societies existing in different political and social conditions. Yet he also says that his political conception of justice, in a democratic constitutional regime, is also inevitably moral in the sense that it has a moral effect. Justice as fair cooperation refers to the institutions of society as its specific subject:

> In particular, justice as fairness is framed to apply to what I have called the "basic structure" of a modern constitutional democracy. ... By this structure I mean such a society's main political, social, and economic institutions, and how they fit together into one unified system of social cooperation.[108]

Of course, Rawls is right that social and political institutions are loaded with moral significance like anything else relating to the common life of

---

[108] John Rawls, *Justice as Fairness: Political not Metaphysical*, Philosophy and Public Affairs, Vol. 14, No. 3, (Summer, 1985), p. 224.

people. They all are inconceivable outside of their moral meaning. Institutions and the constitutional regime under which they operate are the embodiment of established moral standards that apply to "everyone." Their "strength" is tested in each interpersonal interaction and is challenged daily in the life of small and large groups alike. In his views on the basic structures of society, as a result of political as well as moral consensus, attached to, objectified and guaranteed in them, Rawls recognizes that the very morality as fairness plays a constitutive role in setting the general framework. It further provides the cooperation between different groups and individuals, channelling their activities through institutions and thereafter; the institutions in turn, as already constituted and developed, set and reproduce certain moral standards.

> The social and historical conditions of such a state have their origins in the Wars of Religion following the Reformation and the subsequent development of the principle of toleration, and in the growth of constitutional government and the institutions of large industrial market economies.[109]

Rawls insists that any effective outlook of political justice should allow for a variety of doctrines, as well as for many contradictory and even incommensurable conceptions of good. Hence, a hegemonic state policy would be unacceptable nowadays. But in the institutions of today's democratic societies the idea of justice as fairness is intuitively implied and interpreted in accordance with existing traditions, so that we can speak of "partial consensus", i.e. one that includes opposite religious and philosophical doctrines that have sustainable support in a constitutional democratic regime.

Here it is obvious in plain sight that Rawls builds on moral categories such as honesty and tolerance, etc., so he can hardly claim metaphysical neutrality, as the very understanding of moral categories is inevitably

---

[109] Ibid. p. 225

metaphysical. At least in the initial version of his doctrine Rawls deliberately removes himself from the metaphysical debate and looks to find a procedure that would not depend on philosophical disputes.

Rawls believes that within democratic thinking there is disagreement between the tradition, starting from John Locke, that gives more weight to freedoms (freedom of thought and conscience, individual rights, right to ownership etc.) and the tradition of Jean-Jacques Rousseau, which gives greater weight to equality and values in the political life of the community. Rawls recognizes that this is a stylized contrast that is considered the basis of the conflict between liberals and communitarians. It is a long standing dispute about the most appropriate forms of institutionalization of the values of freedom and equality. Very often, these two categories are considered to be related as communicating vessels — when the volume in one increases, it is at the expense of the volume in the other. Rawls, however, believes he has found an idea that allows for the unification of equality and freedom — the idea of society as a system for fair social cooperation between free and equal individuals and consequently proposes two principles of justice:

1) Every individual has an equal right to a fully adequate scheme for the same basic rights and freedoms compatible with a similar scheme for all
2) Social and economic inequalities must satisfy two conditions
a) They must be connected with offices and positions open to equality of opportunities
b) They must be of the greatest benefit to those members of society who are at the biggest disadvantage.

Rawls himself does not claim this conception of fairness to be the Truth, nor that it is deducible from any truths, but it is a proposal which could serve as a basis for political consent. It is achievable as every citizen is capable of "testing" whether the major institutions of society function properly and whether they are consistent within the scheme of social cooperation; every citizen can check what benefits he obtains by the institutionalization of such consent, regardless of his private, special interests or his social position.

When Rawls tries to expand the use of the conception of consent, not in some already constituted order but to the process of the constitution and in the establishment of the support frame itself, he needs a perspective which is not provided by an external body but relies on mutually cooperating people. Gone is God and the absolute Hegelian Spirit, as well as the *a priori* independent moral code or even some premised moral imperative; there are no eternal values or natural laws, nor a universal reason, the people's will or another similar instance by which the idea of cooperation would be legitimized. Everything is left in the hands of the contractors and decisions are taken by them in accordance with what they consider their mutual benefit and fair conditions for further interaction.

Rawls is aware that the agreement on the fundamental matters of political justice must be achieved with adequate information on the common conditions, without coercion and in ways compatible with the status of all citizens as equal and free individuals. Morality in the theory of Rawls is emphasized also with the requirement to take into account the condition of the weakest and most vulnerable on the social ladder as a criterion for fairness. Their status should be the concern of all who are better placed in the hierarchy. Moreover, the openness of institutions for "everyone" is undoubtedly a fundamental pillar of any social system pursuing justice. However, there is an undeniable weakness in the way Rawls derives his conclusions by "simulation" in respect to the initial state in which the parties involved in the agreement are presented:

When, in this way, we simulate being in this position, our reasoning no more commits us to a metaphysical doctrine about the nature of the self than our playing a game like Monopoly commits us to thinking that we are landlords...[110]

In order not to allow some people more benefits than others, and to avoid threats, lies, coercion, etc. in the establishment of the pact of public understanding, a "veil of ignorance" is needed. To ensure pure procedural justice Rawls assumes that:

> ... the parties are situated behind the veil of ignorance. They do not know how the – various alternatives will affect their own particular case and they are obliged to evaluate principles solely on the basis of general considerations.[111]

It is presupposed that the parties do not know their place in society, or their class or social status, nor do they know their fate in the distribution of natural resources and capabilities, nor how much strong, intelligent and so on each of them is. Moreover, they do not know their understanding of good, nor their life projects, nor even individual private facts about the living conditions of society, i.e. they do not even take into account the political and economic situation, the level of civilization, cultural development etc. In general, it seems that Rawls' theory proposes that agreement must be reached between people for whom everything human is alien to them and they are almost pure, transcendental subjects but defined as such by their ignorance, tolerance and honesty. Rawls speaks of them as "noumenal persons." It is very interesting then what they would be debating and facing when making a rational choice. Are these "*fully cooperating members of society*"[112] indeed? As many commentators have noted, the "veil of ignorance" is pure fiction.

This is the most unacceptable postulate in John Rawls' theory of justice. As a well-known critic of Rawls' position sarcastically remarked:

---

[110] Ibid, p. 239.
[111] John Rawls. *A Theory of Justice*. Harvard University Press (Cambridge, Massachusetts: 1971), p. 136–137.
[112] Ibid. p. 78.

> For people meeting together behind a veil of ignorance to decide who gets what, knowing nothing about any special entitlements people may have, will treat anything to be distributed as manna from heaven."[113]

Criticism by the communitarians is directed towards the liberal understanding of the subject perceived as always distant from all possible value orientations, free to choose between them without external constraints, "as if he had decided to buy something".

Indeed, it is an obvious and banal fact that individuals and groups communicate and interact with each other because they are different and are aware of their differences and in view of these differences, they build the institutional framework of their contacts. For example, health care institutions are created because there is a difference between the competence of doctors and patients, differences in the health status of different people and groups and because there is specialization in medical services according to various diseases and so on. The same can be said about the police, schools, transportation services and all other public and government departments / institutions. The spirit of institutions is the moral support and guarantee for citizens according to their needs. People need each other and when these needs are recurring and regularly arise, social mechanisms are established with their own rules for fulfilling those needs; the question is how these mechanisms can be hereinafter most efficiently and fairly used. The question is also how institutionalization can foster the undertaking and implementation of responsibilities and not allow the abdication from them. With a just legislation, through which institutional responsibilities are attached to the relevant positions which correspond to the rights of citizens, people's participation in social life is regulated—the inclusion and exclusion of individuals and groups, recognition and sanctions, resource allocation, etc. However, as many critics of Rawls point out, when people have to make decisions behind

---

[113] Robert Nozick. Distributive Justice. *Contemporary Political Philosophy. An Anthology.* Ed. by Robert E. Goodin and Phillip Pettit, Blackwell (Oxford: 1997), p. 224.

the veil of ignorance, what principles will constrain them? It is not about anything else but a basic principle of distribution, i.e. distributive justice as such. But even if we ignore these critical considerations and accept that Rawls' theory also provides smooth operations from the outset of the organization of institutions and their system, then other questions come to mind, not just relating to organizational, technological or political matters: institutions created for whom? Used in the name of whom? In whose interest? Whom do they favour and who do they ignore? The simplest answer is "to benefit all!" However, it is impossible due to the inevitable constraints of the whole's resources and the continuous challenge of their distribution. The moral answer to these questions, although it seems clear and simple, namely that the social mechanisms must work in the interest of those who need the services and resources provided by the institutions in a certain order, is not as unambiguous as it seems. First, behind the other invariably looms the Third. As we have seen in previous chapters, justice is never fair if it does not take into account the uniqueness of each one, i.e. if you do not overlap with the moral good, understood as responsibility for the Other in his uniqueness. Furthermore, if society, considered as a whole, is composed of forces, each seeking its own advantage and its own security, albeit under the umbrella of "partial coincidence of interests", then the structure of institutionalized social relations is neither derived from morality, nor does it support it. It is rather the opposite—it is a compromise with the interests of each of the participants. The requirement for equality and freedom of all citizens leads Rawls to think of the fairness of procedures as a means of neutralizing the antagonism and working toward solidarity. Nevertheless, neutralization and tolerance, as well as procedural rules, can ensure neither morality, nor solidarity. Peace would once again be achieved at the cost of compromises as due to the conflict and mutual limitation of claims; otherness would remain behind the "veil of ignorance" and the Other would be reduced without residue to the

Third, whose "normality", however, would always be in question because of the continuous "deviation from the norm". The problem here lies in the fact that individuals and groups are seen as autonomous and even, as Rawls himself says, "noumenal" persons, each of them monologically self-centred:

> My suggestion is that we think of the original position as the point of view from which noumenal selves see the world. The parties qua noumenal selves have complete freedom to choose whatever principles they wish; but they also have a desire to express their nature as rational and equal members of the intelligible realm with precisely this liberty to choose, that is, as beings who can look at the world in this way and express this perspective in their life as members of society. They must decide, then, which principles when consciously followed and acted upon in everyday life will best manifest this freedom...[114]

Rawls maintains that subjects choose their goals or viable projects monologically, rationally and autonomously by calculating their interests and controlling their claims in respect to claims by others by relying on the original agreement. But if the participant in this agreement is individualized before he/she enters into any relations, even before choosing his/her goals, they would be "no one"—a being that is beyond the particularity of the situation, man without qualities or authorization.

Rawls draws on Kant's concept of autonomy, according to which people are reasonable and free beings who can manage their life:

> To act from the principles of justice is to act from categorical imperatives in the sense that they apply to us whatever in particular our aims are.[115]

Even classical liberal theorists emphasize that when freedoms participate in a system formation, they are limited, although ultimately restrictions are imposed to protect freedom itself. Constitutional or statutory rules aim to guarantee for all individuals the opportunity to express

---

[114] John Rawls. *A Theory of Justice*. Harvard University Press (Cambridge, Massachusetts: 1971), p. 255.
[115] Ibid. p. 253.

judgments and act according to their reasonable nature, i.e. to provide the most favourable conditions for everyone to carry out their life projects, guaranteeing the most important social goods. This means that everyone has the right of autonomy to determine their personality, rejecting any obedience to the principles of someone else and everyone has the right to pursue their own goals. One can be free only if they recognize the same right of freedom of every other. This is Rawls outlook on tolerance. Everyone has the right to carry out their project, if the institutions guarantee public order and security. Knowing the stability of the fair constitution, members of a well-ordered society are also convinced that no restriction on the freedoms of the intolerant ones is necessary, except when they threaten the freedoms of others. For example, Rawls supports the secular state, where everyone is entitled to their religion, as long as it does not prejudice the equal right of religion of others. However, Axel Honneth notes:

> For the principles of justice he develops are initially intended only for a negative purpose, namely to protect the individual within the community against social and economic sanctions which would constrain him when practically exploring his individual life goals.[116]

In Rawls we see a negative definition of the Other—as a limitation. The prescriptions or norms of society are also seen negatively—as prohibitions, and not in the light of responsibilities as a source of positive motivation. Freedom is more "freedom of ...", i.e. independence, than "freedom for ...", i.e. connecting with others through responsibility.

---

[116] The Limits of Liberalism: On the Political-Ethical Discussion concerning Communitarianism. Chapter 14. *The Fragmented World of the Social. Essays in Social and Political Philosophy by Axel Honneth*. Ed. Charles W. Wright. State University of New York Press (New York: 1995).

In his outlook on social cooperation, Rawls underlines three main points: [117]

1) Cooperation is distinct from merely socially coordinated activity, for example, from activity coordinated by orders issued by some central authority. Cooperation is guided by publicly recognized rules and procedures which those who are cooperating accept and regard as properly regulating their conduct.

Thus priority is simply given to another type of universalization replacing personal charisma or personal dependence with "neutral" procedural regularity. The distinction between the I and the Other is put aside, out of the scope of norms and rules, and so itself falls within the territory of indifference, making tolerance possible, as it is not engaging with otherness; all that is required is loyalty to the procedures.

1) Cooperation involves the idea of fair terms of cooperation: these are terms that each participant may reasonably accept, provided that everyone else likewise accepts them. Fair terms of cooperation specify an idea of reciprocity or mutuality: all who are engaged in cooperation and who do their part as the rules and procedures require, are to benefit in some appropriate way as assessed by a suitable benchmark of comparison. A conception of political justice characterizes the fair terms of social cooperation. Since the primary subject of justice is the basic structure of society, this is accomplished in justice as fairness by formulating principles that specify basic rights and duties within the main institutions of society, and by regulating the institutions of background justice over time so that the benefits produced by everyone's efforts are fairly acquired and divided from one generation to the next. Individuals interact namely by virtue of the general rules which help establish symmetrical and reciprocal relations. But as

---

[117] John Rawls, *Justice as Fairness: Political not Metaphysical*, Philosophy and Public Affairs, Vol. 14, No. 3, (Summer, 1985), p. 232.

much as it benefits relations, this type of mediated interactions also impedes them. Undoubtedly, they are the source of contemporary alienation and meritocracy, where again profit and distributive justice are the guiding principles. Profit separates rather than unites—what is mine and what is yours, and where the exact border lies, even when sharing is fair and equitable, especially when profit itself are at stake and the highest goal.

2) The idea of social cooperation requires an idea of each participant's rational advantage, or good. This idea of good specifies what those who are engaged in cooperation, whether individuals, families, or associations, or even nation-states, are trying to achieve, when the scheme is viewed from their own standpoint.

It is therefore presumed that the "units" of society, regardless of whether they are families, individuals, groups, nations, etc., are teleologically determined—they have to "rise" towards the goal, but the objectives must be such as to be achieved through shaping, processing and rational application of the concept of individual rational gain or good.

As Rawls himself confesses, "Thus, justice as fairness deliberately stays on the surface, philosophically speaking."

We would say that not only *surface* as *superficiality*, but *inconsistency* is the most appropriate word for Rawls' theory.

Rawls insists that the only alternative to the principle of tolerance is the authoritarian use of state power. This is the enemy, whom Rawls tries to fight in his *Theory of Justice*. However, according to our critical stance herein, the principle of tolerance cannot underlie as a fundamental principle in a policy of differences and a humanistic social theory, because it eventually destroys the possibility of social cooperation. In this sense, it saws-off the bough on which it rests.

Rawls himself, in response to criticism by communitarians attempts to correct the hard-line neoliberal Republican idea of justice. He begins to speak of two moral forces—the sense of justice and the concept of good that make individuals equal and free. In this context, the morality of individuals is their readiness for dedication to a sincere cooperation within society.

> In the case of social cooperation, this good must not be understood narrowly but rather as a conception of what is valuable in human life.[118]

Rawls will further recognize, willingly or not, that the notion of good must also include religious and philosophical views of the world, *"by reference to which the value and significance of our ends and attachments are understood"*. So it seems the veil of ignorance is slightly lifted with the "tolerant" assumption that *"the perception of persons as free and equal"* is also a fundamental intuitive idea taken as implicit in the social culture of a democratic society (which is of course metaphysical in its essence).

3.2. The Communitarian notion of justice

In the preface it was mentioned that in Western social philosophy two main trends are outlined: liberal and communitarian. As a representative of the former, we draw on John Rawls's theory of justice, and for the latter—the theory of Axel Honneth.

Honneth is considered a follower of the Frankfurt School and of Critical Theory that engages in the problems of emancipatory struggles for greater justice. Based on the corresponding conceptions of justice and good, this trend seeks to interpret and evaluate social struggles as struggles for recognition.

Honneth, like Rawls, starts from the idea of constitutional democracy as a social and political regime of modern Western society, corresponding to the modernization and industrialization, to individualism and the alienation within its totality. He defines the essence of the epoch pursuant to this outlook as:

---

[118] Ibid, p. 233.

Sociality and Justice: Toward Social Phenomenology 235

> One of the experiences which decisively shape consciousness in contemporary Western industrial societies is the perception of an accelerated process of personal individualization. Although this process has been evaluated in both positive and negative terms, the individual's increasing detachment from pre-given social forms has come to be understood as a determining feature of our age, even to the point of heralding a new social epoch. [119]

This accelerated individualization is seen in the liberation from traditional role expectations, in the expansion of the field for individual expression and in the erosion of values, which in pre-modern lifestyles created a sense of community. Consequently, and in keeping with this tendency, individuals strive even more for autonomous behaviour and personal achievement. Thus, individuals in our contemporary society are in a social situation, different not only from the pre-modern but from the modern one too:

> In philosophy, the idea of "post-modernism" which arose from a critique of reason was the first reaction to these changed social conditions. This approach understands the specific process of the accelerated pluralization of individual life-orientations to be a result of the definitive overcoming of universalistic moral principles; and, in an affirmative mode, declares this to be the liberation of consciousness from false "generalities".[120]

Unlike the premises concerning sovereign individuals-atoms, from which John Rawls draws his "political ethics", Honneth relies, in his own words, on the "intersubjective conditions of human socialization." In the process of self-creation, i.e. in the formation of a practical attitude towards himself, the modern person needs recognition consisting of:

1) Emotional support and care
2) Respect

---

[119] The Limits of Liberalism: On the Political-Ethical Discussion concerning Communitarianism.Chapter 14. *The Fragmented World of the Social. Essays in Social and Political Philosophy* by Axel Honneth. Ed. Charles W. Wright. State University of New York Press, 1995
[120] Ibid.

3) Social assessment

A lack of recognition along any one of these coordinates is experienced as injustice and motivates the struggle to obtain such recognition.

Honneth references Hegel, who from his early works distinguished between family, civil society and the state. According to Honneth the three circles in which individuals live their life together, correspond with the three dimensions of recognition in modern society mentioned above.

Honneth believes that the struggle for recognition, which gives meaning to the lives of individuals and groups, challenges the accepted social standards by which people judge and form their expectations. The various members of society are attributed their status, functions, meanings and according to them their identity. In fact, Honneth is more interested not in the forms of recognition, but on the contrary, in forms of non-recognition, such as racism, sexism, neglecting minorities etc., as they provoke the claims of individuals and groups for mutual understanding and rights. This type of discourse that logically privileges negation (in this case non-recognition, which in turn must also be non-recognized to ultimately achieve recognition of the unrecognized), is a reiteration of the Hegelian concept of negation of negation. The process should finally reach a positive result favouring not only the previously disadvantaged, but society as a totality. Communitarians are often called "holists" as they are believed to prioritize the social whole. As in Hegel's logic, here too negation is the driving force of development and negation of negation reaches the synthesis, so totality is the arch framing all human efforts which gives them meaning. This totality is called human community.

Honneth soberly emphasizes that the various forms of non-recognition are included in certain power relations which they also express. They are imposed from outside and attribute certain identities to subjects who cannot identify themselves autonomously. Their voices are neglected or marginalized. Ignorance or underestimation by others is internalized, so that they live with a sense of helplessness, inadequacy, inferiority, etc. This in turn contributes to the perpetuation of injustice towards them. In appropriate circumstances, the marginalized and unrecognized in society have different ways of raising their claims to recognition, but this inevitably leads to challenging the conventional order and to social conflicts. We can see here the Hegelian logic, whereby within the system there is a clash of opposing claims, forces, interests and positions, arriving finally at their reconciliation. In Honneth's theory, truce between opponents is achieved through mutual recognition, rather than through the victory of one and the establishment of a relationship of domination between master and slave. Reconciliation synthesis is presented in Honneth's theory as social solidarity and mutual recognition and the claim of the other is seen in light of the supportive behaviour of the rest of society. In Hegel's philosophy relations of domination are also sublated into civil society.

It is well known that Honneth aims to explore the "moral grammar of moral conflict",[121] as presented in the book he is most renowned for: *The struggle for recognition. Moral grammar of social conflicts*. He is careful not to be ranked with supporters of Hobbesian theory who believe that struggle is the main feature of social life, thus he replaces "struggle" with "dialogue" and offers his theory of social interaction which rests upon the intersubjective relationship. He associates the roots of his conception with Greco-Roman antiquity where for the first time in theoretical thinking, historic relations between citizens of the polis, whether harmonious or agonal, received attention. However, the dialogue of this epoch was nothing but disputatious, where the arguments of opponents often contributed to the reinforcement of one's own position. Honneth sees these

---

[121] This is the title of the book that made Honneth's name known to the public: Axel Honneth. *Kampf um Anerkennung. Zur moralischen Grammatik sozialer Konflikte*, Suhrkamp, Franfurt am Main, 2000.

relations as mere struggle for recognition. Contrary to the liberal paradigm, in Honneth's theory, individuals are not isolated from each other, hence when discussing their condition they should not be guided by an individualistic but rather by a communicative concept of individual freedom. Consequently, they see the achievement of their own freedom as dependent on the attainment of the freedom of the other. A communitarian theory of justice thereby focuses not on a calculation of life benefits based on chance, nor on the distribution of goods that guarantee freedom but on the quality of social relations and binding reciprocity. Hegel's authority on the matter led him to support the notion that individuals are interdependent and this interdependence is constitutive of them as moral beings and acting subjects. After Hegel, our knowledge about the intersubjectivity increases and the human subjects become more and more aware of the supportive experience of mutual recognition.

Honneth also tries to revise the notion of the good, understood as "the common good" of the polis which, as purported in Plato's theory, sets the measure of every idea and every existence. Good is not given once and for all, nor is it a predetermined rule or norm, but rather is the process of becoming of the community and achieves legitimacy obtained through institutionalization of communication, that is, of interactions and rights.

Axel Honneth does not embrace either the liberal ideal of equal rights, or the communitarian one of communities prospering because of a common value orientation. Honneth's position is that the autonomy of the individual must be preserved and maintained. On this point, he agrees with Rawls who in turn agrees with Kant that it is correct to follow of the individual's autonomy as a moral principle. Even if the personal identity of the subject trough autonomy is formed according to the social community standards, the freedom of actions is guaranteed first of all by the law. Complying with ethical values of the world which the individual inhabits and accepting them with no external coercion namely ensures the individual freedom of action and interaction.

Since it is obvious that for Honneth the relations of recognition are reciprocal, i.e. mutual, we are curious as to how such mutuality is achieved. Honneth argues that the true object of his conception of justice is not so much subjective freedom of action as the social spheres of communication. Honneth notes very clearly that it is the state that takes measures through which the binding mutuality of intersubjective relations can be protected and guaranteed. In this manner his conception of justice, in his own words, loses its character of a distributive theory and accepts its form of normative communicative theory since the principles of state guaranteed social conditions for mutual recognition are substituted for the principles of fair distribution.

As in Hegel's *Philosophy of Right*, in Honneth's theory of justice the egalitarian right, typical of liberalism, loses its monopoly position. Under conditions of modernity, the addressee of the deliberations on justice is always the democratic state with reference to the rule of law, but with limited power. Honneth insists that most relations of recognition have the nature of private relationships that defy legal regulation. Honneth sees the advantage of his conception in the multiplication of normative principles, as being in accordance with the areas of communication. Therefore, according to him, together with the law we must also take into account areas of work and emotional attachment. In this sense, besides the basic principle of equality of rights the principle of love, that is, the justice of demands, ought to be added as well as the justice of achievements or the fair division of labor. Each of these principles is valid in its own area but nevertheless all of them together imply the possibility for individual autonomy and thus they determine what in the contemporary situation could be called "social justice".[122]

---

[122] Ibid., p. 30.

What Honneth actually wants, instead of recognition as a formal guarantee of rights and freedoms, is to extend the task of the rule of law as regards social guarantees onto relations of recognition. This point raises a pertinent question which arises from such strong demands whereby any claim on a democratic state must be considered legitimate and it must be expected to be satisfied.[123] How far should the state intervene and what guarantees can it provide for certain rights? Apart from constitutional freedoms, should it commit to their material provision too? It seems that in Honneth's conception, obligations of the state tend to increase indefinitely and with this an expansion of expectations in the state control of relations. Accordingly, the question of responsibility arises, which, as strange as it sounds, is absent in this communicative conception of freedom.[124]

With the help of Hegel's historicizing method and the idea of progress, Honneth speaks of a reformist function of his theory which through its engagement with the future determines the present as moral, but a present worthy of improvement and existing relations in terms of practices and institutions. Furthermore, this present is just to some extent, but requires more justice. Relations of recognition should not be thought of as random interactions, but as relatively stable models of communication, which reciprocally make the experience of recognition possible for the participants. This presupposes, however, the existence of moral norms to whose validity they would adhere:

> In this sense, the relations of recognition are a form of binding reciprocity in which obligations have lost their binding character having become self-explanatory components of habitual practices [125]

---

[123] Christo Todorov. Freedom and/or Justice. Critical Comment on Axel Honneth's *Justice and Communicative Freedom. Critique and Humanism*, v. 22, 2006, p. 36 (my translation from Bulgarian)
[124] Ibid., p. 38.
[125] Ibid., p. 27

Honneth sees the real task of his theory of justice in the guarantee of equal opportunities for participation in the constitutive relations of recognition. Pluralization of contacts and of areas of functioning multiply the dimensions that individuals learn to see as opportunities for self-realization. However, individuals acquire a stable knowledge of their own claims and abilities when they see them reflected in the behaviour of their partners in interaction. Ultimately, Axel Honneth associates expanding freedom and accordingly the need for increased justice with the acceptance of the challenges made by the unfree and unrecognized. The sense of injustice overlaps with the moral sense of not being socially recognized, i.e. by others and on the level of institutionalized rights and freedoms.

On this point and contrary to Honneth's recommendations Levinas would say that to be recognized by others, one must, in the first place, question his own abilities and behave responsibly and not make claims for recognition; he must participate in the lives of others, not because of their recognition of him, but because of his care for them:

> For me, the original acknowledgment of the other and the beginning of meaningful resonates through the "Thou shalt not kill!" The word is very important: Care for the death of the other is the beginning of the acknowledgment of the other.[126]

The struggle for recognition and the claims for more rights for oneself is an extremely selfish purpose, according to the measure of Levinas' philosophy. In Honneth's theory, the self-realization of others must be actively supported by me and this is the definition of my solidarity with them, but in fact the main motive for this kind of solidarity is the possibilities it opens for my own self-realization.

---

[126] Florian Rötzer. *Conversations with French Philosophers*. Emmanuel Levinas. Humanities Press, New Jersey, 1995, p. 64

The I, according to Levinas, is responsible for everything that happens to it, including its non-recognition by others. However, the recognition or non-recognition of its own merit and rights is none of the Ego's business but of the others. The Ego's task is to be able to respond in such a way that allows it to apply its abilities for the others and to participate in activities beneficial to them. Its rights would then be invested because of the responsible behaviour with which it is expected to act. In this way, the question of freedom and justice is raised, i.e. as regards institutions, standards, distribution of power and resources, assignment of responsibilities, the control over them and the evaluation of results. Justice always implies not simply arithmetic equality or levelling, but ordering people according to the urgency of their needs and responsibilities. The good that the I is motivated to do for others cannot be associated with profit for itself (although in the light of justice, this is also important). Good cannot be inspired by the universality of laws, rights and freedoms, but by the faces of others.

Conclusion

The distinguishing feature of modernity is the denial of the divine origin of community in favour of the claim that community life is derived from the intelligibility of human beings. Reason becomes the principle which replaces divine authority. This interpretation therefore separates secular from religious authorities. Modern secular government relies on autonomy, rights, reciprocity, laws; i.e. on the modern constitutional state and the promise of justice for all. However, this promise has not been fulfilled. Late modernity has led to the pursuit of financial, market and business independence from the monopoly of central state power. The particular group and individual autonomy has reached a state that was foreseen as a threat from the outset: a war of everybody against everyone; *my rights against yours*. The continuing reform of the legal foundation of rights and the demand for relations that are symmetrical and reciprocal at any cost (as an expression of meritocracy and contractualism) attest to continued alienation instead of justice and solidarity in the community. These failures certainly contribute to a postmodernist query of the assumptions on which modernity is founded. Postmodernity emphasizes pluralism, diversity, locality, seeking to escape from the dictate of the principle of hegemony of the universal and from obedience to a single sovereign power. However, the new status feels like a crisis as a result of the absence of the moral authority of the state. In the past the admittance of the universality of each regional or individual choice or claim depended on it.

As is well known, and as we have already said here, the pre-modern community was established on personal dependence. The command from the master—the head of the family, feudal, king, emperor, etc.—was unifying, but it was a unity of subordinates. In modernity, personal dependence upon relations is replaced by impersonal dependence—all functions are integrated into the system of the state. It becomes the organizer of structures and regulator of activities. State organization (as any organization) is a form of power. It creates a common social space that overlaps with a certain territory where all subjects under its jurisdiction belong. These subjects are also the heirs to its national customs and history. In this way, the state establishes a common social horizon of receptivity, understanding and memory, common standards of communication and interactions, "implicit" arrangement of positions, common meanings for everything that goes on inside its borders. By setting the framework for all transactions and categorizations, the state creates a "consensus" with respect to the network of shared evidence that forms the national *doxa*. Positions in the common space under the jurisdiction of the government are perceived as more real than the actual individuals occupying them. Obedience is universalized—people recognize one another through the inclusion in and mediation of the state. Individuals become replaceable occupants of offices, positions and functions in the entity of the state. Of course, the differences, according to the duties and responsibilities that create the hierarchy, are recognized, but they cannot take the individuals beyond the relations of symmetry and reciprocity towards the Impersonal Third, namely, the entity of the state. Individuals are reduced to elements of the governing mechanism, to functions in the system, to parts of the whole, to cells of a single organism and these cells can be replaced in the interest of survival, preservation and reproduction. Thus everyone owes his/her life to the whole and through the whole life becomes meaningful. The logic of the whole is the logic of circularity or a return to oneself: the meaning of life is the struggle for life; the sense of freedom is freedom itself; the meaning of the totality is totalization itself; man is also a purpose for himself, as is the nation, and so on.

Throughout modernity where personal domination is replaced by the impersonal, the state monopoly empowers those who speak on its behalf, to take decisions that are valid for all. Equality of citizens of the state does not allow the figure of the Other to appear in his otherness, because the Other is the same as me—a citizen with the same rights as me. One of the major contributions of Kant's "Copernican revolution" lies not only in the formulation of the categorical imperative as a universal fact, but also in the discovery of the respect to the Other. However, for Kant, and long after him, the meeting of the I with the Other remains, in its most important aspects, a meeting with one's own Self. In Hegel's theory, in the emancipatory movement the particularity of the other must be included in the further course of history, but the significance of otherness is reduced to its role in the constitution of universal subjectness. With the latter, every Ego can be identified. The universal subject of the Enlightenment remains substance throughout the entire period of modernity all the way to the Hegelian dialectic. Even where the other is recognized as my *Alter Ego*, it is the Other, similar to me. In Husserl's transcendental phenomenology we see how the Other obtains some advantage because he is transcendence compared to immanence but transcendence constituted in the Ego's own subjectness as a condition for the correctness of the world. In the phenomenological tradition the Other is transformed into a mirror in which the I is reflected and through its image in it, it returns to itself, attaining self-consciousness. The Other does not possess his own otherness, since it is imposed on him as a quality with reference to my Self—either as a similarity or as a difference. The Other is the mediator in the transition from naivety to self-reflection. In the meeting with the other person each of us discovers his own Self in his genus and universality.

Levinas, however, does not think that people can be recognized in their importance on the basis of universality only, or substantiality, or common essence. He even insists that such unity through universality is devastating in terms of the difference, between the One and the Other, a difference which he wants to emphasize, preserve and elevate. Levinas is suspicious of totality and reciprocity, so essential to the modern way of thinking. He considers dialogue, at least initially, as an asymmetric relationship. Proceeding from the ideas we have for dialogue which have their foundations in Greek antiquity and understood as a discourse that opposes another discourse, we start by asking ourselves whether Levinas speaks of a dialogic relationship between the Other and the I. In contrast, we should say rather that Levinas describes something as transforming the monologue of the sovereign and self-empowered universal subject into dialogue with others. The question is how is such a transformation possible.

As per Heidegger's definition, phenomenology is the study of what exposes itself, which reveals or manifests itself: how do things show themselves to be what they are? However, can we ask the same question in reference to people, i.e. to ask how people show what they are? Is the way in which they expose themselves the same as the way things are exposed? If we use Husserl's terminology, this question would be formulated as follows: what is the intention which directs me toward the other person and what kind of entity satisfies or fills this intentionality of my consciousness? This is exactly the question Levinas tried to answer with his philosophy of non-intentional consciousness and he underlined that the Other is not an entity in the world but is a face and has a transcendent dimension. It was called "beyond being".

Unlike silent objects, people communicate. Communication should not be understood in terms of the model of Platonic dialogue which lacks embodiment. On the contrary, if we want words to be more than just noise, they must be made sensible by our deeds. Consequently, we constitute the world and our destiny with each other. In each meeting between human beings, they relate to each other not in the way that objects are present in the world; the meanings and connections between objects

Sociality and Justice: Toward Social Phenomenology 247

are determined by the intentionality of consciousness of the Self. The conversation with the Other, every single conversation, happens in the questions and answers. In monologue, the I asks the questions and responds to itself. In dialogue, the interlocuters do not coincide. They do not coincide in monologue either, because the questioning naive I is not the same as the thinking I that has found the answer for itself. This disparity allows monologic philosophy to speak of the identity of the I—as a departure from one's Self, seeing oneself in the Other as a mirror, and returning to oneself. Monologue, however, is internalized dialogue. Conversation between people begins with the mere presence of the Other before me and the silent appeal of the Other heard my me. Of course, I can approach the Other intentionally, according to my own goals, values, beliefs, fears, hopes, interests, etc, i.e. as in our biased approach to objects and events in the world. They are interpreted in my horizon and thus made meaningful and rationalized. But then the otherness of this single, unique other, would remain outside my sight. Under the pretext of a conversation with the Other, the I remains alone with itself in its horizon. In the presence of the Other there is an unarticulated and even anonymous call on his part in his meeting with me. As if there were some inexplicable confidence in my Self that I will not leave the Other without a response and treat that Other in a way I treat the things around. Rather I will be responsible for his human presence as if his fate to be a man or not depends at this point on me. I can choose not to answer him, but this is still an answer of sorts. This inevitable responsibility that the Other with his presence lays on my shoulders, which is neither desired nor expected, nor is it a conscious assumption of responsibility, represents for Levinas human subjectivity or rather subjectness. Its beginning is otherness, imprinting itself with no intention on my side as a trace in me. However, from then on, the Ego consciously chooses its behaviour, becoming an active subject. My passive sensitivity is not a naïve or pre-predicate knowledge. It is not even knowledge, nor intentional consciousness, but the non-intentional internalising of the challenge made by the alterity of the Other which awakens my conscience and my responsibility. When this happens, the Other is accepted as face and provokes my humanity, i.e. morality. Levinas defines as moral only the relation with the Other as face. This unspoken appeal from the Other which can not be identified with anything uttered by him nor with anything implicit or explicit as a quality in his presence, is calling me to decide his destiny at this point or, similarly, to participate in the joys and sufferings of his life, i.e. in the construction of his fate. This is precisely the responsibility that falls on me, even against my will. The situation may be such that I reject his appeal, considering that only a rejection would be in his interest. However, the challenge of the call by the Other to me is precisely in the fact that I have to decide—and I am even obliged to decide with an obligation from which there is no escape. It is not just something that affects my Self, but which primarily affects the Other in his deepest identification: belonging to humanity. Therefore, none of us is responsible for its own Self only nor is the Self merely a sovereign being; the I is always responsible for the Other.

Usually we do not trust completely with childlike naivety and do not leave our fate entirely in the hands of the Other, nor do we answer the Other openly and unreservedly. In everyday relations we treat each other according to social conventions and norms which reduce caring for the Other from a perpetual responsibility to conscientiousness in following common sense. All norms and conventions, including legal ones have a dual function—they facilitate our relations and make them smoother, more balanced and less burdensome, but also protect us from exposure, from complete openness and vulnerability or from aggressive expansion, thereby preventing unjustified violence. Otherwise, our dependence on one another would be unbearable, and our relationship would be ineffective. In conventional forms, however, the care for the

Other, is both averaged and mediated and is neither unseen nor open, but is concealed in everyone's right.

Levinas considers morality as the infinite responsibility of the One for the Other, the utopian in all utopias, but simultaneously speaks of an earthly morality. Looking to protect the possibility for morality, Levinas turns to the philosophy of human rights. Sadly, he concludes that with regard to human rights, we are in a state of crisis.

Since the 18th century, when it first appeared in Western European bourgeois society, the discourse on human rights, on dignity for everyone, on freedom, equality before the law, the right to life of everyone, etc., there was a recognised need to acknowledge the primordial meaning of both the individual and the rights providing his defence. Today with regards to human rights, it is commonly accepted that it is not about one or another particular jurisdiction, but about something legitimizing law itself. When we discuss justice, it does not coincide with what is set out in the clauses of the various codes. We mean morality as a measure of the justification of one or another law provided for by legislation. In a sense, human rights precede any power, any distributive, criminal, administrative and civil justice and any criteria for the contribution and recognition of individuals and groups. These human rights are inalienable and are not bestowed upon man is as with a title, or a reward, or privilege, and so on. They are an expression of the absolute value of everyone, regardless of the time and place in which he lives, regardless of the natural and social conditions, where his life is lived and which they secure and guarantee. As if they nullify every individual's belonging to mankind, in order to highlight not simply his *differentia specifica* or some attribute, which can be found only once within the multitude of individuals, but in his uniqueness. This uniqueness, as Levinas says, is the fact that every person is an "I". Everyone should be given the opportunity to speak on his own behalf as an "I". However this cannot be done without the Ego being referenced to others:

> I like the second formulation of the categorical imperative which asks us to "respect ourself and the others". In this formulation we are not pure universality but are in the presence of the other. You know that people's rights are not something new and we can trace them back to Cicero. What I find interesting here is that the rights of the other supersede my own. This is very important. We must realise that the rights of the other do not commence with the defence of my own rights.[127]

However, for human rights to be guaranteed, not just on paper, but in practice, how can the multitude of individuals be reconciled with the uniqueness of each of them? Does this not affect the dignity of the unique Other to be classified under universalizing human rights? Isn't peace, established on the basis of the Charter of Human Rights, unstable and without guarantees? Of course, any peace is better than the best war. However, peace, seeking stability through government power, in politics, means abiding by laws through the use of force. Thus justice relies on politics with its strategies and tactics, thereby opening the path for a totalitarian state that tramples on human rights or cynically mocks them, by promising them or postponing them to some indefinite future. To have genuine peace, human rights should be seen not from the perspective of freedom for everyone, because then the freedom of one is always a restriction on the freedom of the other and peace is achieved as a reciprocal negation that strikes a compromise. Freedoms themselves need peace in advance which is not just a lack of aggression and the presence of tolerance, but is the meeting with the Other—meeting and lack of indifference to him, a desire for peace as the most important condition for peace. The most important thing here is approaching the Other, which is not a return of the self to itself in ego-centrism, but the answer that I give to the Other in the protection of his rights. Good, as responsibility, is an attitude completely different from neutrality and tolerance, i.e. residing in the midst between love and hate; good is the desire for peace with the Other in the recognition of him as a face. Moreover, this peace precedes

---

[127] Christian Delacampagne. *Entretiens. Philosophy. Emmanuel Levinas.* Editions La Decouverte et Joural Le Mond (Paris: 1984), p. 146., own translation.

Sociality and Justice: Toward Social Phenomenology 251

any agreement, any consensus-seeking or any contract and is more stable and better guaranteed than the peace maintained by the State. However, in this peace human rights are the rights of the Other and I am responsible for them:

> Their original manifestation as rights of the other person and as duty for an I, as my fraternal duty—that is the phenomenology of the rights of man.[128]

If the Other is perceived only through categories and universals, ignoring corporality and uniqueness, this means mortifying him, reducing him to the concept we have of him—this means to perceive him within the Whole with which we identify ourselves and to subdue him to the world of my Self. Universal justice, which gives rights to everyone in the entity of the State is, in fact, injustice. The other is not excluded from the genus and generic categories, but he cannot be present in his uniqueness and otherness only through them. The search for justice does not seem to avoid the risk of mortification of the other by reducing him to a link in the chain, the cog in the mechanism, an item in the system, a part of the whole, a cell in the organism, a number in the sequence; the search for justice is constantly exposed to the danger of becoming terror over the other. However, most importantly, this option has an alternative and that alternative is the hope for community. Justice is the guarantee for the community. Justice does not speak the language of indifference and neutrality, nor does it conceal brutality, wars and coercion in order to present as an ideal the balance of powers, or the reciprocity of actions and counteractions or the reconciliation of damages and compensation. Indeed, things happen in the established order as a regime of unbiased judgments issued under the laws of existence and survival. The order of existence and survival, however, if it becomes an end in itself, is evil. On the contrary, going towards the Other is an infiltration of humanity into

---

[128] Emmanuel Levinas. The Rights of Man and the Rights of the Other. *Outside the Subject.*, Transl. by Michael B. Smith, Stanford University Press (Stanford: 1994), p. 125.

being, meaning to go beyond one's own survival.[129] Humanity does not consist of the impersonal prudence of one's might and the strengthening of one's own positions and power, but in the relation to the Other as face. Justice comes from love but it does not mean that the severity of justice will not turn against love, understood as responsibility. It is rather such an inverted condition that we are constantly witnessing. Politics, left to itself, has its own determination which consists in privileging power for the sake of power. Love must always supervise it. For justice to remain justice, the intervention of Good is needed. The only absolute good, the only absolute value is the human ability to prioritize the Other. This is the ideal of holiness. Furthermore, as Levinas claims, my responsibility for the other (**sociality**) is endless, because my reconciliation with the Other (**justice**) can never be completed once and for all.

---

[129] See Emmanuel Levinas. Philosophy, Justice and Love. *Entre nous: Thinking-of-the-Other*. Columbia University Press, 1998, p. 114.

Index

A

a priori 16, 28, 43, 134, 184, 210, 226
absolute 19, 33, 46, 69, 72, 75, 87, 150, 151, 164, 165, 180, 212, 226, 249, 252
abstraction 35
activity 24, 31, 54, 62, 66, 68, 75, 89, 102, 108, 109, 119, 132, 134, 136, 138, 142, 145, 146, 157, 196, 199, 207, 232
addressor, addressee 30, 132, 134, 193, 196, 197, 199, 200, 201, 203–205, 220, 239
anonymous 29, 38, 40, 60, 62, 65, 104, 152, 183, 195, 200, 206, 247
appeal 21, 60, 76, 79, 83, 85, 100, 106, 115, 119, 124, 126, 130, 131, 137, 157, 170, 179, 190, 200, 205, 206, 209, 219, 247
appearance 12, 109, 111–113, 116, 141, 146, 158, 164, 180, 208
arbitrariness 17, 21, 89, 91, 94, 125, 130, 139, 162, 175, 187
Aristotle 22, 66, 127, 195, 202
asymmetrical 25, 27, 33, 34, 51, 100, 106, 137
authentic 17, 22, 44, 61, 64, 80, 116, 118, 160, 209
autonomy 19, 20, 21, 50, 68, 162, 177, 179, 181, 182, 194, 196, 200, 202, 206, 212–214, 217, 221, 230, 231, 238, 239, 243

B

Balibar, Étienne 71
barbarism 174, 177, 217
Bauman, Zygmunt 7, 8, 10, 17, 47, 140, 141, 209, 211, 213
Being 38, 45, 54, 55, 59–63, 73, 77, 81, 82, 87, 88, 90, 96, 112–114, 121–123, 126, 127, 143, 144, 147, 148, 160, 161, 222
beyond 7, 11, 13, 30, 32, 42, 45, 46, 56, 63, 65, 75, 81, 83, 85, 88, 94–96, 100, 102–104, 115, 120 124, 126, 128, 135, 137, 140, 143, 145, 147, 165, 178, 180, 222, 230 244, 246, 252
Bible 61, 93, 159, 164
Blanchot, Maurice 55, 81, 193
Bourdieu, Pierre 8, 11, 13, 32
Buber, Martin 23–26, 33, 57, 133, 137, 140
bureaucracy 40, 42, 149, 191, 206

C

calculation 95, 102, 238
Camus, Albert 45, 85
care 12, 44, 50, 55, 56, 58–60, 66, 83, 86, 129, 135, 158, 160, 170, 177, 182, 185, 210, 228, 235, 241, 249
categorical 21, 42, 73, 178, 179, 185, 198, 200, 230, 245, 250
choice 15, 57, 101, 121, 129, 142, 200, 213, 214, 227, 243

citizen 7, 10, 40, 70–73, 75, 94, 162, 214, 225, 245
civilization 8, 42, 80, 173, 174, 227
closeness 26, 65, 116, 117, 126, 132, 140, 142, 145, 164, 210
coercion 8, 74, 89, 144, 152, 163, 166, 170, 177, 208, 226, 227, 239, 251
command 74–77, 94, 99, 125, 127, 128, 135, 141, 143, 162, 184, 200–202, 206, 209, 212, 220, 243
communitarian 10, 13, 20, 217, 234, 238
community 7, 10, 11, 16–20, 23, 26, 33, 34, 49, 51, 63, 73, 77, 82, 94, 96, 116, 117, 133, 143, 144, 152, 157, 173, 180, 182, 205, 218, 225, 231, 235, 236, 238, 243, 251
conatus essendi 61, 96, 158–160, 163, 176, 177
conception 17, 19, 20, 26, 32, 33, 36, 38, 46, 58, 63, 68, 88, 145, 162, 163, 178, 185, 217, 221–223, 225, 226, 232, 234, 237, 239, 240
conflict 8, 15, 69, 142, 154, 155, 163, 187–189, 191, 222, 225, 229, 237
consciousness 18, 19, 24, 36, 37, 53, 62, 73, 81, 82, 87, 88, 91, 94, 112, 117, 123, 127, 142, 157, 176, 185, 206, 235, 245, 246, 247
constitution 15, 17, 22, 37, 63, 115, 162, 175, 179, 184, 189, 200, 210, 218, 226, 231, 245
construction 180, 248
conversation 14, 27, 28, 31, 34, 62, 63, 82, 98, 100–102, 106, 109, 112, 114–117, 121, 132, 134, 137, 146, 159, 183, 188, 247

culture 9, 23, 27, 30, 33, 38, 40, 53, 59, 67, 75–78, 80, 81, 88, 119, 127, 193, 206, 216, 234

D

Das Man 38, 62, 79, 133, 144
death 41, 44, 54, 64, 65, 80, 85, 86, 87, 88, 89, 90, 94, 95, 96, 97, 103, 118, 126, 128, 135, 137, 150, 162, 163, 168, 169, 178, 241
defence 13, 49, 90, 91, 94, 178, 249, 250
Descartes, René 39, 67, 68, 70, 72, 104, 105
despotism 21, 25, 75, 134, 183
destruction 33, 40, 93, 98, 112, 150, 157, 163, 171, 216
determinism 50, 167, 169, 171, 175
dialectics 100, 104, 127, 195
dialogue 16, 18, 23–26, 31, 57, 82, 99, 101, 121, 132, 137, 215, 237, 246
dictate, dictature, dictatorship 150, 154, 167, 174, 175, 243
difference 14, 15, 18, 19, 25, 26, 28, 31, 55, 74, 80, 84, 86, 88, 95, 101, 106, 107, 108, 111, 114, 126, 132, 179, 194, 198, 214, 220, 228, 245, 246
discourse 9, 12, 14, 16, 21, 27, 28, 34, 48, 50, 70, 104, 107, 147, 165, 173, 182, 195, 197, 201, 202, 205, 215, 236, 246, 249
duty 43, 163, 176, 185, 202, 251

E

Ego 33, 63, 84–86, 89, 96, 114, 117, 142, 242, 245, 247, 249
election 75
empirical 13, 18, 19, 63, 68, 71, 73, 88, 149, 175, 179, 198, 202
enemy 18, 177, 233
eschatology 96, 221
Europe 39, 41, 50, 65, 73, 81, 173
existence 19, 30, 31, 35, 37, 39, 41, 43, 44, 46, 47, 52, 53, 55–58, 63, 65, 73, 76, 79–82, 85, 87, 92, 95–97, 103, 105, 110–112, 117–119, 124, 131, 136, 141, 149, 155, 157–159, 178, 182, 184, 194, 211, 220, 238, 240, 251
existential 47, 61, 86, 90, 92, 95, 96, 120, 219
existentialism 38, 41, 44, 46, 48, 119

F

face 25, 31, 40, 44, 48, 51, 61–63, 65, 83, 85, 86, 92, 94–97, 100, 101, 103, 106, 115–117, 119, 126, 132, 135–137, 141, 144, 152, 154, 157–159, 162, 165–168, 171, 173, 174, 177–181, 184, 185, 191, 192, 193, 200, 204, 205, 210, 220–222, 246, 248, 250, 252
faith 33, 39, 42
finite 64, 68, 70, 86, 101, 178
formal 10, 20, 22, 51, 52, 140, 144, 148, 169, 190, 240
formalism 140, 180, 188, 190
Foucault, Michel 81, 83, 193
fragmentation 10, 13

freedom 7, 15, 17, 20–22, 38, 43, 47, 49, 50, 55–57, 60, 62, 66, 69, 72, 75, 78, 79, 82, 83, 88, 89, 91, 93, 101, 117, 129, 130, 131, 136, 138–140, 144, 150, 152, 156, 161, 163, 165, 171, 173, 176, 177, 179, 181, 183, 184, 188, 190, 192, 194, 196, 197, 199, 200, 202, 206, 214, 215, 225, 229, 230, 231, 238–242, 244, 249, 250
function 23, 26, 34, 54, 66, 81, 86, 108, 111, 113, 115, 124, 131, 156, 170, 177, 187, 215, 225, 240, 248
future 40, 86, 88, 91, 147, 199, 201, 205, 222, 240, 250

G

Gadamer, Hans-Georg 26, 27, 66, 67
God 32, 43, 55, 67, 68, 71, 72, 74, 76, 77, 83, 88, 97, 103–105, 117, 124–127, 145, 164, 179, 181, 204, 206, 211, 212, 214, 226
good 14, 43, 45, 56, 65, 68, 74, 78, 85, 91, 102, 121, 124, 138, 160–162, 168, 169, 170, 172, 173, 175, 182, 184, 233, 234, 238, 242, 250, 252
Greece 49, 173, 195, 212, 213
group 9, 10, 11, 14, 15, 17, 19, 22, 73, 94, 116, 142, 145, 182, 215, 219, 243

H

Habermas, Jürgen 26, 27
Hegel, Georg Wilhelm Friedrich 19, 28, 68, 77, 80, 86, 93, 112, 120, 123, 154, 169, 180, 183, 191, 236–240, 245
Heidegger, Martin 37, 43, 44, 45, 50, 52, 53, 55–61, 64, 76, 79, 80, 85–87, 92, 93, 107–112, 118, 120, 121, 124, 125, 128, 131, 132, 135, 145, 158, 246
heteronomy 20, 21, 105, 179, 194, 195, 200, 211
history 24, 33, 34, 42, 45, 49, 62, 63, 70, 74, 78–80, 82, 91, 95–98, 112, 120 121, 132, 144, 145, 155–157, 160, 164 ,169, 173, 174, 178, 210, 223, 244
Hobbes, Thomas 149, 150, 159, 161–163, 167, 217
holiness 29, 119, 160, 172, 181, 210, 252
Honneth, Axel 223, 231, 234–241
hope 7, 33, 89, 90, 96, 251
horizon 26, 35, 37, 62, 64, 79, 100, 132, 136, 145, 156, 158, 217, 244, 247
hostage 62, 117, 135, 139, 141, 203
humanism 18, 42, 44–46, 49, 50, 57–59, 66, 118, 173
humanitas 50, 56, 58, 65, 76, 173
Husserl, Edmund 27, 33, 35–38, 50, 63, 80, 82, 85, 118, 123, 145, 245, 246

I

idea 20, 31, 37, 46, 65, 69, 76, 102, 113, 114, 136, 137, 171 173, 214, 225, 226, 233–235, 238
identification 10, 12, 15, 17, 26, 46, 56, 61, 81, 83, 84, 92, 112, 113, 127, 129, 149, 182, 188, 220, 248
ideology 44, 45, 146, 173, 215
image 72, 78, 97, 101, 103, 107, 116, 166, 180, 182, 245
immanence 24, 33, 63, 69, 77, 126, 128, 154, 245
imperative 18, 21, 73, 89, 105, 164, 172, 174, 178, 179, 181, 183–185, 193, 197–202, 205, 212, 221, 222, 226, 245, 250
indicative 179, 193, 197, 199
individual 7, 9, 10, 11, 14, 15, 17, 19–22, 32–34, 38, 39, 41, 44–49, 57, 60, 67, 70–72, 74, 75, 81, 87, 89, 90, 92, 94, 95, 116, 129, 136, 142, 144, 147, 149, 155, 163, 171, 174–176, 178, 179, 185, 186, 189, 191, 192, 195, 197, 207, 213–215, 217–221, 223, 225, 227, 231, 233, 235, 238, 239, 243, 249
infinity 65, 68, 93, 125, 127, 128, 154, 178
institution 62, 185, 186, 187
intentionality 29, 36, 37, 54, 82, 100, 102, 112, 116, 123, 124, 180, 246, 247
interest 8, 33, 62, 65, 86, 95, 118, 150, 155, 157, 163, 174, 175, 178, 182, 216, 229, 244, 248
intersubjectivity 11, 28, 37, 100, 139, 238

irresponsibility 17, 78

J

judge 43, 95, 102, 114, 130, 133, 141, 145, 166, 172, 185, 187, 189, 195, 202, 205, 207, 221, 222, 236
judgement 43, 90, 94, 148, 185, 195
justice 10, 14, 18, 21, 22, 26, 28, 29, 41, 49, 51, 60, 91, 93, 99, 101, 102, 114, 117, 119, 124, 142, 144, 148, 151, 155, 161, 164–168, 170–172, 182, 183, 185, 187–189, 191–193, 195, 197, 208, 210, 217, 218, 221–227, 229–234, 238–243, 249–251

K

Kant, Immanuel 18, 20, 21, 32, 38, 68, 71, 72, 120, 169, 172–181, 183, 186, 196–200, 202, 204, 205, 217, 230, 238, 245
Kierkegaard, Søren 38, 46, 47
knowledge 12, 28, 30, 31, 36–39, 41, 43, 44, 46, 64, 67, 69, 77, 94, 112, 114, 116, 119, 123, 126, 130, 134, 136, 145, 156, 168, 176, 180, 186, 188, 211, 238, 241, 247
Kojeve 123

L

language 14, 24, 25, 30–32, 35, 41, 43, 44, 58, 76, 80, 86, 92, 99, 100, 107–111, 113, 115, 118–120, 123–125, 131, 145, 147, 183, 185, 203, 204, 206, 221, 251

law 10, 11, 15, 16, 18, 20, 21, 29, 39, 65, 74, 89, 99, 149, 152, 164, 165, 172, 174–176, 178, 180, 181, 185, 187–192, 195, 196, 199, 200, 202, 204, 207–211, 213, 214, 216, 220, 222, 238–240, 249
legitimate 151, 164, 166, 168, 240
Levinas, Emmanuel 11, 18–20, 25, 26, 28, 34, 35, 37, 38, 46–50, 53–68, 70, 76, 78–82, 84–93, 95–105, 107, 109, 111, 113, 116–118, 120, 121, 123–127, 130, 131, 133, 135–140, 143, 144, 145, 148–151, 153–155, 157–162, 164, 165, 167–174, 176–186, 190–192, 199, 200, 202, 204–206, 210, 220, 221, 241, 242, 245–247, 249–252
liberal 10, 13, 20, 40, 154, 164, 165, 167, 170, 171, 214, 215, 217, 218, 222, 223, 228, 230, 234, 238
listening 54, 80, 109, 110, 118, 200
logic 9, 14, 26, 36, 48, 67, 128, 153, 154, 177, 186, 201, 236, 237, 244
logos 76, 100, 101, 114, 116, 123, 124, 145, 205
Løgstrup, Knud 219
Lyotard, Jean-François 81, 192, 193, 195, 200, 203–205

M

Marx, Karl 32, 196
meaning 11, 12, 14, 22, 27, 31, 35–37, 40, 41, 46, 52, 54, 55, 57–59, 61, 70, 76, 79–81, 84, 88, 90–92, 98, 101–103, 106, 108, 109, 111–113, 115, 119, 121, 124, 126, 129–132, 134, 138, 139, 144, 146–148, 151,

156, 157, 178–180, 182, 187, 190, 194, 198, 200, 204–207, 211, 221, 224, 236, 244, 249, 252
meeting 24, 26, 32, 33, 48, 56, 63, 82, 101, 105, 114, 127, 129, 131, 133, 136, 140, 159, 178, 179, 181, 210, 228, 245, 246, 250
metaphysics 37, 42, 43, 45, 46, 58–60, 111
method 25, 28, 240
Mirandola, Giovanni Pico della 46
modernity 7, 9, 16, 17, 31, 32, 39, 42, 69, 81, 152, 177, 195, 211, 213, 239, 243, 245
monologue 31, 98, 109, 132, 246, 247
moral 14, 17, 19, 21, 25, 28, 32, 48, 49, 55, 62, 66, 68, 77, 83–85, 88, 94, 98, 114, 117, 123, 128, 130, 131, 134, 136, 138–142, 145, 149, 152, 155, 158, 160, 161, 163–165, 168, 169, 172, 176, 178, 181, 182, 187, 189, 192, 198, 199, 202, 208, 209, 211, 214, 218–224, 226, 228, 233, 235, 237, 238, 240, 241, 243, 248

N

narration 125, 193
nature 8, 28, 33, 38–40, 45, 47, 57, 59, 62, 66–68, 72, 77–80, 89, 91, 102, 114, 148, 151, 156, 158, 162, 169, 174, 177, 180, 198, 202, 214, 227, 230, 231, 239
negativity 18, 48
neutrality 14, 16, 207, 208, 216, 224, 250, 251

norm 16, 184, 192, 198, 202, 205, 207–209, 213, 215, 216, 220, 221, 230, 238

O

object 24, 25, 29, 31–33, 35, 36, 62, 71, 75, 90, 94, 101, 108, 111–113, 134, 137, 147, 150, 151, 180, 198, 199, 239
obligation 14, 74, 83, 96, 165, 189, 193–195, 199, 202, 204, 210, 213, 214, 221, 248
One-for-the-Other 62, 98
ontology 37, 52–55, 57–60, 80, 91, 99, 113, 114, 120, 124, 136, 159, 161, 205
onto-theo-logy 72, 111, 118
opposition 7, 9, 12, 15, 16, 45, 64, 65, 70, 79, 88, 149, 154, 160, 176
order 9, 11, 12, 13, 23, 26, 32, 43, 51–53, 60, 67, 72, 74–76, 83, 89, 90, 93, 104, 107, 109, 111, 115, 116, 119, 125–127, 130, 134, 136, 138, 145, 148, 149, 152, 155, 156, 159, 161, 163, 170, 177, 178, 181, 183, 184, 189, 192, 193, 197–199, 201, 203–206, 208, 209, 212, 213, 217, 219, 220, 222, 223, 226, 227, 229, 231, 237, 249, 251
Ortega-y-Gasset, José 78
Other 11, 12, 15–35, 37, 38, 47–49, 51, 53, 56–59, 61–67, 69–71, 76, 77, 79, 80, 83–90, 92–108, 110, 114–118, 120, 123, 124, 126–132, 134–138, 140–148, 150–152, 154–174, 176–182, 184–187, 190–193, 200, 201, 203–208, 210, 216, 218–

222, 229–232, 237, 238, 241, 242, 245–252
particularity 10, 13, 18, 49, 56, 100, 174, 175, 180, 186, 199, 209, 230, 245
passivity 75, 89, 220
past 46, 52, 86, 90, 97, 121, 133, 185, 243
peace 60, 95, 148, 150, 153, 158–161, 163, 168, 169, 176, 177, 181, 185, 192, 221, 250
perception 13, 29, 31, 37, 38, 108, 110, 112, 115, 136, 137, 179, 234, 235
perspective 10, 14, 16, 18, 22, 27, 28, 34, 35, 37, 39, 56, 57, 61, 62, 71, 75, 76, 88, 90, 99, 104, 106, 112, 113, 132, 133, 135, 146, 153, 155, 156, 172, 177, 181, 185–187, 191, 199, 206, 207, 213, 220, 221, 223, 226, 230, 250
phenomenology 27, 28, 33, 35, 37, 47, 50, 82, 118, 123, 159, 245, 246, 251
Phenomenology 35, 118, 120, 123
philosophy 7, 14, 16, 18, 20, 24, 27–32, 34, 36–38, 41, 42, 44, 46–50, 52–56, 58–62, 67, 69, 70, 73, 76–80, 82, 104, 112, 115, 118, 120, 121, 123, 124, 127, 130, 137, 142, 145, 150, 154, 155, 161, 162, 172–175, 181, 185, 186, 191, 193, 196, 198, 200, 202, 204–207, 214, 217, 219, 234, 235, 237, 241, 246, 247, 249
pluralism 9, 10, 12, 154, 243
polis 22, 162, 195, 197, 212, 213, 237, 238

political 12, 14, 40, 42, 52, 66, 71–73, 75, 77, 81, 89, 101, 120, 130, 148, 149, 152–155, 161, 162, 169, 171, 179, 183, 195, 196, 203, 208, 210, 214, 215, 217, 219, 222–227, 229, 232, 234, 235
politics 9, 17, 49, 70, 89, 99, 124, 142, 153, 155, 160, 161, 163, 168, 169, 171, 173, 184, 186, 196, 210, 250
possibility 42, 55, 80, 82, 87, 95, 111, 115, 144, 148, 154, 155, 159, 166, 175, 195, 207, 216, 221, 233, 239, 249
post factum 222
postmodernity 7, 17, 211
power 8, 40, 42, 60, 61, 72–74, 76, 81, 83, 86–88, 95, 101, 110, 120, 131, 134, 136, 139, 142, 144, 148–152, 154, 156, 157, 160, 163, 165, 166, 168, 170, 172, 173, 187, 191, 193, 194, 200, 201, 203, 206–208, 212, 216, 233, 236, 239, 242–244, 249, 250, 252
practice 15, 31, 49, 57, 146, 157, 169, 196, 210, 250
prescription 125, 130, 192–202, 204, 205, 209, 211–213, 220
present 14, 24, 27, 29, 31, 36, 48, 49, 51, 54, 62, 73, 78, 84, 86, 90, 95, 97, 104–106, 110, 117, 128, 147, 179, 182, 194, 198, 210, 212, 220, 222, 240, 246, 251
principle 8, 10–12, 14–16, 21, 24, 27, 30, 33, 35, 38, 41, 69, 74, 99, 116, 151, 170, 175, 177, 190, 197–199, 207, 215, 218, 224, 229, 233, 238, 239, 243

progress 39, 46, 69, 81, 112, 152, 173, 174, 240
property 136, 147, 149, 157, 163, 197

R

Rawls, John 217, 218, 222–228, 230–235, 238
reason 7, 8, 31, 32, 42, 43, 45, 46, 68–70, 73, 77, 81–83, 99, 103, 104, 106, 121, 123–125, 127, 129, 130, 145, 151, 153, 154, 156, 157, 161, 169, 173–181, 183, 184, 186, 197–200, 202, 205, 217, 243
reciprocal 11, 25, 28, 33, 51, 82, 99, 100, 137, 140, 143, 165, 181, 207, 208, 232, 239, 243, 250
recognition 8, 14–16, 19, 32, 69, 83, 94, 112, 115, 120, 134, 156, 169, 190, 192, 206, 221, 222, 228, 234–237, 239–242, 249, 250
reflection 12, 17, 24, 28, 44, 49, 63, 84, 92, 112, 117, 127, 142, 153, 173, 201, 211, 212, 220, 245
respect 9, 14, 18, 41, 91, 94, 99, 102, 106, 115, 129, 142, 156, 157, 162, 164, 165, 168, 169, 171, 175, 176, 178, 190, 192, 206, 222, 226, 230, 244, 245, 250
responsibility 11, 17, 19, 22, 25, 26, 28, 38, 43, 47, 49, 50, 55, 58, 61, 62, 64, 66, 68, 76, 78, 80, 82–84, 89, 91–93, 96, 97, 99, 103, 114, 116, 117, 126, 129, 130, 138–143, 151, 155, 164, 165, 167, 170, 172–174, 181, 182, 184, 185, 187, 189, 191, 192, 201, 203, 204, 208, 210, 213, 219, 222, 229, 231, 240, 247–250, 252
Ricoeur, Paul 185–192
right 7, 10, 13–15, 17, 21, 41, 51, 67, 71, 73, 74, 76, 84, 91–96, 100, 103, 105, 139 142 147, 148, 150, 151, 162, 163, 165, 170, 171, 175, 192, 207, 214–216, 221–223, 225, 228, 231, 232, 236, 238, 239, 241–243, 245, 249–251

S

said 28, 30, 31, 84, 100, 107, 109, 111–113, 126, 127, 133, 134
Sartre, Jean-Paul 37, 38, 50, 57, 58, 63, 65, 79, 105
saying 28, 100, 107, 110, 116, 123, 124, 128, 132, 133, 135, 137, 204
science 35, 39, 52, 186, 197, 198
sense 7, 19, 22, 28, 29, 42, 44, 54, 66, 72, 77, 79, 89, 93, 105, 109, 110, 112, 127, 133, 138–140, 147, 152, 154, 161, 166, 170, 172, 180, 186, 195, 199, 201, 205, 209, 219, 223, 230, 233, 235, 237, 239–241, 244, 248, 249
Shestov, Lev 44, 45
sign 15, 33, 108, 115, 126, 132
silence 47, 80, 108, 109, 111, 114, 125
slave 43, 70, 75, 101, 150, 237
social contract 149, 151, 162, 163, 168, 173, 177
sociality 11, 17, 19, 27, 28, 34, 46–51, 57, 65, 81, 105, 116, 118, 124, 143, 145, 158, 169, 210, 221, 252

society 7, 10–13, 16, 26–29, 33, 34, 38, 39, 48–50, 62, 81, 89, 90, 92, 94, 103, 141, 142, 144, 145, 151, 154, 161, 162, 167, 170, 173, 177, 178, 182, 184, 191, 197, 205, 210, 213–215, 217, 219, 221, 223–225, 227, 229, 230–237, 249
Socrates 23, 49, 139
sovereignty 70, 72, 75, 112, 219
state 7–9, 11, 12, 41, 49, 71, 74, 97, 104, 105, 145, 150, 153, 161–163, 165–168, 170–173, 175, 177, 184, 187, 192, 197, 206, 207, 210, 215, 216, 217, 219, 224, 231, 233, 236, 239, 240, 243–245, 250, 251
subject 12, 19–21, 24, 25, 27, 28, 30, 32–35, 39, 41, 46, 54, 62, 63, 66–70, 72–76, 78, 80, 81, 83–85, 88, 90, 93–96, 98, 113, 125, 128–131, 136, 138, 140, 156, 165, 172, 175, 178, 181, 184, 185, 190, 191, 195–197, 206, 212, 214, 215, 218, 219, 223, 228, 232, 238, 245–247
subordinate 8, 71–74, 130, 158
substance 19, 70, 129, 245
survival 54, 55, 60, 86, 97, 119, 129, 142, 150, 158, 169, 177, 214, 244, 251
system 22, 23, 37, 40, 47, 48, 50, 61, 62, 68, 89, 90, 93, 108, 113, 116, 117, 125, 131, 141, 143, 144, 146, 153–155, 157, 158, 175, 177, 191, 197, 223, 225, 226, 229, 230, 237, 244, 251

T

theory 15, 26, 27, 38, 47, 50, 52, 68, 73, 107, 120, 131, 149, 151, 162, 163, 168, 169, 191, 196, 210, 217, 223, 226, 227, 229, 233, 234, 237–241, 245
Third 12, 28, 51, 62, 91, 96, 103, 105, 106, 116, 123, 124, 127, 132–134, 140, 141, 143, 144, 146, 162, 164, 171, 183, 186, 187, 189, 208, 220, 221, 229, 244
Thou shall not kill! 5, 8, 23, 35, 39, 40, 42, 43, 185, 224, 225, 234, 249
time 8, 22, 34, 38, 39, 41, 42, 46, 47, 49, 50, 61, 64, 65, 69, 72, 78, 84–89, 92, 93, 95–97, 111, 119, 127, 130, 136, 137, 140, 141, 152, 159, 163, 168, 173, 180, 189, 196, 205, 209, 213, 217, 222, 232, 237, 249
totalitarianism 8, 9, 17, 154, 174
totality 7, 9, 11, 12, 14, 22, 26, 27, 31, 32, 34, 35, 39, 45, 55, 56, 63, 69, 73, 80, 91, 127, 144, 148, 149, 151, 153, 154, 157, 162, 169, 171, 180, 186, 197, 215, 234, 236, 244, 246
trace 96, 117, 145, 247, 250
tradition 7, 20, 24, 26, 27, 29, 30, 37, 50, 59, 67, 118, 125, 131, 145, 162, 164, 165, 176, 200, 211, 212, 217, 225, 245
transcendence 20, 31, 33, 36, 48, 63, 64, 77, 79, 84, 93, 97, 102, 126, 127, 128, 136, 154, 178, 180, 245
transcendental 18, 27, 32, 36, 37, 68, 71, 72, 103, 202, 206, 227, 245

truth 23, 30, 38, 45, 47, 53, 54, 58–61, 64, 67, 69, 73, 81, 86, 93, 97, 101, 102, 108, 111, 113, 114, 116, 118, 119, 121, 127, 130, 133, 139, 158, 161, 176, 192, 195, 196, 201, 202, 209

U

understanding 11, 13, 17, 19, 21, 23, 29, 30, 32, 34, 35, 38, 46, 52–54, 57, 58, 64, 75, 78–80, 82, 85, 94, 99, 104, 110, 111, 112, 115, 117–119, 123–125, 127, 129, 130, 132, 134–137, 144, 145, 156, 176, 178, 179, 182, 193, 201, 204, 206, 207, 223, 224, 227, 228, 236, 244
uniqueness 11, 49, 85, 94, 116, 126, 129, 138, 146, 147, 166, 169, 171, 173, 182, 219, 220, 229, 249–251
unity 9, 12, 22, 26, 27, 32, 40, 71, 73, 126, 138, 150, 153, 215, 243, 245
universal 7, 8, 10, 13, 15, 17–19, 21, 26, 27, 31–33, 45, 47, 48, 67, 68, 73, 79, 81, 90, 94, 130, 134, 145, 149, 153, 166, 172–174, 176, 179, 186, 199, 202, 205, 209, 214–216, 219, 220, 226, 243, 245, 246
utopia 97, 120, 152, 222

V

value 44, 46, 47, 80, 120, 160, 172, 173, 174, 179, 192, 228, 234, 238, 249, 252

violence 25, 42, 60, 87–89, 143, 148, 150–152, 155, 156, 159–161, 163–169, 174, 176, 177, 183, 187, 188, 189, 192, 208, 213, 221, 248
virtue 8, 17, 22, 36, 39, 112, 155, 160, 181, 185–187, 195, 232
vision 167

W

war 41, 70, 95, 118, 149, 150, 155, 159, 160, 161, 163, 165, 169, 177, 216, 243, 250
Weber, Max 151, 187
West 33, 74, 98, 169, 204
whole 10–12, 14–17, 19, 20, 22, 26, 29, 32, 33, 49, 51, 53, 61, 62, 66, 68, 69, 75, 83, 86, 90, 107, 127, 137, 144, 145, 149, 151, 153, 177, 180, 182, 186, 188, 195, 197, 205, 207, 210, 214, 215, 219, 229, 236, 244, 251
word 28, 44, 57, 58, 66, 75–77, 85, 86, 99, 100, 102, 108, 110, 115, 116, 125, 126, 134, 139, 140, 157, 162, 164, 198, 204, 233, 241
world 9, 24, 25, 29, 32–36, 38–40, 43, 46–48, 52, 53, 55, 56, 61, 62, 63, 67, 77, 80, 81, 83, 84, 86, 89, 92, 93, 96, 97, 100–104, 106, 107, 110, 111, 114, 115, 119, 124, 126–128, 132, 134–136, 139, 146, 149, 151, 156–159, 171, 174, 178, 180, 182, 184, 206, 217, 222, 230, 234, 238, 245, 246, 251

ibidem-Verlag

Melchiorstr. 15

D-70439 Stuttgart

info@ibidem-verlag.de

www.ibidem-verlag.de
www.ibidem.eu
www.edition-noema.de
www.autorenbetreuung.de